FAILURE OF JUSTICE

A Brutal Murder, An Obsessed Cop,
Six Wrongful Convictions

JOHN FERAK

Bestselling Author of BODY OF PROOF

WILDBLUE
PRESS

WildBluePress.com

Failure of Justice published by:
WILDBLUE PRESS

P.O. Box 102440
Denver, Colorado 80250

Copyright 2016 by John Ferak

978-1-942266-47-1 *Paperback ISBN*
978-1-942266-48-8 *eBook ISBN*

Interior Formatting and Book Cover Design by Elijah Toten
Totencreative.com

Other Exciting WildBlue Press Books by Jon Ferak

DIXIE'S LAST STAND: *Was It Murder Or Self-Defense?*

http://wbp.bz/dixie

BODY OF PROOF: *Tainted Evidence In The Murder Of Jessica O'Grady*

http://wbp.bz/bop

FAILURE OF
JUSTICE

Contents

ACKNOWLEDGMENTS   1

INTRODUCTION   4

CHAPTER 1: THE PROWLER   10

CHAPTER 2: A CHILLING DISCOVERY   24

CHAPTER 3: AN OLD FAMILIAR FACE   37

CHAPTER 4: FBI'S KILLER PROFILE   46

CHAPTER 5: THE HOG FARMER P.I.   60

CHAPTER 6: JOANN'S SAGA   74

CHAPTER 7: BACK IN NEBRASKA   84

CHAPTER 8: THE NON-SECRETOR   91

CHAPTER 9: JOSEPH'S TALE   96

CHAPTER 10: INFORMANT REVISITED   108

CHAPTER 11: ALABAMA, HERE WE COME   123

CHAPTER 12: GLASS OF ICED TEA   136

CHAPTER 13: THE SNITCH   149

CHAPTER 14: DEBBIE'S DILEMMA   153

CHAPTER 15: THE POLYGRAPH TEST   161

CHAPTER 16: DETECTIVE WANTS OUT   172

CHAPTER 17: CONVINCING KATHY   178

CHAPTER 18: THE ALL-SEEING EYE   193

CHAPTER 19: JOANN'S CONFESSION   202

CHAPTER 20: NO PLEA DEALS   209

CHAPTER 21: THE OLD WEST COURTHOUSE   215

CHAPTER 22: APARTMENT UNIT 4   231

CHAPTER 23: THE PILLOW   241
CHAPTER 24: 'THAT OLD WOMAN'   253
CHAPTER 25: LIFE OR DEATH   265
CHAPTER 26: TRIALS REMAIN   273
CHAPTER 27: GLIMMER OF HOPE   291
CHAPTER 28: UNEXPECTED TWIST   297
CHAPTER 29: STARTING OVER   304
CHAPTER 30: THE OLD SUSPECTS   313
CHAPTER 31: REVELATION TIME   319
CHAPTER 32: WICKED LIFE   327
CHAPTER 33: BEYOND ALL DOUBT   341
CHAPTER 34: JUBILATION   351
CHAPTER 35: POTHOLES AHEAD   355
CHAPTER 36: RITNOUR'S WRATH   367
CHAPTER 37: BACK IN SOCIETY   373
CHAPTER 38: TROUBLE AT TARRANT   383
CHAPTER 39: LIGHT BEHIND DARKNESS   386
CHAPTER 40: LASTING TRIBUTE   397
EPILOGUE   413

ACKNOWLEDGMENTS

I would be remiss if I didn't take the time to single out a number of people who went above and beyond the call of duty in helping me produce *Failure of Justice*.

First, my publisher, WildBlue Press, led by co-founders Steve Jackson and Michael Cordova. This marks my third book with WildBlue Press, and I have been incredibly fortunate to have gotten to know Steve and Michael and many other fine members of the WildBlue Press team over these past few years. Along those lines, I must single out my copy editor Mary Kay Wayman for her strong attention to detail. Mary Kay had a profound impact on shaping and editing the content and the story flow of *Failure of Justice,* and for that I am especially grateful. Additional recognition goes out to WildBlue Press designer Elijah Toten for coming up with an excellent book cover. I also want to thank Ashley Butler, who leads the WildBlue Press communications team and works hard to promote the content of all the WildBlue Press authors.

I would also like to thank my wife, Andrea, and our three children, Libby, JD and Caroline, for being overly supportive in letting me pursue my passion of writing nonfiction. Without your strength and encouragement, I would be nowhere.

I have worked on writing *Failure of Justice* for more than two years, first taking up the project in January of 2014. Along the way, I've reviewed somewhere in the neighborhood

JOHN FERAK

of 10,000 court-related documents, police reports, plus countless newspaper articles that date back to 1985.

I feel indebted to a number of people who were helpful and gracious with their time as I tried to make this book project possible:

Tina Vath, a police investigator from Beatrice; Randy Ritnour, a former Gage County prosecutor; Pete Klismet, retired FBI special agent; Beatrice Police Chief Bruce Lang; Beatrice Police Lieutenant Mike Oliver; Ernie Chambers, an Omaha state senator; Jon Bruning, former Nebraska attorney general; Artis Milke, an employee at the Beatrice Library; Scottsbluff lawyer Maren Chaloupka; Nebraska author Merle Henkenius; Lincoln attorneys Herb Friedman and Toney Redman; Gage County District Judge Paul Korslund; and Beatrice attorney Lyle Koenig.

Additionally, a special word of thanks also goes out to members of the Helen Wilson family, particularly Helen's daughter-in-law Edie Wilson and Helen's granddaughter Jan Grabouski. They both helped me better understand the life of Helen Wilson.

I also want to thank the *Lincoln Journal Star* for granting me permission to republish a handful of photos and also to *Beatrice Daily Sun* editor Patrick Ethridge for his help as well. Both newspapers did an exceptional job over the past many years in covering the many twists and turns that arose during the Wilson murder case, a tragedy like no other in Nebraska.

Most of the quotations that appear throughout *Failure of Justice* come from court testimony, police reports, lawsuit depositions, written statements about the case provided directly to me, numerous interviews I've conducted, newspapers articles, press conference speeches, minutes of state legislative hearings.

***

Failure of Justice is dedicated to public defender Jerry Soucie, a true crusader for Nebraska's wrongly condemned.

INTRODUCTION

A decade ago, my duties as a regional reporter at Nebraska's largest newspaper allowed me to roam small towns and communities in three primary counties surrounding Omaha/ Douglas County: Cass County, Saunders County and Mills County, Iowa, which is just across the Missouri River. My duties were to cherry-pick for stories of magnitude to a wide-reaching audience, not just of interest to the locals.

And that's what led me to a white-haired, no-nonsense former Army veteran named Jerry Soucie. He worked in the capital city of Lincoln as a statewide public defender, but his job often put him on the road bringing him into Nebraska's small-town courthouses. He had a combative style about him that many of Nebraska's police officers did not like.

In the spring of 2006 a terrorizing double murder happened along a gravel road inside a two-story farmhouse. Blood was sprayed everywhere, and several red ammunition shells were left at the scene. Everybody near the tiny town of Murdock knew the victims, a middle-aged farm couple who were slaughtered in their upstairs bedroom on Easter Sunday night. About a week later, the local Cass County Sheriff's Office arrested two relatives for the shotgun slayings. There was great relief across the region and people expressed their gratitude toward the sheriff and his fast-working handful of investigators.

Six months later, I drove to the historic Cass County Courthouse in downtown Plattsmouth to report on a stunning development. The prosecutor was dismissing double murder charges against Soucie's indigent client, Nick Sampson. Charges against co-defendant Matt Livers were dismissed weeks later as well. Largely thanks to Soucie's aggressive and tireless crusade to prove his client's innocence, the local prosecutor realized he had a giant mess on hands. Those two cousins who had been dished up by the sheriff's office were not the real killers at all. It was a stunning news story to cover, and I was there every step of the way. The farmhouse tragedy in Murdock was chronicled in my first published book, *Bloody Lies: A CSI Scandal in the Heartland*, 2014, The Kent State University Press.

Until the double-murder case debacle occurred in Murdock, most of Nebraska had been in a state of denial when it came to social justice topics such as false confessions, wrongful convictions and DNA exonerations. Even I was naïve. Little did I realize that the small-town miscarriage of justice in Murdock had only scratched the surface when it came to false confessions and wrongful convictions in America's Heartland.

Sometime in 2008, as I recall, Soucie hinted during a phone call that something huge was brewing behind the scenes of Nebraska's criminal justice system. I pressed for details, but he wouldn't divulge anything. He just assured me that when the story broke, the news would be like an atomic bomb exploding. And he was right. It was a history-in-the-making episode. Three men and three women, dubbed the "Beatrice 6," were having their long-ago murder convictions set aside in the 1985 murder of a widow.

Once again, Jerry Soucie was at the front lines of unearthing the truth. He helped achieve exonerations for not just one, but an astonishing six people in a lone murder case.

The exonerated Beatrice 6 were:

Debbie Shelden, a learning-disabled Beatrice resident who was a distant relative of the murder victim.

JoAnn Taylor, a North Carolina native, who had undergone psychiatric care for repeated instances of delusional behavior.

Kathy Gonzalez, a former Beatrice resident, who had lived in the apartment unit above the victim.

James Dean, a young man from a dysfunctional family, who had no serious brushes with the law.

Tom Winslow, a high school dropout who battled chronic depression and was easily manipulated.

Joseph White, an Alabama native who proudly had served his country in the military.

In the 1980s, these six loosely acquainted individuals in their twenties had one thing in common: They were living in Beatrice, Nebraska. These were people who didn't attend local churches, and they certainly weren't members of the Lions, Jaycees or Kiwanis clubs. They were disenfranchised, troubled souls. They were just the right people to fall prey as scapegoats for a brutal murder that the town – and relatives of the victim – desperately wanted solved. They will forever be known as the Beatrice 6.

It was a remarkably tragic story – six people in their prime whose lives were ruined, all caught up in a web of deceit, all because of a series of faulty assumptions by one man, a former Nebraska police officer, with a burning desire to solve the murder himself. Innocent people became brainwashed into believing they shared some blame, thanks to the help of a psychologist who moonlighted as a sheriff's deputy. Rather than roll the dice with the risk of being sent to die in that barbaric method of capital punishment, the state's electric chair, most of these weak-willed individuals fell over like a stack of dominos. The infamous case involved not just one false confession but four.

At the time of this book's publication, the Beatrice 6 case marks the largest mass exoneration case in the country due to newly tested DNA evidence, but I'm guessing many of you aren't familiar with the case.

Crimes that happen in Nebraska rarely draw wide national interest. The Heartland is often mocked by the national press as fly-over country, so when major crime news breaks there, it usually only gets reported by local and regional news outlets. The best news coverage chronicling the unraveling Beatrice 6 case came from reporter Joe Duggan, of the *Lincoln Journal Star* newspaper, not the state's largest newspaper, which was where I worked from 2003 through 2012. I was never involved in any of the coverage at the *Omaha World-Herald* because Beatrice was not considered part of my specialized coverage zone. And so it went.

A few years ago, I returned to live in Wisconsin where I write for the USA TODAY NETWORK-Wisconsin Investigative Team. The plight of the Beatrice 6 largely faded out of the public spotlight back in Nebraska. And that's where my interest in the case grew. I reached out to Soucie, the Nebraska public defender, who had a leading role in securing the exonerations for the Beatrice 6. He was extremely gracious with his time, sending me a copy of a computer disk containing several thousand original police reports and court transcripts of the Beatrice case. From this material, in January of 2014, I began my research.

The story was unlike any other wrongful conviction I had ever researched or read about. There are seven victims in this crime: the kind-hearted older woman, Helen Wilson, who was callously murdered, plus the three men and three women who became a burden for the Nebraska taxpayers as wards of the state's general prison population for many years. They, too, are truly victims of a gross miscarriage of justice such as had never been seen before. I have tried my best to portray the lives of all seven victims in an accurate, but sympathetic light.

Hopefully, you will gain a better understanding of how one small-town good ol' boys club, otherwise known as the Gage County Sheriff's Office, has thrived for decades. That sheriff's department, with the political cover of fellow county officials employed at the courthouse across the street, continues to cover for its own.

As you read *Failure of Justice*, it's also my sincere hope that you take away favorable impressions of the conscientious members of the City of Beatrice Police Department, the Nebraska State Patrol investigators and the Nebraska Attorney General's Office. These individuals had direct roles in the ultimate outcome of the Helen Wilson murder investigation. Through their own skills and professionalism, they realized that the Sheriff's Office investigation was nothing short of a disaster of epic proportions. In my estimation, these public servants were shining stars who rose to the occasion and they deserve to be recognized for going above the call of duty, even when facing enormous public pressure to accept the status quo and move on.

Lastly, I want to direct my comments to the victim's family. I can't fathom the pain and agony you have endured over the past thirty-one years. You waited years for an arrest to be made. You sat through courtroom proceedings and you heard lurid and gruesome details, not realizing these horrific stories had been concocted by a cagey sheriff's investigator blinded by his own incompetence. He brought you a sense of closure, a feeling that justice was served. We now know he wasn't a hero at all. In reality, his interrogative methods bullied weak-willed people into repeating his own convoluted theory of the murder. I don't have any expectations that the more stubborn-minded relatives of the victim will change their long-standing beliefs about the murder after reading this book. Perhaps, though, they and others like them will become more open-minded about the travesties of justice that can arise anywhere in America, including small towns where police officers can be your friends and next door neighbors.

Hopefully, readers of *Failure of Justice* will be more mindful that false confessions tend to be magnified in states where elected prosecutors and small-town sheriff's departments can run around using the death penalty as an interrogation threat. As a consequence, weak-willed, mentally challenged people are sometimes prone to confessing to a brutal crime, even murder, with little regard as to whether their confession meshes with the actual crime.

The recipe for disaster known as the Beatrice 6 involved an inept investigator, an opportunistic sheriff, a mischievous shrink, and a lazy, power-hungry prosecutor who ruled over Gage County with an iron fist for more than twenty-five years.

CHAPTER 1
THE PROWLER

Tucked away in America's Heartland along the Big Blue River sits an aging blue-collar community accustomed to hearing its name, Beatrice, mispronounced as an old-fashioned name for a woman. Properly addressed as Bee-AT-triss, this small city is nestled in deep southeastern Nebraska, bordering Kansas, a couple of counties over from the murky waters of the Missouri River. The region is dominated by livestock and farming. Summers are hot. Winters on the Great Plains can be downright wicked. Landowners since the first pioneers have faced howling winds and bitter cold.

Beatrice's claim to fame is the Homestead National Monument of America, marking the area's role in the settlement of the American West. Since the mid-1800s, settlers passed through the area on the famous Oregon Trail, many on their way to stake a claim in the federal government's land giveaway. After Congress passed the Homestead Act of 1862, the first application filed was for a piece of land west of Beatrice that is now part of the national monument.

During the last half of the twentieth century, Beatrice fought hard to retain its small-town charm. The population remained relatively stable, hovering around 12,000. Industries such as a dairy plant and windmill and metal manufacturers were longtime employers, but for decades the backbone of the local economy was a state-run institution for persons diagnosed with profound and severe mental retardation. The care facility first opened in the late 1880s as the Institution for Feeble Minded Youth. The forty-acre tract later became known as the Beatrice State Home. Today, it's called the Nebraska State Development Center.

A fascinating footnote about Beatrice: The community is the self-proclaimed "lawn mower capital of the world." Several companies that make lawn mowing equipment are clustered near the city's industrial park. If Beatrice residents don't work at the state mental institution, chances are they or someone they know work in the lawn mower industry.

Beatrice has long been regarded as a pleasant place to call home and, overall, a safe community with very few incidents of violent crime. During the 1980s, a stable city police force consisting of twenty to twenty-five officers provided round the clock courteous service for the citizens.

But even this quaint city forty miles south of Lincoln, Nebraska's capital, was not immune from the stain of the occasional undesirable element. Downtown Beatrice saw its share of riffraff and aimless drifters who patronized the local watering holes and occasionally caused mayhem. Civic leaders and the local churches decried a certain element of the bar culture. Some taverns were a haven for attracting troublemakers, alcoholics, drifters, and dopers. Such customers generally consisted of the uneducated, the poor, unskilled laborers, people with no sense of meaning or purpose in life. Some authority figures loathed the so-called dregs of society who tended to be frequent visitors to the local jail and kept the city's cops constantly busy, being at the forefront of many of the community's crimes.

In 1983, a series of frightening late-night home invasions put residents of Beatrice on edge. The targets of these crimes were all older women who lived alone. That June, a seventy-three-year-old was sitting in her living room, knitting and watching television just before going to bed. Suddenly her life flashed before her eyes as she found herself face-to-face with a young man wearing a full-length stocking cap, with tiny holes cut out for his eyes. He brushed a twelve-inch knife against the older woman's neck, holding the weapon just below her ear. This parasite of a human being was sexually aroused. He clasped his hand over the older woman's mouth to keep her from screaming.

He moved in for the attack, the zipper on his pants wide open. As the attacker tried to pull up her nightgown, the woman bravely fought back. She brushed away his knife. Then she kicked him in the groin. The man felt immediate, intense pain. He tumbled backward and fell on the living room floor. When he got off the floor, he whimpered and tucked the knife back into his belt. He no longer lusted for rape. Instead, he bolted straight for the door and ran out into the night. Thanks to the cloak of darkness, the prowler managed to get away, police reports show.

Obviously, this particular woman was lucky. She escaped with only small minor cuts to her thumb. Flustered, she told Beatrice police officers that her attacker appeared tall and thin. He wore a dark shirt and khaki pants, she thought. Over the course of several days, detectives aggressively investigated the attempted sexual assault, but police had little else to go on. These were the days before cellphones and video surveillance cameras were everywhere.

No one was immediately arrested for the attack. Six weeks passed before another horrifying incident.

Around 10:00 p.m. that night, a woman in her seventies who lived on Ella Street suddenly heard a strange noise. Curious, she wandered through her house to investigate. When she flipped on the light switch, there was a prowler creeping around her garage. The light startled him, and he made a mad dash into the night, police reports show.

Later that night, another elderly woman was in a chair minding her business inside her house on Bell Street. She was caught in total shock when a masked intruder appeared at her side. He clutched her throat. He wedged his knees between hers. This was life or death, she sensed. The eighty-two-year-old screamed loudly. Her shrieks of panic startled the would-be rapist, whom the woman described to police as being about twenty years old with straight blond hair parted down the middle. He jumped off her and darted for the door.

Yet another violent rape was averted in Beatrice. The distressing news, of course, was that it seemed the late-night prowler who pulled a knife on one of his victims that night was not finished terrorizing elderly Beatrice women. By August, this so-far frustrated predator was growing more brazen. He seemed fearless about being caught. He decided to return to the residence on Elk Street where he had hidden inside a woman's garage, only to be scared off when she turned on the light. This time, the seventy-one-year-old was fast asleep when he made his move. At 12:40 a.m. a sudden and jarring noise awoke her. She lifted her head, but quickly dismissed the sound. She turned over and fell back asleep not knowing the attacker had cut a hole through her back screen door. Once inside the dark house, he sneaked into her kitchen. He was careful not to make any loud commotion. There in her kitchen, he pulled a long steak knife from one of the drawers. He tiptoed through the darkened home until he came to her bedroom door. He flipped on the light switch. The woman awoke. She saw the stranger towering over her bed, his face concealed with a rag he stole from her garage. The predator lunged at her. He brushed the knife against her throat.

"If you scream, I'll kill you," he growled.

Even faced with grave danger, she screamed her lungs out anyway. She hoped everyone in Beatrice would hear her. As she tried pushing her attacker away, he punched one of her eyes. Luckily, she freed herself from his grip and fended him off. She escaped from her bedroom and hustled outside. Dazed, the rapist ran out the door, turned away again.

The victim suffered minor cuts to her neck, left thumb and right little finger, but luckily she was not seriously harmed. Another courageous and determined older woman had managed to escape the grip of this young attacker. But no matter how many times he was turned away that summer, there seemed to be no stopping his behavior.

***

All four of those incidents transpired within a six-week period. It was a tough ordeal for the city's police force, who didn't know when the serial predator would strike next. The police did not want fear and paranoia to rule their normally safe and peaceful town. Above all, the cops did not want every elderly woman in town to be consumed with fear as they went to bed every night.

Officers knew they were trying to nab an abnormal perpetrator. It was uncharacteristic for the small-town force to be challenged by a sexual deviant with an appetite for older ladies. Perhaps he was a troubled teenager who attended the local high school, some officers suggested. Whoever he was, the police suspected he was sure to try to invade the home of another woman when she least expected.

But then … that did not happen.

No more older women were victimized inside their residences that fall and winter. Then Beatrice made it through all of

1984 without a single such home invasion. Some officers thought the predator skipped town. Others figured he landed in jail or ended up in prison for an unrelated crime such as a residential burglary. In fact, if a different town's cops had arrested him, the chances would be good that those officers had no knowledge of the rape attempts in Beatrice.

In any event, all remained nice and quiet in Beatrice as the city celebrated the Christmas holidays and welcomed New Year's Day 1985. Snowplows kept the paved streets easily passable for travelers that winter. Children loved the cold weather because it meant snowball fights and snow angels. Overall, residents in the Heartland were resilient as always -- not just in braving the cold, but embracing the chill with mittens, insulated jackets and warm stocking hats as a part of life in the cold-weather region.

As the winter dragged along, February 5, 1985, would mark one of its coldest nights on record. But it wasn't the extreme chill that would burn that date into the community's consciousness and bring Beatrice widespread infamy some years later. It was the traumatic violence that night that visited Unit 4 of an unassuming apartment building on the town's main thoroughfare.

***

Mrs. Helen Wilson had dark gray hair. She stood about five feet tall, weighed about 110 pounds, and was regarded as a fiercely independent woman. She was also a longtime widow. Her husband, Ray, died of a heart attack during the 1960s, when he was only fifty-four. After burying her husband, Helen Wilson never remarried. In fact, her close friends and family were absolutely sure that she never had any male suitors or romantic acquaintances in the years after her husband's untimely death. Helen Wilson was known as a dignified, helpful lady around Beatrice. She had a sharp mind and liked to stay active. On Sundays, she volunteered in the children's nursery at her Methodist church. For leisure, she played bingo several nights each week at the local church halls. She usually bounced between the local Catholic Church and the Fraternal Order of Eagles Club.

Two of Wilson's three grown children still remained in Beatrice, but one of her sons lived far away, at the other end of the state. Regardless of distance, the Wilsons stayed a close-knit family. In January 1985, as Helen Wilson was approaching her sixty-ninth birthday, she boarded a bus to visit her son Larry, who lived in Scottsbluff, near the Wyoming border. The Beatrice woman was excited to spend time with family. "When we picked her up, she was wearing this little crocheted beret type hat with a plastic lining she had made," recalled Wilson's daughter-in-law Edith "Edie" Wilson of Scottsbluff.

"Come to find out she had washed her hair that morning and it was in rollers. She wore the hat to cover the rollers. When she took off the hat, her hair was still wet from wearing the plastic. Later she became very sick from this."

Still, the visit was a great time to bond with her faraway family. While in western Nebraska, her grandson Mark graduated from a welding technical school out in Casper, Wyoming. Wanting to savor the memories, Helen snapped numerous keepsake photographs of her smiling grandson posing with his diploma. That would also be one of the last times Helen Wilson was happy.

Unfortunately, Helen developed a terrible, nagging cough during her two-week stay in western Nebraska. As her cold persisted, Helen contemplated seeing a doctor. "I didn't want to call him on the weekend so I kind of talked her out of it

… At one point she said, 'I wish someone would just shoot me,'" Edie Wilson recalled years later.

The next day, Saturday, was crazily busy around the Wilson household in Scottsbluff. Two of Helen's teenage grandsons, Shane and Tadd, competed in a wrestling tournament, and both earned their win into the championship finals for their respective weight divisions. Larry Wilson knew this was an extraordinary accomplishment so during a break in the matches he rushed back home to pick up his mother. They made it back to the high school just in the nick of time so she could cheer on both of her grandsons from the bleachers. Both of the Wilson boys won their wrestling weight classes that day and the family was in a joyous mood. "I can still hear her laughing proudly as they won," Edie Wilson said. "Again, out came the camera and a lot of pictures were taken with the boys and their medals. These were to be the last pictures she took and were taken of her."

The next day Helen Wilson decided to return to Beatrice.

"On Sunday morning, she wanted to go home and see her own doctor and sleep in her own bed," her daughter-in-law said. "We took her back to the bus station. She slipped Larry twenty dollars just like she always did when she left."

Several hours later, the large Greyhound bus rolled into the depot in Lincoln, Nebraska. Wilson wore her beret and clutched her suitcase as she saw her relatives there to welcome her. She was relieved to get a ride back to Beatrice, the final leg of her long journey.

Wilson lived at 212 N. Sixth St., a three-level brick apartment building near the heart of downtown Beatrice. Most people around the community knew the structure as the former Lincoln Telephone & Telegraph Co. building. Beatrice's Sixth Street is otherwise known as U.S. Highway 77, the main thoroughfare for motorists heading into and out of town. The apartment building made of high-quality masonry brick was built around 1900. During the 1980s, the complex was bordered by the green space of Charles Park, Beatrice Public Middle School, professional offices, a funeral home and a few smaller apartments. A church sat across the street.

This brick building on the edge of downtown Beatrice, Nebraska, was the former Lincoln Telephone & Telegraph Company building. Photo/Beatrice Police Department

Wilson had lived in the building since the mid- to late 1970s, and it served her needs. Her apartment was within walking distance of numerous downtown retail stores and shops. She grew comfortable living here. It was home. In addition, her sister, Florence, and Florence's husband, Ivan "Red" Arnst, lived right next door, in Unit 5, also on the second-floor level. When you entered the unlocked building and scampered up a short flight of carpeted stairs, Wilson's apartment was the very first door in the second-floor hallway. The names of the tenants were etched on their doors and also on the building's mailbox for postal deliveries.

Wilson's apartment was a simple and economical four-room unit. In her small kitchen had a stove, a refrigerator, cabinets, and her trusty coffeepot. A large bay window in her living room overlooked the sometimes busy traffic passing along U.S. 77 in the distance. She kept her apartment immaculate and decorative. However, one of the drawbacks of living even on the second and third floors was the potential loss of personal privacy. If residents failed to shut their drapes or blinds at night, people walking along Sixth Street could peer into those units and view a tenant's activities, especially if the unsuspecting renter had his or her lights on.

Less than two blocks south of the old telephone building was Court Street, otherwise known as State Highway 136, and the handful of drinking establishments that operated in the vicinity of Sixth and Court Streets. A place known as the R&S Bar was about four blocks southwest of Wilson's apartment building. A friendly watering hole known as The Little Bar was just two blocks away. Wilson did not frequent the local drinking establishments, but the local riffraff who did would pass by her apartment building as they headed to and from the bars, day and night.

That first Sunday night in February 1985, Wilson towed her suitcase in hand into her apartment building. She trudged up the brief flight of stairs. Finally, she stared down the narrow illuminated hallway. At long last, it was a relief to be home, though she knew she was very sick.

***

Two days later, it was February 5, and Wilson's nagging cough had not let up. In fact her health was becoming progressively worse. At about 6:00 p.m. that Tuesday, her sister Florence cooked up some hamburgers next door and brought them over for Helen's supper. Florence and her husband regularly cooked Helen's meals. They also ran errands and fetched her groceries, reports show. After Wilson ate her burger, her son Darrell, who lived in Beatrice, paid her a visit. While there, he drank two cans of Miller beer that he found in his mother's refrigerator. Mother and son sat with the television on in the living room, where Helen also kept a bowl of fruit and another with baked cookies. Later on, Darrell's wife, Katie, came over after she finished her regular Tuesday night bowling league. Darrell and his wife both expressed deep concern about Helen's poor health. Since they knew she was stubborn, they promised to call her around midnight to make sure she took her daily dose of medicine. They didn't want her to end up in a hospital bed. Wilson gave them a warm smile as her son and her daughter-in-law left her apartment at approximately 9:45 p.m. They shuffled down the short flight of stairs and drove home. Outside, it was unbearably cold. Temperatures had plunged below zero. Practically nobody was out wandering the streets of Beatrice that awfully frigid Tuesday night.

With her family gone, Wilson retreated to her back bedroom. She slipped off her clothes and put on a blue nightgown. She wore a pair of calf-length nylons and booties to keep her legs and feet warm. Before going to bed, she removed her dentures. She put her false teeth on her bedside table. The cluttered table also contained a washcloth, a handkerchief, an empty glass, a piece of fruit, and a Kmart-brand tissue box. The weary widow with the nagging cough turned off her bedroom light. She snuggled into her cozy warm blankets and drifted off to sleep.

As the night wore on, Wilson's sleep was likely disrupted by her severe, persistent cold. A sea of white tissues would be found uncharacteristically littering the floor around her bed. But the rest of her apartment remained immaculate, just the way Wilson always tried to keep her place.

***

As far as the other tenants were concerned, that Tuesday night was uneventful in the three-story apartment building. Of course, this was not a fraternity house. Renters were not accustomed to keg parties, stereos blaring rock 'n' roll music or obnoxious noise complaints. The tenants who resided in the old Lincoln Telephone & Telegraph building were typically the elderly or younger single working women. People who lived there minded their own business. Night after night, residents slept soundly and comfortably, and February 5, 1985, didn't seem any different, except for the blistering cold winds howling outside the sturdy brick building as the temperature plunged to minus 7 degrees.

Then, without warning, a strange sequence of events struck the normally well-maintained apartment building. The hallways on all three levels suddenly grew dark as a cave. For reasons unknown at the time, the power went out. The abrupt, middle of the night mechanical failure also left tenants without precious heat, though most didn't immediately notice because they were already sound asleep. However, when they awoke the next morning, February 6, they knew something was amiss because their apartments felt cold as a meat locker.

***

Before most of Beatrice woke up that Wednesday, a young aimless drifter with pock holes or some other kind of marks on his face wandered into the Gas 'N Shop around 6:00 a.m. The gas station was a short distance from the old telephone building. The twenty-one-year-old clerk behind the counter, Jerry Rowden, was alone when he spotted the unfamiliar customer with shaggy, dark brown hair dangling past his ears. The young man, about the same age as the clerk, approached the front counter to pay for one bag of Doritos. To his embarrassment, two more bags of Doritos concealed in the customer's long, tan-colored Army bomber jacket fell to the floor. The clerk glared and asked if he intended to pay for them. Yes, the man who looked like a drifter meekly replied. He reached into his pockets and scrounged together enough money to pay for all three Doritos bags. Afterward, the young man walked out the Gas 'N Shop and headed west.

A few weeks later, the store clerk was asked for his best recollection about the suspicious snack-food thief. During that interview with Beatrice police, the Gas 'N Shop clerk remembered something else that stood out, something dark and eerie. The employee thought he saw stains of blood on the young man, police records state. However, these were the days before retail stores had nonstop video surveillance cameras recording. The police had to rely upon the clerk's memory. Unfortunately, too much time had elapsed for the clerk to remember any more specific details about the young man's appearance. Not helping matters, the police furnished Rowden with a woefully outdated photo of a young man they were seeking, from when he was fourteen or fifteen. The gas station clerk studied the photo and told them that "the facial features were familiar but the hair was not, and he was then advised that the photo was approximately seven to eight years old," police reports state.

FAILURE OF JUSTICE

***

At the apartment building in Beatrice on that frigid morning, Florence Arnst hadn't heard a peep from her ailing sister next door. She knew Helen's lingering cold showed no improvement.

Shortly after 9:00 a.m. on Wednesday, February 6, Florence told her husband, Ivan, that she was going next door to check on Helen. At the door, Florence called for her sister. Her beckoning call drew no response. Fortunately, Florence had a spare key. She reached into her pocket and opened the door. When she walked into the unit, Florence did not notice anything out of the ordinary. However, the elderly woman's eyesight was failing miserably. As she walked through the apartment, Florence overlooked the fresh bloodstains on her sister's bedroom walls and the bedsheets that were in disarray. When she checked the bathroom, Florence didn't find her sister there, either. Eventually, she walked past the living room a second time and realized to her surprise that her sister was lying on the floor. Helen appeared to be sleeping, she thought. But something did not seem right. Florence summoned her husband to check on her sister's well-being. His eyesight was far better.

Right away, he saw that his sister-in-law was nude from the waist down and lying stretched out on her living room carpet, her face completely concealed. Towels covered her head. A thick, winter scarf was tightly wrapped around her eyes and face and used to gag her mouth. Ivan "Red" Arnst bent down. He touched her body, trying to determine if his sister-in-law, who brought so much warmth into the world, was still alive.

CHAPTER 2
A CHILLING DISCOVERY

At 9:29 a.m. that cold morning, the local police radio system relayed a possible "10-65" at a residential property not far from the Beatrice police station. In cop and paramedic lingo, a 10-65 call meant a death. Beatrice Police Sgt. John Scholl heard the call and hit the gas. Three minutes later, his squad car arrived at 212 N. Sixth St., the old telephone company building. There, Ivan Arnst ushered the officer into Unit 4. A pair of ambulance paramedics already there had recognized the situation was hopeless and tragic. Arnst's sister-in-law, Helen Wilson, was dead, sprawled across her living room floor -- and this did not appear to be a natural death. The elderly widow's nightgown was yanked up above her crotch. Her face pointed west. Her feet positioned east. Bath towels restrained her hands and wrists. The winter scarf that was wrapped around her face

Helen Wilson was approaching her sixth-ninth birthday when she was slain in February of 1985. The community of Beatrice, Nebraska, was terrorized by the details of her ritualistic murder.

twice had cut off her oxygen supply. Back in the bedroom, near the foot of her bed, officers found a black-handled steak knife and traces of blood on the sheets and one of the walls.

Evidently, the attack had migrated from the back bedroom to the carpeted living room floor where the victim was slain. Perhaps the widow submissively complied with her sadist attacker's demands in order to save her life. The police found no drag marks or signs that the attacker had pulled her into the living room. Her rugs were not torn, tattered or otherwise in disarray. The attacker apparently wasn't interested in robbery. At the time her body was found, Wilson was still wearing her gold-colored Timex wristwatch and two of her rings.

Wilson's underwear had been slipped off her body, the crime scene showed. The underpants were not torn and cast aside, but rather placed gently on a nearby couch.

Helen Wilson's blankets were ruffled and blood was evident on her covers when the Beatrice Police Department was summoned to her apartment on the morning of February 6, 1985. Photo/Beatrice Police Department

As for the knife, it came from one of the kitchen drawers, police determined. And yet the knife did not appear to have been used to inflict any bodily harm. Wilson had not suffered any apparent stab wounds to her body. Indeed, the crime scene was both disturbing and puzzling to decipher. A plastic flashlight was recovered from a bedroom dresser, but Wilson's son later told police that he had seen the flashlight on a living room table during his visit just hours before the brutal attack.

Although she seemed about the least likely person in Beatrice to be murdered, Helen Wilson became her city's first homicide victim of 1985. A sexual predator of the worst kind imaginable had robbed her of her wonderful life. The town had lost a loving and caring mother, grandmother and great-grandmother. Within the sanctity of her small four-room apartment, a subhuman sicko had desecrated her body and then run off under the cloak of darkness just before dawn.

**

Shortly after 10:00 a.m. Edie Wilson answered the phone at the Green Stamp Redemption Center in Scottsbluff where she worked. It was Uncle Red – calling from Beatrice, 450 miles away. "I knew it was bad because he never called me," she said. "He told me Helen had died. I assumed it was from the bad cold she had and never thought twice about it. I told him I would let (her son) Larry know and we would be home to Beatrice as soon as possible."

Before the family hit the road, Larry spoke on the phone with his sister, Jan Houseman, in Beatrice. She relayed that their mother might have been murdered. It made for a long drive, Edie Wilson remembered. "We never turned on the radio because we were afraid of what we would hear," she said. "It would be better to come from family."

A large contingent of relatives rushed back to Beatrice. Helen's only surviving brother, Mel Jones, who lived in Las Vegas, hopped on the first airplane available. Everyone gathered at the Beatrice home of Jan and Wayne Houseman. "We were hugged by everyone," Edie Wilson remembered.

With all the adults present, one of Helen's grandchildren broke the distressing news to the family: Helen Wilson had died after being raped. Everyone was mortified.

It was now up to the Beatrice Police Department to avenge this heinous murder and apprehend her killer. Fortunately, the community and the Beatrice Police Department had a solid relationship. Residents would bombard local detectives with calls and tips over the next several days.

***

Shortly after Helen Wilson's body was found that day, veteran Beatrice Police Chief Donald Luckeroth rushed to the crime scene. Luckeroth was homegrown. He had joined the Police Department in 1956 as a patrolman, became a lieutenant around 1965 and became chief in 1974. He had substantial training and expertise in polygraph work. During the 1980s, many police departments relied extensively on polygraph machines to solve felony crimes. After all, the blockbuster breakthrough known as DNA technology remained years away from being a game-changing, dynamic force in the criminal justice arena.

Inside the widow's apartment, the chief scanned the living room where her body lay. Luckeroth surveyed the bedroom, where rumpled bedsheets showed signs of a bloody struggle. By midmorning, Luckeroth summoned three of his most seasoned and dependable investigators. The chief warned other officers not to let any unnecessary visitors or guests into the apartment. Unit 4 was being classified the scene of a homicide.

As the investigation unfolded, the Beatrice police soon discovered a disturbing clue on the lower level of the apartment complex, where a missing fuse was found to have caused the darkness that blanketed all three apartment hallways. Unbeknown to police, an angry first-floor tenant had already dialed up the building's owner that morning, clearly unaware of Helen Wilson's murder on the floor above. The tenant complained to the landlord that her unit had no heat. The owner, also oblivious to the slaying, dispatched her trusty handyman to investigate the furnace problem. When the police probed the matter, they learned that someone had moved a stepstool near the furnace to yank wires from an electrical transformer. This action caused a number of apartments to lose their heat sometime during the previous night. The same culprit also apparently messed with the fuse box, causing all the hallway lights to go dark.

But who tampered with the wires and the fuse box? The circumstances pointed to the unknown killer, still roaming at large.

***

Back in Unit 4, police officers delicately placed towels across the carpet inside Wilson's apartment. The cops did not want the crime scene compromised. That day, the elected criminal prosecutor for Gage County, County Attorney Richard T. "Dick" Smith, along with his chief deputy and the Gage County sheriff, stopped by the apartment to tour the morbid scene. As the investigation unfolded, one of the sharp-eyed city cops saw some hairs near the victim's body. These hairs were deemed useful in the hopes of hunting down the killer.

FAILURE OF JUSTICE

The Nebraska State Patrol was summoned to assist the small-town police force with the murder investigation. By early afternoon, a state trooper arrived with a hand-held video camera. He recorded the disturbing scene of Helen Wilson's body on the floor. Another cop snapped about two dozen photos. These were the days before digital cameras could save and store thousands of images. In 1985, crime-scene photos were developed in an ancient, dark photo lab.

In the widow's kitchen, police found her black purse and a torn five-dollar bill on the carpet along with a single key on a plastic ring. Actually, there was an abundance of loot around the apartment, altogether more than $1,300 in cash and other currency. According to police reports, authorities recovered nine twenty-dollar bills, three hundred-dollar bills, two fifty-dollar bills, another set of thirty twenty-dollar bills, plus a number of money-market certificates and several uncashed checks. The money was easily located within the top dresser drawer in the bedroom. Why didn't the attacker stuff his pockets with her money when he had a golden opportunity?

In time, however, the discovery of the ripped five-dollar bill on Helen Wilson's carpet would take on a life of its own and play a tremendous role in the outcome of the case.

***

During a day that would forever haunt Beatrice, Detective Sam Stevens rushed over to the dark-colored brick building on that snow-covered Wednesday morning. "It was probably one of the coldest days I remember. It was way below zero early in the morning," Stevens recalled later. "When I got there, I remember there were several patrolmen there, and I don't know if the county attorney was there yet or not, but I remember seeing him there."

That afternoon, authorities placed paper bags over the dead woman's hands. They took such precautions to preserve any scant physical evidence left underneath the victim's fingernails during her struggle. To keep the crime scene fully intact, police cut away the living room carpet underneath the victim. Wilson's body, carpet and all, was delicately carried out of the building.

By midafternoon, a station wagon arrived in the parking lot of Lincoln General Hospital. There, the undertaker unloaded Wilson's body and wheeled it on the steel gurney into the pathology wing of the hospital. There, Dr. John Porterfield and two of his well-trained assistants performed the autopsy. The paper bags were removed from the victim's hands and upon doing so, the pathologists noted that the fingernails on the right hand contained lots of blood. Wilson's left arm was broken at the elbow. Tweezers were deployed to remove the foreign hairs left on her blue nightgown by the killer. Her nylons and foot booties were slipped off and secured in a special evidence bag for proper safekeeping.

The autopsy was revealing. Wilson had suffered excruciating chest fractures to her sternum, plus several broken ribs. She was raped and badly beaten before she died. Sadly, the crime was more repulsive than anybody had fathomed. The widow's body also had been sodomized shortly after her death, autopsy reports showed. Porterfield notified police that he had found a large amount of sperm inside the body. It also turned out that Wilson's declining health was worse than her relatives realized. Pneumonia had settled into her left lung, Porterfield stated. The pneumonia made it especially difficult for Wilson to gasp for air as her predator tightened the scarf around her neck. "The scarf acts as a gag within the mouth," the pathologist's report stated.

On the other hand, the green and pink bath towel used to restrain her hands was only tied in a half knot, the pathologist noted. "This towel easily slips from the hands and would not appear to have been an effective restraint."

Wilson died from suffocation, Porterfield concluded. He ruled her death a homicide though the precise time of her demise was not certain. The pathologist estimated time of death at between 10:30 p.m. and 2:30 a.m., but this was clearly a best-guess scenario.

In all likelihood, a young adult male was the culprit, Porterfield duly noted, based on the presence of so many lively sperm inside the victim's body. He was also confident in his finding that the abhorrent perpetrator had committed necrophilia.

***

As part of their routine, the Beatrice cops canvassed the entire apartment building. Police knocked on the doors of every unit to account for all the tenants. Perhaps somebody had seen a strange man scoping out the victim's apartment or peering into Helen Wilson's window. But police struggled to find any strong leads. The victim's brother-in-law, Ivan Arnst, remembered he watched *The Tonight Show With Johnny Carson* and then retired to bed around 11:30 p.m. However, he wore two hearing aids and was unable to hear even the ringing of his sister-in-law's phone through the apartment walls, according to police reports.

A woman in her mid-sixties who lived directly below Wilson told police she never heard any commotion or shrieks coming from the homicide victim's unit. The tenant recalled going to bed shortly before 1:00 a.m. However, she did recall hearing a noise around 11:00 p.m., but thought it sounded like the two beauty school students who lived next door to her.

During subsequent interviews, those two young women told police they had returned to their lower-level apartment at 9:30 p.m. and 12:15 a.m., respectively. Both insisted that all the hallway lights were working properly at the times they got back. Additionally, no unusual characters lurked around the building when they returned home, the police were told.

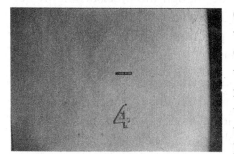

Helen Wilson, like other tenants residing within the former telephone building, had her name on the door of her apartment. Photo/ Beatrice Police Department

Officers eventually canvassed the top floor. One of those renters was a young woman named Kathy Gonzalez, who said she had gotten off work and come home around 6:00 p.m. Gonzalez, age twenty-five, told police she had done laundry inside the building at around 9:00 p.m. At that time, the hallway lights functioned fine. Gonzalez told police she went to bed around 10:00 p.m. The police asked if she recalled any suspicious characters lurking around her building. Gonzalez recalled there had been one well-dressed door-to-door insurance salesman a few months ago, in the fall of 1984. He had short hair and glasses, and looked to be in his early forties, but other than that, nobody else came to mind. The police deemed her interview satisfactory. They moved on to interview others.

Still, the Beatrice Police Department did not take any chances of overlooking critical evidence. Some officers searched a filthy trash bin behind the apartment building. The bin reeked, but the cops had a job to do. One brown-paper sack buried deep within the bowels of the trash bin caught the attention of an officer. The sack contained miscellaneous letters, papers, a belt, and two bras, one of them bloodstained. The letters within the bag included the name and an old address of a woman named Kathy Knehans – the maiden name of Kathy Gonzalez, the third-floor tenant that city detectives already had interviewed. For the time being, the paper bag was preserved. The bloody bra was put into a special bin for safe-keeping back at the Beatrice Police Department.

Meantime, the homicide investigation pressed onward.

***

There initially was a strong belief at the Beatrice Police Department that Wilson's rapist and killer might be a deviant homosexual. The police aggressively pursued that angle because the scarf had been wrapped around her face, concealing her identity, and the killer had engaged in sodomy with the body after she died, as the autopsy proved.

The police theorized that this dangerous rapist was unable to bottle up his demented and twisted sexual fantasies, perhaps fueled by hard-core X-rated pornography.

Within days of the murder, police descended on the Beatrice Book Store, a regular book store in town that carried a limited amount of X-rated materials. The bookstore operator was asked about any customers who bought sexually explicit bondage books or homosexual-themed magazines. The manager replied that he had several regular customers he knew were gay. And he determined for police that his store had only sold four different sets of X-rated bondage books over the last several months, according to police reports. Officers revealed to the manager that their suspect in Wilson's murder was probably a slender young white man, perhaps in his early twenties. However, the manager assured the detectives that none of the customers who recently bought any bondage books fit that description. In any event, the manager told detectives he would keep a careful eye on any future customers who had an appetite for kinky sex magazines in light of the widow's murder.

To their credit, the Beatrice Police Department remained hardy in their pursuit of the elusive killer. Detectives surmised Helen Wilson's killer might even want to clear his conscience. Perhaps he desired to show up at her funeral to pay his respects. The cops huddled with the Harman Mortuary Chapel, the local funeral home handling the arrangements and burial. All funeral home visitors, except the family, would exit through the east chapel door at the Beatrice mortuary, police reports state.

In a tragic coincidence, shortly before her death Helen Wilson had scheduled an appointment at Harman Mortuary to begin the process of pre-paying for her eventual funeral. According to her daughter-in-law, the meeting had been set for Friday, February 8. As it turned out, Saturday, February 9, was the day of her funeral.

Obviously, the mourners already knew that the circumstances of Wilson's death were revolting. The details of her killing had made the front-page of the daily local newspaper.

"Closed casket – no public viewing," read Wilson's obituary notice in the *Beatrice Daily Sun.*

Even still, some distraught relatives were able to view her body anyway, notably the homicide victim's only surviving brother, Mel Jones, and her daughter-in-law Katie Wilson, who lived in Beatrice and was the last person to see her alive, other than the killer.

"Uncle Mel went to the mortuary and saw his sister," Edie Wilson vividly remembered years afterward. "He advised us not to see her as this would upset us more because of her injuries. Katie did go to see her, but the rest of us followed his advice. This made it hard to say goodbye and realize she was gone."

During the funeral service, Beatrice Police Lieutenants Gary Wiebe and William Fitzgerald discreetly staked out the east chapel door. From a safe distance, the pair of detectives snapped photographs of unfamiliar faces that might warrant additional scrutiny. Next, the cops hustled out to the rural cemetery near Pickrell, a tiny village about fifteen minutes away.

Grieving family members were keenly aware that the funeral was swarming with police officers on the hunt for the killer. Squad cars from the Beatrice Police Department and the Gage County Sheriff's Office lined the funeral route, the Wilsons said.

"This made it very hard to accept her death and concentrate on the death," Edie Wilson pointed out. "Everything seemed so unreal, like we were in a movie."

As for local authorities, they hoped the killer would show up for the burial ceremony. While there, a brown or tan Mercury Comet 1974 model caught their eye. It was a local car, with Gage County license plates. The driver drew heightened curiosity because he had a large Band-Aid slapped across the left side of his face. An unknown woman accompanied him, the police reported. Detectives ultimately determined the man with a bandage was not a viable suspect.

***

If the killer had stayed away from the funeral service, police thought perhaps he might prefer to visit the cemetery once it grew dark, after Helen Wilson was laid to rest.

That night, the Beatrice cops placed an artificial bouquet of flowers near the granite headstone inside the Pleasant View Cemetery. It contained a voice-activated tape recorder, police reports show. It seemed like a brilliant investigative idea, but would it snare their elusive killer? Officers took turns conducting covert surveillance outside the rural cemetery during the next few nights, hiding out in an RV. Officers waited and watched to see if Helen Wilson's rapist-murderer had grown remorseful.

CHAPTER 3
AN OLD FAMILIAR FACE

Several hours before Helen Wilson endured an agonizing and cruel death at the hands of her rapist, Michael Hyatt was spending the afternoon scooping piles of snow from his driveway near Cedar Elementary School.

Out of nowhere, an old familiar face walked up his street. At twenty-two, Bruce Allen Smith still resembled the scrawny pencil-thin young boy with sandy-colored hair and hazel eyes with whom Hyatt developed a friendship during adolescence. Eight years prior, Smith and Hyatt attended public school together in Beatrice. However, the friends were separated around 1977 when Smith was sentenced to the state's Youth Development Center in Kearney, Nebraska. He came out of a dysfunctional home and had a chaotic upbringing, court records show. By age fifteen, he had racked up a number of juvenile criminal infractions around Beatrice. Police reports show Smith was involved with illegal fireworks, property damage and stealing gasoline. By 1985, Smith was in his early twenties and lived primarily in Oklahoma City with his mother. Even though he had not lived in Beatrice for years, Smith still dropped into town from time to time. Back in the day, Smith lived on South Second Street. His grandmother once lived in an older brick apartment building near the downtown, police reports show.

By 1985, Smith and Hyatt were both down on their luck. Both were unemployed, though Hyatt seemed better off in general. At least he had an automobile, unlike Smith, who told him February 5 that he had just dropped in to visit relatives, arriving on a bus from Oklahoma. That afternoon, Hyatt and Smith rekindled their friendship. These two long-lost buddies hopped into Hyatt's car. They cruised around town and caught up on their lives. During the drive, Smith openly talked about his bleak circumstances, admitting he was flat broke. He needed to scrounge up enough money to buy a bus ticket to get back to Oklahoma City. In fact, Smith became so desperate during their joyride that he hawked his wristwatch to Hyatt for a few extra bucks. By midafternoon, Hyatt dropped off Smith near the downtown street corner of Fifth and Court Streets. They made plans to meet up later that evening for a round of beers at one of the downtown taverns.

Bruce Allen Smith grew up in Beatrice, Nebraska, but was sent off to a juvenile detention facility around the time that this photo was taken. Photo/Beatrice Police Department

That evening, Hyatt, along with another young man and two women in their twenties, met up for drinks at the R&S Bar. Hyatt desired to hook up with one of the young women, though he wasn't having any luck wooing her at the bar, police records reflect. As the foursome enjoyed one another's company and their drinks, Bruce Smith casually walked in and joined them. The taps flowed. Hyatt bought Smith several drinks that night, remembering that his friend from Oklahoma City was hard up for cash.

During his five-hour stay at the bar, Smith's mind raced with lustful thoughts of sex. From his bar stool, Smith turned to Hyatt and remarked, "I haven't had any for quite some time, and I'm fucking horny," records show. At one point, Smith divulged to Hyatt that he got an erection as he surveyed the young women at the R&S Bar. Smith boasted of his burning desire to land "a piece of ass" one way or another.

Inside the bar, the two former classmates gravitated to the billiards table. There, Smith and Hyatt wagered several rounds of beer over games of pool. Sometime after midnight, Smith was heavily inebriated as he stumbled out of the bar and climbed into the passenger seat of one of the women's cars. It was dark and extremely cold. The others piled into Hyatt's car. Both vehicles sped to a trailer court near Blue Springs, about fifteen miles from Beatrice, where the two women lived. At the trailer park, the women hosted an after-hours party. As for Bruce Smith, he crawled into one of their beds to pass out from his excessive drinking. At one point, Smith rustled out of his slumber and tried to rape one of the women inside the trailer, reports show. She grew furious. She yelled and rejected his sexual advances. The situation grew ugly, and a young man from an adjacent trailer tossed Smith out. The simmering tensions soured everyone's party mood.

It was now well after 3:00 a.m. on February 6. Being the peacemaker, Hyatt agreed to leave with Smith, and the men drove off along with another friend of Hyatt's, Richard Styers. The trailer park party dispersed without any more blows or flying fists. Sometime around 3:45 a.m., Hyatt dropped off Styers at a friend's house back in Beatrice. Then Hyatt rolled up to the downtown intersection of Sixth and Court Streets, where he let Smith out of his car. As Hyatt drove off, he saw the young man staggering north, in the direction of Beatrice High School.

It was unbearably cold, minus 7 degrees, and the bone-chilling wind made it even colder. Smith wasn't dressed for the frigid weather. He wore blue jeans, brown leather motorcycle gloves, hiking boots, and a tan-colored denim jacket. Smith lacked a hat or stocking cap to guard against frostbite. Where would Smith find warmth on his walk? A familiar three-story apartment building would have been one of the first properties he encountered. He knew it ... It was the same building where his grandmother used to live.

***

After Hyatt read about the gruesome killing of Helen Wilson in the Beatrice newspaper, a chill ran up his spine. He immediately suspected the young man he had dropped off in the area late that night, Bruce Smith, court records show.

Hyatt even told the local cops that his old classmate – who had said he'd just arrived in town on February 5 -- seemingly drifted out of Beatrice again on February 6, after Wilson was killed. Hyatt kept replaying Smith's remarks from their night of drinking in his head. Smith wanted to land "a piece of ass" that night, one way or another, Hyatt told police. Hyatt also had seen Smith turn into a ball of rage when he was tossed out of the trailer park party.

Even though Hyatt assumed Smith skipped town immediately after the slaying, that wasn't the case. While the Wilson autopsy was being conducted in Lincoln, Smith wandered into the Homestead Paint and Paper Co. in Beatrice. Originally, Smith had tried to visit the Job Corps office next door, but it was already closed for the day.

At the paint store, Smith struck up a conversation with the female owner. He was broke, except for some loose change in his pocket that he boasted about winning earlier in the day while shooting pool at the R&S Bar. For the next forty-five minutes, Smith loitered around the paint store, according to police reports. He indicated he was looking for work, trying to make some extra money. He talked about having a wife and a small child back in Oklahoma City. But his presence gave the female owner-manager the willies. He looked unkempt. And, he acted flirty even though the paint store owner was in her early sixties. In any event, she told Smith to write down his name, phone number and contact information. He did so.

That was a wise move on the owner's part. The scrap piece of paper containing Smith's name and contact information was then handed over to the Beatrice police as part of their developing murder investigation. The scribbled piece of paper proved Smith was in town at the time of Wilson's rape and murder. Bruce Allen Smith was moving up the ladder and emerging at the top of the list of murder suspects.

***

As the homicide investigation progressed, the Nebraska State Patrol visited the bus station in Beatrice for clues. Back in those days, hard copies of customers' receipts were not saved by the bus company. However, a person believed to be Smith had, in fact, showed up at the Beatrice bus depot a few days after the homicide. At the time, Smith did not have enough money to make it to his final destination of Oklahoma City. Instead, he settled for a bus ticket to Wichita, Kansas, the police learned.

Meanwhile, another promising police lead came from the Daylight Donut Shop in Beatrice. A former teenage girlfriend of Smith's told police he had called her around 10:30 a.m. (which would have been about an hour after Helen Wilson's body was found). That same afternoon, the ex-girlfriend and one of her female friends went riding around with Smith. They saw several scratches across his face, according to police reports. When they asked what happened, Smith claimed he just got into a fight with Michael Hyatt, his former schoolmate.

As the investigative leads continued to point toward Smith, detectives re-interviewed Hyatt. The young man vehemently denied he ever got into any fight with Smith on the night of the homicide. Hyatt distinctly remembered Smith had no absolutely cuts or lacerations to his skin or face when Hyatt dropped him off that night less than two blocks away from the apartment complex where Wilson was savagely raped and suffocated.

As the police dug into Smith's background, they came across an interesting coincidence. A 1977 Beatrice City directory indicated that Smith had a grandmother named Ruth A. Garrison who lived at the same apartment building as Helen Wilson. Police surmised that Smith would have been familiar with the layout of the building, along with its various female tenants. Detectives put forth a modest attempt to track down Smith's grandmother, but ultimately came up short. A local woman with the same name worked at the

Best Western Motel, but she was not Smith's grandmother. She was only thirty years old. The relative sought by police was a seventy-five-year-old widow. Eventually, the Beatrice police realized Smith's grandmother had moved to Auburn, a peaceful Nebraska community an hour's drive away. The police didn't develop this lead any further.

As the murder investigation wore on, Beatrice police were hampered by the fact that Smith was long gone. By late February, police in Oklahoma City were notified that Smith might be back in their area. The call triggered heightened curiosity. According to police records, Oklahoma City homicide Detective Ron Bonny relayed that Smith was also on his radar as a possible suspect in an unsolved Oklahoma City murder from March 20, 1984. In that crime, a young white woman in her mid-thirties was tied up and bound with a knotted chord. Her neck had ligature marks. Her hands and feet were also tied. Like Helen Wilson, she, too, was a victim of a violent rape and it also looked like a knife was involved. Smith had lived in proximity to the 1984 unsolved murder, and Smith associated with some friends who lived nearby, Bonny told the Beatrice police. In Oklahoma City, Smith had been charged with a rape in 1981, when he was nineteen years old. Bonny noted there was not any scientific laboratory follow-up conducted in the 1981 rape case. And for reasons still unclear, Smith was never prosecuted in Oklahoma's courts for the rape.

At any rate, Nebraska and Oklahoma appeared ready to work together to flush out their suspicions about Smith's role in Wilson's murder. A lot of strong circumstantial evidence pointed toward Smith. When the police eventually interviewed Smith's mother, she said she figured her wayward son was in Edmond, about thirty miles from Oklahoma City.

About a month after Helen Wilson's slaying, Nebraska State Patrol Investigator Terry Becker, who was stationed in nearby Falls City, and Beatrice Police Lieutenant William Fitzgerald hit the road. They embarked on a more than 400-mile journey to Oklahoma City. The objective: to question Smith and obtain his blood and hair samples.

Once in Oklahoma, the Nebraska investigators got off to a slow start. First, it wasn't easy to figure out Smith's whereabouts as he apparently had no permanent address and instead constantly bummed around the homes of acquaintances. But by March 7, the detectives had staked out a van backed up to the corner of a house in Oklahoma City. A woman who answered the door at the residence confirmed that Bruce Smith had in fact spent the previous night sleeping in the van. But Smith was already gone and the woman answering the door claimed she didn't know where he went, reports state. Later that afternoon, a reliable local police informant alerted Oklahoma City Detective Ron Bonny that Smith might show up at an Arby's fast-food restaurant in Edmond. Smith was known for showing up sporadically after closing time to help clean the joint for extra cash. The stakeout of the van was abandoned. The police officers raced toward Edmond. As far as strategy, the detectives chose to downplay that Smith was under investigation for a murder back in his hometown of Beatrice. Oklahoma City's Bonny agreed to take the lead in approaching Smith. After all, he was a local Oklahoma City detective and this was his turf. The two Nebraska investigators in hot pursuit of Smith were relegated to being bystanders.

Sure enough, the tipster was right. Smith was inside the Arby's. The plainclothes Oklahoma City detective approached Smith and coaxed him to come back to the Oklahoma City Police Department. At the station, Smith signed a consent waiver letting police take a vial of his blood, plus saliva, head hairs, and pubic hairs, according to police records.

Reports, however, do not indicate Smith was ever questioned by the Nebraska detectives.

The biological specimens from Smith were handed off to Joyce Gilchrist, a crime lab technician for the Oklahoma City Police Department who later would make a name for herself in the forensic science community nationally.

If the lab samples proved a match to the crime-scene blood and DNA evidence, Bruce Smith would be tied to Helen Wilson's rape and murder. It would be a great relief to everyone to announce an arrest. The vile attack on an elderly widow had shocked the conscience of the Beatrice community. In Oklahoma, it seemed as if the weight of the world rested on the shoulders of Gilchrist, the crime lab technician.

CHAPTER 4
FBI'S KILLER PROFILE

Days before Nebraska investigators drove south to Oklahoma City two other Beatrice cops arrived at the Omaha airport to pick up a highly regarded and welcomed helper.

FBI Special Agent Pete Klismet Jr. had spent four years in the U.S. Navy, including two tours of submarine duty during the Vietnam War in the 1960s. In the 1970s, Klismet worked as a police officer in Ventura, California. He joined the FBI in 1979 and by 1985 was part of an elite group of special agents selected to receive exclusive training as behavioral profilers. Klismet

FBI Special Agent Pete Klismet, at right, is shown in this photo with former FBI Director William Sessions. Back in 1985, Klismet flew into Nebraska to come up with a detailed behavioral profile surrounding the widow's unsolved murder. There was only one perpetrator responsible for the crime: an angry white male, who was in his early twenties, Klismet determined. Photo/Pete Klismet

became the profiling coordinator for the FBI's branch covering Nebraska and Iowa. At the time he got the call in Helen Wilson's murder, Klismet worked in the FBI's bureau in Cedar Rapids, in far eastern Iowa near the Mississippi River, an area known as the Quad Cities.

By the time Klismet flew into Nebraska, the widow's perplexing murder had gone unsolved for three weeks. The befuddled police in Beatrice held out a ray of hope that Klismet's valuable insights would steer them toward the unknown killer. Once his plane landed in Omaha on February 26, the cops exchanged pleasantries. They grabbed Klismet's luggage and walked with him through the airport terminal back to their squad car. They had a one-hundred-mile drive ahead of them, plenty of time to chat in the car about the many hurdles that the investigation faced. Back in Beatrice, the FBI profiler received a warm greeting from Beatrice Police Chief Don Luckeroth. His department put Klismet up at the local Best Western hotel for two days.

The profiler met with a number of stumped investigators, including the chief. Klismet gathered up police reports and interview statements, and reviewed crime-scene photos. All of this material would be crucial toward his final behavioral analysis.

After he flew back to his office in Iowa, Klismet worked closely with the FBI's behavioral science unit in Quantico, Virginia. His final psychological profile report wouldn't be submitted to the Beatrice chief for a few months.

Obviously, the FBI profile wasn't ready a little more than a week later, by March 7, when Nebraska State Patrol Investigator Becker and Beatrice Police Lieutenant Fitzgerald were anxiously sitting around the Oklahoma City Police Department awaiting word on the serology test results from the crime lab.

Blood-type serology was considered the top scientific method at that time to solve crimes in which a perpetrator left blood, hair with follicles or semen. There are four main human blood types: A, B, AB or O. In addition, people are either classified as secretors or non-secretors depending on whether their blood type can be detected in such secretions as semen or saliva; by far, the majority of people are secretors (85 percent). People classified as non-secretors are more prone to encounter a variety of health risks, research has shown.

Wilson's rapist left plenty of semen at the crime scene. Scientific tests that had been performed earlier on the evidence by Dr. Reena Roy, a serologist for the Nebraska State Patrol's crime lab in Lincoln, revealed the killer possessed type B blood and he was a non-secretor. Only about one in ten people carried such a rare blood type at the time, according to police reports.

At 7:30 p.m. on March 7, 1985, Becker and Fitzgerald were alerted that the test results on Smith's samples were ready, and the men went to consult with the Oklahoma City crime lab. Becker summed up Gilchrist's report to them in his investigative reports:

"Lab technician Joyce Gilchrist with the Laboratory in the Oklahoma City Police Department indicated that subject Bruce Smith had Type B blood and was a secretor, which eliminates Bruce as a suspect."

Dejected, the Nebraska investigators had smacked into a brick wall on their promising lead. After all, Bruce Smith's friend in Beatrice assured police that he had dropped off Smith about two blocks away from Helen Wilson's apartment building at about 3:30 a.m., near the time of the murder. Smith was also drunk and lusting after sex, reports state. And furthermore, Smith was familiar with the victim's apartment building, given that his grandmother used to live there.

Though such circumstantial evidence against Smith was strong, the forensic science failed to match up, according to Oklahoma City's Gilchrist, and she was the crime lab's expert.

What did all this mean? It meant Bruce Smith wouldn't be coming back to Beatrice, Nebraska, in handcuffs. He would not be arrested in Helen Wilson's murder.

***

After staying overnight in Oklahoma City, Beatrice Police Lieutenant Fitzgerald took it upon himself to scrounge up Smith's suspect kit: blood samples, pubic hairs, scalp hairs, saliva, and fingerprints. On March 8, he and the Nebraska State Patrol's Becker made the frustratingly long six-hour drive back to Nebraska. Back at the Beatrice police station, their colleagues learned the bad news.

Smith's specimens were put into a climate-controlled evidence storage refrigerator for safe-keeping. They would eventually wind up in the Police Department basement, along with dozens of hair and blood vials from numerous other local suspects in the Helen Wilson case.

March 1985 came and went. No arrests appeared imminent. Still, the police detectives persevered with their interviews, and careful attention was given to every possible suspect's blood type serology.

***

By Memorial Day, about three and a half months after the killing, the FBI notified the Beatrice police chief that its behavioral profile regarding the unknown rapist-killer was available for review.

"It is requested that you keep the contents of this profile confidential, and use it only for purposes of investigative assistance," the FBI advised. "In the event you develop a suspect, or require additional information, it would be appreciated if you would contact SA Klismet in the Cedar Rapids Resident Agency."

The FBI behavioral profile was revealing. For one thing, there was no obvious reason Wilson had become a victim of violent crime, the FBI analysis said.

"It is our opinion that Helen Wilson was not the victim of opportunity, but was selected by the subject as a result of surveillance activity, possibly having seen her through the windows of her apartment from the street or having seen her go into the apartment complex," the FBI profile said. "It is also possible that the offender was known to the victim."

And there was the money situation. Wilson kept considerable cash, stocks, bonds and other money market certificates in her apartment unit. Her attacker very easily could have stolen this money. Oddly, he did not. Her apartment was not found in disarray. No drawers were ransacked by the killer. "This would all be consistent with robbery definitely not being the motive for this attack," the FBI profile theorized.

Moreover, the steak knife found at Helen Wilson's bedside came from her kitchen, and relatives assured police she never slept with a knife at her bedside for protection. She never had any reason to be deathly afraid or believe her life was in danger, the FBI concluded. "It would appear this knife was used by the subject to gain control of the victim inside her bedroom, and in the infliction of several defensive wounds on the victim."

From the FBI's perspective, Wilson's attacker had to be the same twisted young man who had terrorized other elderly women in the Beatrice community during the summer of 1983, roughly a year and a half prior. The FBI noted that those three other women all lived alone and were all within a few blocks walking distance of Wilson's apartment building. "If a circle were drawn on a map around all four residences, there would only be a distance of approximately four city blocks between any of the four residences," the FBI stated.

FBI Special Agent Pete Klismet Jr. advised police in Beatrice, Nebraska, that Helen Wilson was the target of a vicious sex crime carried out by a lone deviant young man. Her apartment was not left in disarray. Photo/Beatrice Police Department

The FBI suggested Wilson's attack could have occurred between midnight and 2:30 a.m. on February 6, 1985. The federal law enforcement agency mostly relied on the autopsy reports of Lincoln pathologist Dr. John Porterfield to reach this conclusion.

As far as the crime scene, there were only a couple of noteworthy clues, a toppled footstool and an ottoman in the living room.

"Sexual penetration after death was likely," the FBI also noted.

The FBI suggested a number of characteristics could be assumed about Helen Wilson's killer: He may live alone. He may reside close to the murder scene. He's probably unemployed. If he works, it's unskilled menial labor. He doesn't have a job that is uplifting or career-oriented. "He has a terrible self-image and is likely confused about his own sexual identity," Klismet stated in his analysis.

As for the eighteen-month gap between the last known attempted rape in August of 1983 and the rape-homicide of February 5-6, 1985, the attacker may have left town for a new job, joined the military or been busted for prowling somewhere, the FBI posited. There was a strong possibility Wilson's rapist-killer resented or hated older women, the analysis said. He probably had a terrible relationship with his own mother and was a latent homosexual. He may have endured physical abuse or psychological tormenting from his mother, a grandmother, an aunt, or some other older female relative while growing up, though not necessarily sexually, the FBI profiler predicted.

The FBI concluded that Wilson's killer would be living with his mother, an aunt, or a grandmother when he was finally identified. As part of his extensive analysis, Klismet examined and rejected a number of alternative scenarios, including the possibility that two people committed the late night break-in, rape and murder within apartment Unit 4.

"The crime appears to have been committed by one single male individual," Klismet declared. "The only contributing factor to the possibility of a second suspect would be the large amount of semen found inside the victim. However, this could also be consistent with the suspect having had intercourse with the victim on more than one occasion, indicating he spent a considerable amount of time inside the victim's apartment. Consideration in this analysis must also be given to the three previous assaults on older women in the immediate area."

Here's what else Klismet told Beatrice cops to watch for:

In all likelihood, their suspect was a white male, short or of medium height, in his early twenties. He was thin, a high school dropout who was considered a loner and viewed as odd or wimpy when he attended high school. Athletics or team sports were of no interest to him. He came from a broken home and owned a limited stash of pornography. He probably spent time at a detention facility as a juvenile or young adult. He underwent counseling and saw a psychologist after high school. He engaged in fetish burglaries or window peeping. Even if he had not been arrested for such deviant behavior, he certainly did it without being caught. He was sloppy. He dressed poorly. He had bad hygiene. If he owned a car, it was filthy on the outside and inside. It would be a beater in need of constant repairs.

Interestingly, the FBI analyst concluded that the rapist did not intend for his victim to die. Still, he had to be someone at ease with spending time inside the apartment building and the surrounding neighborhood. After all, the autopsy indicated he may have stayed an hour or longer in Unit 4. From the FBI's perspective, perhaps he was someone who used to get Wilson her groceries, fetch her mail, or take her on errands. Whoever he was, he had a well-planned escape route and exhibited no fear of being caught. In fact, the FBI stressed, the theory of two accomplices working together to terrorize Wilson did not seem plausible.

"Most significant among these reasons is the likelihood that one of the two offenders, if there were two, would probably have elected to take money," the FBI pointed out. "We can state with almost total certainty that this crime was committed acting alone."

The FBI profile validated the hard work done by the Beatrice Police Department, reinforcing that detectives were on the right track. Many of the dark and disturbing characteristics that the profile attributed to the killer pointed to someone just like Bruce Allen Smith.

Smith never finished high school. Smith spent time in a Nebraska youth jail facility. Smith came from a broken home. Smith had issues with his mother. Smith's grandmother once lived in the same apartment complex as Wilson. Smith's physical traits were a match with the FBI's profile of the unknown killer. Some police reports listed Smith as five-foot-seven, while others pegged him as tall as five-foot-eleven. Smith's weight was listed at 140 to 145 pounds.

But by now, the Beatrice police had ruled out Smith as a suspect because the Oklahoma City crime lab analyst said his blood specimen did not match the blood type of the perpetrator. Even if Smith fit the FBI profile like a glove, which it seemed he did, the Beatrice Police Department accepted the lab test results and decided to move on and pursue other suspects.

Despite the inability to make an arrest, it was hard for residents to fault their hometown detectives and hard-working police chief, Donald Luckeroth. The department was ingenious and resourceful. But nothing was falling into place. That clandestine cemetery stake-out of Wilson's gravesite over the course of three nights, using the hidden tape-recording device inside the flower bouquet, did not yield results. The killer did not show up at her grave to pay his respects, as the detectives hoped he might.

With the killer still on the loose, Beatrice residents were mystified and their small-town police force remained under the microscope. But it was not the local press or the mayor giving the Beatrice Police Department heat. "The only real pressure we had was from the daughter of the lady that was killed," Luckeroth remarked years later, referring to Janet Houseman. "And she didn't think we were doing enough."

As more time passed, the chief continued to hear an earful from Houseman. She lived in Beatrice, where she and her husband operated a dry-cleaning business. "We talked to her, and we had the FBI profile," Luckeroth said. "And they visited with her a little bit. She wasn't satisfied with what they were doing either."

Keep in mind this was 1985 – the same year that Michael J. Fox and Christopher Lloyd starred in their blockbuster movie, *Back to the Future.* But this wasn't Hollywood. This was real life. The Beatrice Police Department couldn't climb into a DeLorean and magically jump the clock forward another twenty or twenty-five years to take advantage of more sophisticated investigative tools. These small-town detectives mostly relied upon old-school investigative instincts. Crime labs were primitive compared to those with today's modern and constantly evolving technology. In 1985, it wasn't practical for detectives to crack a murder investigation thanks to cellphone records, video surveillance tapes or computer forensics. Smartphones and the Internet were years away from becoming household fixtures in American culture. And although Wilson's killer left behind considerable sperm and body hairs, the science of DNA was in its infancy and still being researched. A number of years later, DNA evidence would gain legitimacy in America's judicial system, but not in 1985.

***

As if the task of solving Wilson's senseless murder was not tough enough, the Beatrice Police Department also had stiff competition – from one of their own former detectives, who felt unappreciated by the force. Without consulting the department, he set out to pursue the murder case for his own personal satisfaction.

At 8:45 a.m. on March 3, 1985, police reports show, Norman Steinberg of Bell Street in Beatrice walked into the Police Department. He asked to speak with veteran Detective Sam Stevens, who was about fifty. At the police station, Steinberg relayed the following story:

Two days earlier, a "well groomed" young man had shown up at the home of his mother, Bessie Steinberg, age sixty-one, seeking information about the people who lived directly north of her house. "She stated that the man did show some identification but that she could not read the name through the plastic in the wallet," police reports stated. The man drove a red pickup truck and peppered her with several questions. The courteous younger man proclaimed he was investigating a recent homicide in Beatrice and "that he was directly responsible for solving the homicide in connection with the lady at Gas 'N Shop in Beatrice." Bessie Steinberg remembered the man said he was thirty-six and a former police officer who had taken up farming.

"He stated that he was investigating the homicide but requested that she not give this information to anybody about him being there because it would be a couple of days before he could get his private investigation license at which time he was going to talk to the family of Helen Wilson and then do the work on it but he had to wait until he got his license from the state," police documents state. "Mrs. Steinberg stated that she became frightened because she didn't know the gentleman."

The woman later confirmed that the young man who showed up at her doorstep went by the name of Burt Searcey. To his way of thinking, Searcey happened to be the one person residing in Gage County, Nebraska, who possessed the necessary investigative sleuthing skills to solve Wilson's murder and bring justice to her grieving family. Of course, Searcey overlooked the facts that he was not even a cop at the time and that nobody had asked for his involvement in the case.

In his mid-thirties, Burdette "Burt" Searcey was short and slender, had a full head of brown hair and a bushy mustache, and wore large eyeglasses. Searcey was known for being fidgety, and he liked to gab. During the six years or so he spent with the Beatrice Police Department, he took credit for solving one of the city's most gruesome homicides, 1980's notorious Gas 'N Shop murder.

According to Beatrice Police Department records, here's a summary of the key events surrounding that violent crime on April 13, 1980:

Shortly after 6:00 a.m., a call went out from police dispatch to check out the Gas 'N Shop. When officers arrived at the convenience store, they saw no signs of commotion or chaos. No money was stolen from the register. The on-duty cashier's purse and coat remained behind the store counter, and the woman's vehicle was parked nearby. But Joyce Wiles -- a local woman who was twenty-seven, married, with four children -- was missing. There was no sign of her anywhere, until about two weeks later when a local farmer made the grim discovery of her decomposing body. Wiles had died of multiple stab wounds to the neck, chest, and legs. Although the victim was bound, the autopsy found that Wiles had not been sexually assaulted.

At the time of the Wiles murder, Searcey was a Beatrice patrolman and one of many police officers trying to unravel the stunning crime that left the community unnerved.

As the investigation ensued, gas station customers told police about a man at the scene who had seemed angry. He had been inside the Gas 'N Shop talking to Wiles from around 3:00 a.m. until 5:00 a.m. He also promised to see Wiles later, multiple witnesses told police.

By late that April, one witness told Searcey she had seen "commotion" coming from a vehicle with a burned out taillight and loud exhaust system when she passed that particular car on the outskirts of town. Searcey showed the woman a lineup of various vehicles and even started the engines. The witness positively identified the vehicle of Sherman Warford as the one she saw around 5:30 a.m. at the intersection of Sixth and Sargent Streets, which was in proximity to the row of hedges where Wiles' slain body was dumped. Police recovered a drinking glass at the dump site. Warford's son told police his father drank from that glass on the night prior to Wiles' murder. Tests revealed the lead suspect, Sherman Warford, had an extremely rare blood type, Hh, and he was a secretor. Serology testing on the glass showed someone with Hh blood grouping, who was a secretor, had used the glass.

Warford, thirty-nine, denied any involvement. He was given a lie-detector test and failed, reports show. Initially,

Warford was charged with first-degree murder. Eventually, Warford was allowed to plead guilty to the lesser crime of manslaughter. He was released from prison in November 1986. All told, Warford served about six years of prison time for the gas clerk's kidnapping and fatal stabbing.

Despite taking enormous pride in helping clear the Gas 'N Shop murder, Searcey was displeased with his career on the Beatrice police force. He did not have faith in his superiors, including some fellow detectives. In 1982, Searcey, who then was thirty-four, resigned on a sour note. "He worked for me at the Police Department for several years," Luckeroth said years later. "He wasn't a team worker. He kind of worked for the county attorney. And we didn't get the information that we were supposed to be getting."

Searcey also made sure to let others know about his hostility toward the Beatrice Police Department when he quit the force. "When he left the department, he made the statement that it was a very poor administration," Luckeroth said. "He decided to quit and become a hog farmer. I wasn't sorry to see him go."

CHAPTER 5
THE HOG FARMER P.I.

If you grow up in remote southeastern Nebraska, your life's ambitions and career options are limited, unless you are a rare talent destined for national stardom like Daniel Whitney of tiny Pawnee City, otherwise known as celebrity comedian and actor Larry the Cable Guy.

The last fifty years have not been kind to rural Nebraska's aging smaller towns. In many places, Main Street buildings are decaying. Public schools are up against declining enrollment and the constant threat of consolidations. Young adults continue to migrate toward the state's two metropolitan cities, Omaha and Lincoln, which offer more robust economies and decent paying jobs. Proud little towns with a few hundred people may still have a Main Street watering hole, but those communities are on life support. Many former bars, cafes, and filling stations are boarded up and have weeds littering their properties. Mangy dogs roam wild.

In these parts of the Heartland, young people just don't have the same opportunities in life as their peers born near Chicago or New York City, where skyscrapers reach into the clouds and so do lofty dreams. For young people who desire to stick it out in remote pockets of rural Nebraska, career options tend to revolve around farming, public education and law enforcement. Virtually every county has its own sheriff's office, jail and government courthouse.

Burt Searcey was born in 1948 into a family with a successful grain elevator business whose area of operations overlapped between tiny Pawnee County and rural Gage County. He graduated from tiny Lewiston Consolidated High School in the 1960s. During the 1960 Census, the town of Lewiston had seventy-seven people. After high school, Searcey did not pursue college. He returned to the farm. He welded farm equipment. He scooped grain. He drove a truck. By his late twenties, Searcey managed his own grain elevator business, a nice accomplishment. But farm life tended to be monotonous. Winters on the Great Plains were downright wicked, and the swirling winds were nasty at times. It's no wonder why so many of the pioneers who passed through Beatrice during the nineteenth century hitched up their wagons again and kept moving west.

Down on the farm during the 1970s, in the days before personal computers, smartphones and the Internet, the best way to pass the time and escape the boredom was through the television set. By the mid-1970s, one of the new shows taking America by storm was *Starsky and Hutch*. A pair of adventurous police detectives busted bad guys in the darkest corners of the imaginary town of Bay City, California. Searcey found the show intriguing. He watched it regularly. He began to give serious thought to becoming a police detective just like *Starsky and Hutch*. "It just intrigued me that, hey, I think I can do that," Searcey recalled later. "I love people, and I have ability to deal with people."

With the cop show climbing in national popularity, Searcey put in his application with the Beatrice Police Department. Beatrice was the home of the Gage County Courthouse and the seat of county government. The mostly agrarian county had more than 30,000 residents during the 1930 Census, but that figure had plummeted to about 24,000 people by

1980. In 1977, Beatrice hired Searcey as a city patrol officer. Within a few quick years, he passed through the ranks, rising from patrolman to detective sergeant, the same title as his fictional TV heroes on *Starsky and Hutch*. But Searcey and his police chief, Donald Luckeroth, often butted heads. And by 1982, Searcey chose to leave the police profession altogether. He returned to a life of farming. Initially, he worked at his brother's grain elevator, court records indicate. By 1983, Searcey bought 160 acres of farmland south of Liberty, a village of seventy-five people about thirty-five miles southeast of Beatrice.

When he was a cop with a gun and a shiny badge, Searcey believed his name instilled fear in the minds and hearts of the local riffraff, court documents show. But back on the farm, Searcey was unable to live out his *Starsky and Hutch* fantasies. There were no crimes to investigate out on the farm. He was preoccupied with raising hogs, and missed the action and thrill of being a police detective.

Because he was a chatty fellow, Searcey felt at ease frequenting local bars where the beer taps flowed and cigarette smoke wafted in the air. Searcey preferred to socialize with other upstanding professionals, not those ne'er-do-wells he saw as the burnout crowd.

Many of Beatrice's street people and bottom feeders tended to hang around some of the community's lowly drinking dives. Such social undesirables kept the cops, courts, and mental health professionals busy with their never-ending litany of life's problems. Many were jobless and refused to seek out work. They tended to become drains on the public welfare system. Others bounced between apartments, often stiffing their landlord and leaving the place a deplorable mess in the process.

As a cop, Searcey encountered his share of these freeloaders around Beatrice. These lost souls tended to be high school dropouts. Many turned to drugs. They graduated into petty crime such as shoplifting, burglary and other mayhem and mischief. This lowly element gave Beatrice, an otherwise upstanding and proud community, an unnecessary blemish. Most of Beatrice's residents obeyed the laws. Many citizens were devout Christians and regular churchgoers. They owned homes. They worked steady jobs. They earned an honest day's paycheck. In contrast, the often unemployed members of the local partying crowd offered few redeeming qualities.

***

In early 1985, in the depth of winter's cold, Gage County hog farmer Searcey turned on his radio for the afternoon's commodity reports. He heard a stunning breaking news alert over the local airwaves. An elderly Beatrice woman had been murdered the previous night. In the days ahead, the tragic news of Helen Wilson's shocking homicide remained on his mind. There was something gratifying about solving a high-profile murder case as a police detective. It brought closure to the victim's family and a sense of great relief to the community. Furthermore, Searcey was hardly convinced the Beatrice Police Department was up to the challenge of tracking down the killer. His old adversaries were in charge of the murder investigation. Searcey had the utmost confidence in his investigative skills, court records state. He also had his old network of confidential informants, who roamed the streets of Beatrice. He stewed and pondered his next move. Why couldn't he achieve the glory of solving the widow's murder? Beatrice would be forever grateful. That would be an everlasting badge of tremendous honor.

But there was the one glaring problem. Obviously, Searcey no longer sported a badge. He was not a law enforcement officer, having resigned from the Beatrice Police Department in 1982. Searcey had no official capacity to conduct a murder investigation whatsoever. He had about as much right to investigate a hometown murder as the local plumber, banker or funeral home director. Moreover, he was not even a licensed private investigator.

Searcey testified years later that the slain woman's family sought him out, expressing frustration with the Beatrice Police Department. He said he believed the call came from Jan Houseman, the murder victim's daughter. "She said that if there was anything I could do to help, she would really be happy about that," Searcey said.

Despite his recollection, an official police report submitted during the 1980s indicates the reverse was the case.

"After having been made aware of Helen Wilson being related to Jan Houseman and as a result of my interest in investigation, after having been involved with the Beatrice Police Department for several years and having been a detective sergeant on that department, it was my desire to contact Mrs. Houseman and offer my services to her if desired," Searcey plainly stated.

During his days as a city cop, Searcey had regularly brought his dirty uniforms to Jan Houseman's dry-cleaning business. He developed a friendship with her that way. Jan and her husband, Wayne Houseman, were about fifteen years older than Searcey, and in 1985 the family was in shambles. The murder of their beloved mother under such sickening circumstances left the family outraged and demanding her killer be captured quickly. Desperate, the family set up a $1,000 reward through the American Charter Federal

Savings and Loan in Beatrice for information leading to the killer's arrest. They had used the money found in the murder victim's bedroom dresser to get the fund started. "Many good friends and businesses also contributed to this fund and it grew rather rapidly," Edie Wilson remembered later.

One day, Helen Wilson's children were hunkered down in the Housemans' basement in Beatrice sorting through and dividing up Helen Wilson's possessions when somebody knocked on the door. It was Burt Searcey, and he indicated he was a private detective.

"He was kind of cocky but wanted to take on the case," Edie Wilson said. "He was told that we did not have the money to pay him, but there was the reward money that was over $3,000 by now. He agreed to that. He was a former Beatrice policeman."

Years later, Dick Smith, the Gage County prosecutor at the time of Helen Wilson's slaying, remarked that as far as he knew, Searcey did not have a professional private investigator's license in 1985. So what business did Searcey have investigating the Beatrice murder?

"Good Samaritan," Dick Smith would later testify. "I don't know what you want to call him."

Obviously, it was not long before the Beatrice Police Department caught wind of the so-called Good Samaritan's tactics. Searcey was putting himself in direct competition against his former colleagues by trying to solve the Wilson murder on his own. Members of the Beatrice force were told by their superiors not to cooperate with Searcey's investigative expedition, according to court testimony. As a result, Searcey was not privy to confidential police reports, crime-scene photos, interview statements or the evidentiary clues. He lacked access to the unknown perpetrator's hair and blood samples.

What he saw as a lack of respect only ramped up his efforts to avenge the Wilson murder and solve the case himself, however. Luckily, Searcey still had a few loyal friends on the Beatrice Police Department who kept him in the loop about certain aspects of the murder probe, court transcripts show. Searcey was a congenial fellow, and he had found his access to the case through the heartbroken Wilson family members who ached for justice.

As time wore on, Searcey claimed he obtained a private investigator's license through the Nebraska Secretary of State's Office, though this is a bone of contention. No public record exists to substantiate Searcey's claim, according to court testimony. However, if Searcey sought a P.I. license around 1985, chances are it would have been granted. After all, he had more than five years of experience as a certified Nebraska cop. Furthermore, he had conducted numerous criminal investigations before he left the Beatrice Police Department in 1982.

Still, it's hard to make an arrest when your livelihood is raising hogs. If Searcey were truly serious about cracking the Wilson case, he needed to get back into Nebraska law enforcement somehow, some way.

***

Bars, barbershops, mom-and-pop cafes and high school lunchrooms are prime spots for small-town grapevines to fester and grow like crazy weeds. Local rumor mills are a great pastime, but unfortunately, they often take on a life of their own. Some people who gossip like to make up stories for the attention. Others spread rumors as fact. And gullible people usually don't question the legitimacy of information from the rumor mill because they are more concerned about being some of those in the know, in the inner circle of information.

Competent and experienced police detectives know that using the small-town rumor mill as the cornerstone for a high-stakes murder investigation poses incredible danger and enormous risk. But in 1985, Burt Searcey was no longer a professional cop and he was that kind of risk taker. He was determined to hunt down Wilson's killer, and took information where he could find it. Court records described him as totally "obsessed" with solving the widow's homicide.

Once Searcey gained the confidence of Wilson's reeling family, the rural Gage County hog farmer began to pound the pavement. He banged on doors and rang doorbells around Beatrice in search of answers. Searcey relied on his old police sources and confidential informants to steer him in the right direction. He thought he landed his first major break in April 1985, two months after the murder, when he heard from a Beatrice woman, Dee Milligan, that a local high school student knew who killed Helen Wilson, according to police reports.

Shortly after, Searcey showed up unannounced at the home of Lisa Podendorf, age seventeen. He identified himself as a private investigator probing the Wilson murder. A junior at Beatrice High School, Podendorf hung around with the local party crowd, people who indulged in heavy drinking, drugs and occasional fist fights, according to police reports. Without much prodding, she unloaded a bombshell on the eager private eye. A local partier and druggie named Ada JoAnn Taylor had confessed to her about committing the killing, she said. Taylor was in her early twenties. Podendorf was seventeen. "We got along pretty much at first," Podendorf would say later.

But their friendship faded fast. On one cold, rainy night from a couple years earlier, Taylor and her baby girl needed shelter. Podendorf said she offered to let Taylor stay at her place. "And her baby was crying, and so I was going to fix the baby a bottle of milk, and I smelled the bottle and it smelled like whiskey," Podendorf said.

According to police records, the teenager rinsed out the baby's bottle in the sink. "And I gave the baby some milk," Podendorf said. "And then before the baby went to sleep, I caught (Taylor) in the bathroom with the baby's bottle, and she was pouring whiskey in the bottle. She said that it helped the baby sleep better because she was teething." Besides being known as a fruit cake, Taylor was also vicious, the unofficial private investigator heard. Once, Podendorf said, she was sitting in a car parked near one of the downtown bars with the windows open when Taylor approached with a crazed look. "And she grabbed my arm and she rolled it up in the window," the Beatrice teenager said. "And she kept twisting it and twisting it, and she threatened me. She just said that one of these days I was going to get mine. ... I have seen her pull a knife on somebody."

Searcey was all ears. He saw Podendorf as the bedrock of his case. He trusted everything she had to say. Back in 1985, it was a common ritual for local teenagers around Beatrice to gossip and smoke cigarettes before the high school bell rang. So, according to Podendorf, it was over by Charles Park, near the Beatrice Public Library, where JoAnn Taylor gave a damning confession about her own involvement in Helen Wilson's murder, just a matter of hours after the hideous crime.

Podendorf claimed that Taylor sought her out at around 7:30 a.m. February 6 as both young women braved the extreme cold that Wednesday morning. She told Searcey they were standing across the street from the old three-story Lincoln Telephone & Telegraph building when Taylor struck up the odd conversation. "And she said, 'I know why the police cars were at the apartment building at that time.' ... She mentioned to me that they had killed her, killed this lady," Podendorf said. She claimed that Taylor proudly showed off a few claw marks across the back of her neck as proof of the deadly encounter. At first, Podendorf said, she dismissed the marks. But Taylor was emphatic. "No, me and Lobo did it," Taylor insisted, according to Podendorf .

A week later, Searcey went out and re-interviewed Podendorf . As was his customary practice, the self-employed hog farmer did not bring along a tape recorder, and no pens, pencils or notepads either. Nope. Searcey chose to make no written notes or tape recordings for both of his two interviews with the teenager. The same was true with other people he sought for interviews while probing Helen Wilson's murder in 1985. Instead, he apparently committed their conversations to memory and left it at that.

Thanks to his sources at the Beatrice police station, Searcey learned about a ripped five-dollar bill found on the carpet of Helen Wilson's apartment. Searcey chose to fixate on this clue. He gave it a much higher priority than the scientific serology reports that the Beatrice detectives were using to inch closer toward nabbing the killer. At any rate, Searcey became preoccupied with linking the torn five-dollar bill to one of Taylor's old acquaintances, a man named Joseph White, otherwise known as "Lobo." Searcey came up with the idea that White had methodically torn a piece of money stolen from Helen Wilson's purse to taunt the authorities trying to solve the senseless act of savagery. Searcey became convinced that White dropped the torn money as a crude signature. The crime scene showed Wilson probably had no more than twenty-five dollars inside her purse in the kitchen at the time she was slain.

From that point forward, Searcey made it a habit to ask his interview subjects about Joseph White's supposed trick of shredding money. "Did you ever see him do a trick that would involve tearing any bills in half?" Searcey would ask people.

When he didn't get the answer he expected, Searcey grew frustrated. He pretty much spoon-fed witnesses his desired answer. For example, during one interview with Tom Winslow of Beatrice, Searcey asked whether White ever talked about certain things that appeared on a dollar. Did White ever do a trick in which he would ask the crowd at parties to identify a president, a movie star and then tear the money in front of everyone's eyes?

"Not that I can recollect," Winslow answered.

"But you have seen him tear money in half?" Searcey pressed.

"I seen him tear money in half," Winslow agreed. "He always would stick it in his pocket."

However, Joe Gertisen, operator of the R&S Bar, told Searcey he never saw White actually tear up five-dollar bills in his presence. White was a daily regular at the bar. "However, (Gertisen) is always ending up with numerous halves of dollar bills in his cash drawer," Searcey stated. "Due to the circumstances that he was obtaining numerous torn bills, he then advised his waitresses not to take any more halves of dollars from patrons."

Searcey was vigorously pursuing his own leads on his personal quest to crack the Helen Wilson murder case. He was up against his old nemesis, Sam Stevens, the veteran Beatrice Police Department detective. Decades later, Luckeroth would say he did not regret his decision to hand over the reins of the murder case to Stevens. Since the City of Beatrice had a small force, barely twenty officers, the chief did not have many options to solve the killing. The chief considered Stevens an average detective who brought other positive attributes to the department. "Well, he did a lot of digging," Luckeroth remarked. "But he was kind of the Police Department chaplain."

Sometimes one of those traits, Stevens' desire to minister to criminals, made the chief shake his head. "And he kind of felt sorry for some of these people. And once in a while, he'd promise them something," Luckeroth remembered. "I said (to Sam) 'You can't promise them people anything. The county attorney's the one that's got to deal with that.'"

***

Ralph Al Stevens was born in 1934 in Pennsylvania. After high school, he served overseas in the Air Force, including a stint in Okinawa, where he became an expert at fixing air-conditioning units, documents show. After the Air Force, Stevens settled in the nation's Heartland. His wife came from Wymore, Nebraska, population 2,000 at the time. Wymore was only about a fifteen-minute drive from Beatrice, where Stevens, who went by the name "Sam," chose to put down his roots.

In the 1960s, Beatrice was a stable, nice place to be. The city of 12,000 was dominated by an agricultural-based economy, like most of rural Nebraska. The city's downtown featured a number of retail storefronts, and Nebraskans were friendly, easygoing and polite. At first, Stevens worked as a gas station attendant in that bygone era when full-service attendants pumped your gas, checked your tire pressure and washed your automobile's windows before sending you on your way. Later, Stevens erected and repaired bridges and roads with Gage County's highway maintenance crew.

By 1965, Stevens had found his calling and would spend the next thirty-two years with the Beatrice Police Department. In time, thanks to hard work and perseverance, Stevens was elevated from patrolman to sergeant, then to lieutenant and detective sergeant.

During the late 1970s, a new officer came to the force and later became a source of great tension. About fifteen years younger than Sam Stevens, Burt Searcey was self-confident, ambitious and cocky. Like the chief, Stevens also was not overly sad when Searcey resigned during the summer of 1982 to be a hog farmer. "I think he wasn't making the moves that he wanted on the Police Department," Stevens said.

Even though Searcey made it a point to burn his bridges with the police administration when he left in 1982, he had the audacity to reapply as a Beatrice police officer in 1984. At the time, the city's police commission handled the application process. In turn, members sought input from the veteran chief on whether to rehire Searcey. "I did visit with them, and they said, 'Can you work with him?'" Luckeroth remembered. "And I said, 'Well, I can work with him, but he doesn't work well with the department.'"

Searcey's 1984 application to rejoin the Beatrice police force was rejected. The next year, Helen Wilson was murdered. Stevens and his chief never imagined in their wildest dreams that the former disgruntled colleague would steal their thunder and crack the case. Then again, they were in

72

total darkness about the hog farmer/snooping investigator's unwavering faith and dependence on Lisa Podendorf, the teenage informant who despised JoAnn Taylor.

Searcey kept his investigative leads to himself. There is no evidence to substantiate Searcey's later claims that he passed along Podendorf's information to the Beatrice Police Department.

In 1985, farmer Burt Searcey began advising people around Beatrice that he was a private investigator trying to solve the Helen Wilson murder case. He believed this ripped five-dollar bill left near the door of the murder victim served as the killer's crude signature. Photo/Beatrice Police Department

CHAPTER 6
JOANN'S SAGA

Even before she became entangled in Burt Searcey's murder theory, JoAnn Taylor sensed her life was predestined for doom and gloom because her mother had a brush with the Grim Reaper at age fifteen. JoAnn claimed her mother was actually pronounced dead on a hospital gurney a few years before her birth – only to spring back to life.

"They had everything filled out on her death certificate except the doctor's John Hancock, and they turned around to put the white sheet over her head, and she pulled off the sheet and said, 'No you don't,'" Taylor would later relate. "And she said she scared everybody in that room, which it would. If you had been working over a person's body for two or three hours and you put the sheet over them and they look at you and talk to you, you are going to freak."

***

Ada JoAnn (nee Ledford) Taylor was born to teenage parents on July 30, 1963, in Asheville, North Carolina. Her mother was eighteen. Her biological father of the same age was supposedly related to country music legend Randy Travis and famous NASCAR Winston Cup champion Cale Yarborough, documents indicate. JoAnn's birth father was not destined for fame. He was an alcoholic low-life and a habitual criminal. Before JoAnn was born, he went to prison for killing someone, according to court records. When she was a baby, her teen mother married a thirty-four-year-old man who drove an oil delivery truck. JoAnn said she fell out of her stepfather's truck numerous times as a child.

Home life in North Carolina was rough and tough. Her mother and stepfather constantly quarreled. JoAnn watched their fights through a hole in the sheetrock of her bedroom wall. There were also allegations of incest within the family, court records reflect. When JoAnn was five years old, her parents separated after her half-brother was born. JoAnn and her mother moved to Jacksonville, Florida, only to return to North Carolina some months later.

As a young child, JoAnn grew accustomed to dysfunction. She bounced back and forth between living with her mother and stepfather, who later divorced. When she was in third grade, she returned to live with her mother, who had since remarried. Back in Florida, JoAnn grew up around motorcycle bikers and outlaws. Years later, according to court testimony, she claimed she was subjected to prolonged sexual abuse by her new stepfather, starting at age nine, when JoAnn's mother was not home. When JoAnn complained, her mother accosted her and accused her of enticing her stepfather, court documents show.

However, the abuse JoAnn endured was not just sexual. When she washed dishes, her volatile stepfather in Florida screamed at her and forced her to re-wash all the dishes if he saw that she had missed any food. The family lived in squalor in a dingy, two-bedroom trailer home. As time went on, the abuse escalated. Beatings from her mother "left fist prints on my face as a kid," Taylor later testified. She speculated that she endured regular beatings because she was the only the girl and never really fit into her family. Her mother bore two sons during the early 1970s.

JoAnn longed for a means of escape to take her mind off her miserable childhood. And she found that outlet through an imaginary twin sister whom she named Joleen. Taylor later testified that she regularly heard voices from her invisible twin sister and the two of them talked often. "It was just like she was always there," Taylor said.

***

When JoAnn was about eleven, people at the Baptist church where she sang in the choir noticed numerous purple bruises on her arms, legs and back. Church officials spoke with Department of Family Services representatives, and the adolescent girl was placed into foster care. At first, JoAnn was angry to be yanked away from her mother. "Deep down, I loved my mom."

At thirteen, she quit school after seventh grade. In time, she returned to her family roots around Asheville and stayed with her grandmother. There, she learned about auto mechanics from her step-grandfather. At fourteen, she met a young man at a local roller skating rink. They had one thing in common: Both liked to shoot pool. After a brief courtship, the boyfriend proposed and, within a matter of days, she and William Chris Taylor drove across state lines and arrived in upstate South Carolina. At fourteen, JoAnn should have been in eighth grade like other girls her age. Instead, she was in Greenville, professing her love to a twenty-year-old future convict – in front of the same justice of the peace who presided over the weddings of JoAnn's mother and before that, JoAnn's grandmother, records show.

The young newlyweds moved into a trailer home in High Shoals, North Carolina. The trailer was crowded and a constant source of upheaval. JoAnn's brother-in-law and sister-in-law also shared the cramped quarters. Shortly afterward, her mother-in-law went berserk when she found out JoAnn was only fourteen, and not seventeen, as the woman had presumed. In time, the newlyweds got their own trailer, but it was also packed. A male friend of JoAnn's husband had permission to move in, and, if that was not bad enough, her domineering mother-in-law visited daily. The woman was a religious zealot and a control freak, records reflect. The woman vehemently opposed her son and JoAnn going roller skating or watching movies. It seemed JoAnn could not escape her mother-in-law's control. JoAnn became a textile worker at a local sock factory where her mother-in-law also worked. The two women rode to work daily.

By sixteen, her life in North Carolina was going nowhere fast. Cigarettes became a three-pack-a-day habit for the next decade of her dreadful life. JoAnn's was not a fairy tale marriage. Her husband turned abusive and beat her. The turbulent marriage crumbled when her husband went to prison for attempting to rape a thirteen-year-old girl, according to court records.

With her marriage in chaos, JoAnn sought to reunite with her mother. By now, her mother had moved to New York, not far from Lake Ontario. The reunion was good while it lasted. JoAnn re-enrolled in school, earning mostly Bs and Cs as she finished eighth grade at Sodus Central High School. But she was not happy in New York. Severe depression drove her to slit her wrists during two suicide attempts, according to court documents, and JoAnn underwent a ninety-day voluntary committal to the Rochester Psychiatric Center. There, she befriended an auxiliary police officer with whom she became intimate and soon found herself pregnant. Upon her discharge from the psychiatric ward, JoAnn moved to Williamson, another smaller community in upstate New York. She lived with her new twenty-three-year-old suitor and his family. Unfortunately, JoAnn's dreams of a second shot at marriage were dashed. The young man who got her pregnant had failed to obtain a divorce from his current wife, according to court documents. By the same token, JoAnn was still legally married to a prison convict named Taylor serving hard time back in North Carolina.

Sixteen years old and pregnant, JoAnn found refuge at the Our Lady of Victory Maternity Home in Buffalo, New York. She stayed there for several months, but just before giving birth, she got the itch to move. She relocated to Shreveport, Louisiana, where her mother lived.

In May of 1980, two months shy of turning seventeen, JoAnn delivered a son. Unfortunately, more severe psychiatric problems quickly kicked in. Hospital staff suspected that JoAnn had tried to scald her baby in the neonatal care unit, according to court documents. JoAnn was transferred to the psychiatric ward at Shreveport University Hospital, and her mother took custody of the baby. Upon her release from the hospital, JoAnn moved in with her mother and became preoccupied with finalizing her divorce from her imprisoned husband. She also sank into a deep depression. Whenever her mother called out for her, JoAnn blurted out, "JoAnn is dead!"

Inevitably, JoAnn's mood improved thanks to a newfound love just across the state line in tiny DeBerry, Texas. JoAnn moved to her new sixteen-year-old boyfriend's family farm, court records show. She liked farm life. She helped with chores. She and the new boyfriend soon got engaged, and JoAnn became pregnant again. Then, their relationship collapsed. After the break-up, the pregnant teenager returned to Shreveport, Louisiana, to live in another maternity home. By November 1981, JoAnn's ex-fiance tried to rekindle their relationship. He urged her to move with him to his sister's house in the far southeastern corner of Nebraska.

And that's how JoAnn Taylor, age eighteen, ended up in Beatrice – for the first time, anyhow.

***

Not long after her arrival in Beatrice, JoAnn Taylor's teenage suitor from Texas dumped her for a sixteen-year-old girl who lived thirty miles away in Fairbury, Nebraska. Ultimately, tensions flared one night inside the R&S Bar in downtown Beatrice. Taylor and her estranged lover got into an explosive argument. Another man intervened and came to her rescue. In response, Taylor fell madly in love with her new admirer and moved into his place. However, he left for California by the time she bore her second child, a daughter she named Rachel Leigh, in 1982.

After her daughter's birth, Taylor's life spiraled out of control. She became a heavy drinker. She used prescription drugs including "Yellow Jackets" and other "downers," smoked marijuana, and snorted cocaine, according to police reports. Sometimes she ingested purple microdot LSD laced with PCP, also called "angel dust." Illicit and powerful mind-altering drugs unleashed Taylor's wild side. She began dealing Yellow Jackets to fellow burnouts around Beatrice – people with no real purpose, just aimless drifters.

It wasn't long before her escalating problems with drugs and excessive out-of-control drinking drew the attention of police, Gage County's judicial system and the Blue Valley Mental Health Center in Beatrice. Social service officials took temporary custody of Taylor's young daughter after people in town suspected the little girl was bruised and malnourished, according to court transcripts. Meantime, Taylor started counseling sessions at the Blue Valley Mental Health Center.

She was diagnosed with a borderline personality, which meant she was highly emotionally unstable and could turn explosive and chaotic in a flash. She was put on Mellaril, an anti-psychotic medication for treatment of schizophrenia. Her life remained on the brink of disaster, but her love of her daughter, Rachel, boosted her spirits and kept her going. But the happiness did not last. Gage County's judges found Taylor an unfit parent. Rachel was placed into Nebraska's foster care system. Both of Taylor's children, a son and daughter, had been taken away from her.

After the courts removed her daughter, Taylor struck up a romance with an unemployed redhead in his mid-twenties named Clifford Shelden. He saw her as a lucky catch. Now twenty, Taylor stood about five-foot-seven, medium build, with long, straight dark hair and dark beady eyes. At the time of their romance, they shared a cheap upstairs apartment along with several other burnouts trying to skate by in Beatrice. Shelden had intentions of marrying her and bringing her back to Montana, where his relatives had property, reports state. Taylor, on the other hand, had reservations. She realized nuptials were not right with this man. She refused to marry Shelden, which made him angry and revengeful. Meanwhile, Taylor resumed her education. She enrolled in Beatrice as high school sophomore even though she was already twenty. Sharing lockers and lunch tables with fourteen- and fifteen-year-olds proved too difficult. After giving the Beatrice high school a try, she quickly dropped out.

With more free time on her hands, Taylor started attending regular psychotherapy sessions at Blue Valley. There, she became a patient of Wayne Price, the facility's clinical director. The sessions apparently unleashed her sense of adventure. With her parental rights revoked and no immediate hope on the horizon for a better life in Beatrice, Taylor soon hit the road again.

On March 10, 1983, Nebraska's Blue Valley Mental Health Center responded to request for information from the Clearfield Job Corps Center in Utah regarding former Beatrice patient, JoAnn Taylor. Here's an excerpt of the correspondence sent to health services director, Dr. Alexander Neil:

"JoAnn was initially referred by the Gage County Department of Welfare and her attorney due to an allegation of child abuse. At the time she was seen a history was obtained which indicated a long-term experience with being the recipient of emotional, physical and sexual abuse and a history of disrupted relationships with male persons in her life. She further gave a history of two suicidal attempts the latest being in 1977 following a verbal assault and rejection by her mother."

The Blue Valley Mental Health Center's director, Price, advised Utah's clinicians that Taylor exhibited signs of severe borderline personality, but with psychotherapy she had improved.

"At times her thinking would become rather bizarre and she had difficulty with blow ups. At the time of the blowups she does become quite irrational and explosive both verbally and physically ... JoAnn seems to have little loyalty to others. She is very pleasure seeking and excitement seeking and has lived a very dissocial lifestyle. She does however show a significant degree of potential when she is able to control her extreme emotional outbursts and her marked impulsivity."

Sincerely,

Wayne R. Price, Ph. D.
Clinical Director

***

JoAnn Taylor did not remain in Utah for long. She moved to Boulder, Colorado, where she found work baby-sitting for a female stripper, according to court transcripts. From Colorado, it was on to Hollywood, California. Taylor became a stripper at a gentleman's club in Los Angeles called Coco's Bar, police reports show. Though she made decent money prancing as an exotic dancer and also modeling, she blew through most of her earnings on cocaine and Valium, court records show. Her indulgence in drugs led to a scary near-death experience. On one occasion, she overdosed, but someone quickly revived her with an antidote.

In Los Angeles, Taylor shared an apartment with two friendly young men around the same age as she. They were aspiring nude models in the pornography industry whose real names were Joseph Edgar White and Mark Goodson, but most people called them by their stage names. White starred as "Lone Wolf Bronson," and many friends simply called him "Lobo" or "Snake." Goodson was known as "Skull" and "Widowmaker." White hailed from Cullman, Alabama. He stood six-foot-three with long, wavy dark hair. He barely weighed 160 pounds. Goodson was tall, slender and handsome. He wore glasses and had blond wavy hair. He also had a prior arrest for male prostitution in Nevada, according to police reports.

In L.A., Taylor stuck close to the two male models. One night in Los Angeles when she was heavily intoxicated, she grew hysterical and kicked a Los Angeles police officer in the genitals as he tried arresting her for disorderly conduct. Goodson was also arrested during that incident, police reports state. In 1984, Taylor, now twenty-one, had had enough of the Hollywood Boulevard scene. She took on a new obsession in life: regaining custody of her daughter, Rachel, who was 1,500 miles away in Beatrice, Nebraska.

Taylor shared news of her grand plan with her roommates, White and Goodson, the pair of aspiring X-rated movie actors offered to help. According to court transcripts, White had come into possession of a stolen credit card belonging to a California man in his mid-forties. The three Hollywood misfits used this stolen credit card to purchase one-way airline tickets to Lincoln, Nebraska, transcripts show.

Of all her ill-fated decisions, Taylor's return to Beatrice would take her life on a detour she never, ever, could have fathomed. In the process, she forever changed the life of Joseph White as well.

CHAPTER 7
BACK IN NEBRASKA

On October 12, 1984, a fair-skinned young woman with long dark hair was seen hanging around the Holiday Inn in Lincoln, Nebraska, acting seductively. Beside her was a slender, blond young man with glasses. Another man was armed with a hand-held movie camera. The Lincoln Police Department was called to investigate this unusual activity. After all, the Holiday Inn on Cornhusker Highway wasn't accustomed to being the setting for low-budget pornographic flicks.

Upon arrival, the police officers identified two of the three "filmmakers" as JoAnn Taylor, age twenty-one, and Mark ("Widowmaker") Goodson, age nineteen. The third person furnished identification claiming to be Kindred Ferguson, age forty-five, of Los Angeles, according to police reports. (Unbeknownst to police, Ferguson was the person whose credit card was purportedly stolen back in California.) Anyway, the two men and Taylor did not hide the fact they were at the Holiday Inn producing pornography; they identified themselves as being photo artists who were on their way to Beatrice, reports state. Nobody was arrested that day, but the X-rated filming inside the family-oriented hotel quickly ceased.

Indeed, Taylor was back in Nebraska for the second time in her life. But her efforts to regain custody of her daughter remained murky. In October 1984, Gage County Judge Steven Timm ordered Taylor to undergo more psychological treatment at Blue Valley, where she was previously a patient. She resumed her one-on-one therapy sessions with psychologist Wayne Price. His reports for the courts reflected on the progress, or lack thereof, of Taylor's resumed therapy sessions.

"JoAnn came in much more appropriately dressed, was not wearing her sexually oriented clothing, trying to be more domestic, baking, doing handiwork. Has a new boyfriend and is currently claiming to be pregnant ... She claimed this approximately a year ago before she left for the carnival and indicated that she had miscarried. Had been arrested again, had a fight with a friend, apparently has resolved this. Again told her very clearly and directly about her involvements and the ramifications and consequences of her behavior ... It was also made clear to her that I would not tolerate her being abusive to the staff at the mental health center and she indicated that she would do better. Will see what transpires. Return in two weeks."

– Wayne R. Price, Ph.D., Clinical Psychologist, Nov. 15, 1984.

But Taylor's delusional behavior intensified. Soon, she began spreading preposterous rumors around Beatrice about Joseph White.

"There was a rumor floating around she claimed I was her father," White explained years later. "Only she was just about the same age I was. She had spent several years in California from what I understood or a year or so when I met her out there. But she said she had a two-year-old daughter that they were trying to take away from her in Beatrice. And we came back to Beatrice to see if we could get her kid back for her."

Sam Stevens, the Beatrice police detective, remembered that Taylor and Joseph White were flat broke. They had practically nothing but the clothes on their backs when they dropped into Beatrice in late 1984. "I understand that Joseph was a stripper in California or somewhere," Stevens said. "Somewhere along the line, he picked JoAnn up. She had a kid. I know JoAnn was on drugs. She told me she was on drugs numerous times. She told me she carried weapons, and I believed her. And she was a fighter. She loved to fight. And she loved to drink. And she loved her drugs."

Over the next few months, the Beatrice Police Department dealt with enough police calls involving Taylor to produce several episodes of *The Jerry Springer Show*.

In late October 1984, Taylor threatened to strangle Goodson and declared he would be dead by morning. After he broke free from her chokehold, Goodson called police. He implored the cops to charge Taylor with attempted murder. The police told Goodson they had not witnessed the purported attack. Besides, Goodson was not even injured. Instead, officers gave Taylor a stern lecture not to threaten Goodson anymore.

Within a couple of days, police were summoned to a Beatrice front yard. There, officers found a rope hanging from a large tree and a chair underneath. Taylor's most recent ex-boyfriend, Clifford Shelden, was contemplating suicide, reports state. Shelden told the officers that he longed to marry her, but she was refusing, police reports state. That day, the officers talked Shelden out of hanging himself from the tree.

In mid-November, Taylor accused Mark Goodson of sleeping around with other women. He denied the accusation and threatened to tell the public welfare office that Taylor got pregnant by prostituting herself in California. Taylor exploded like a volcano. She lunged at Goodson's head and tried to choke him again, but he escaped her clutch. When someone at the home called the police, Taylor attacked that woman, kicking her and clawing at her chest. Then Taylor ran out the door just before police arrived. Hours later, Taylor was enraged to find out that Goodson had filed a formal police report accusing her of assault. "You're a dead man," she hollered. "You're a son of a bitch."

Police ordered Taylor to calm down numerous times. This only made her more ornery. "You dumb son of a bitch," she told one of the officers. "You're always standing up for the wrong people. Here I am a pregnant woman getting hit and beat up and nothing is being done about it."

Enough was enough. Two officers grabbed Taylor and put her in handcuffs. They moved her into a holding cell, booking her on suspicion of disorderly conduct. In the sobering confines of the jail cell, she cooled off and regained her composure.

***

In her earlier days in Beatrice, Taylor had become acquainted with a troubled soul named Tom Winslow. The two met during her short-lived attempt at resurrecting her high school experience. He lived on Ella Street, near a grocery store. Like Taylor, Winslow struggled with mental illness. He, too, underwent psychiatric therapy sessions at the Blue Valley facility in Beatrice, according to court records. During the 1980s, Winslow dropped out of high school and found work at a convalescent home. He dated a local girl named Beth "Bethy" Johnson. In 1984, Winslow and Joseph "Lobo" White became roommates, and the two men engaged in sexual experimentation. Once, Winslow's girlfriend walked in on Winslow and White having sex, police reports state. The two young men persuaded her to join in a threesome and she obliged.

Aside from that pursuit of physical pleasure, Winslow's life was anything but fun, though he did have a car. Since many of his friends were broke and jobless, Winslow occasionally gave people a lift or let them borrow his 1973 Oldsmobile, a green two-door with a beige top. These downtrodden friends often shared their tales of woe and despair over beer pitchers and shots of hard liquor at the R&S Bar in downtown Beatrice. The place became a haven for the community's troubled souls. Shortly after landing in town from California, Joseph White became one of the bar's most loyal patrons, though he was not reliable about paying his tab.

***

Taylor took up refuge briefly at Winslow's apartment, but he kicked her out before Thanksgiving 1984. He even went so far as to notify the Beatrice police that problems were imminent if Taylor tried to retrieve her belongings. Days later, more melodramatics ensued. The police were notified that Taylor and her ex-boyfriend Clifford Shelden had gotten into another heated argument and Shelden had tried to overdose, swallowing twenty-five aspirins. When police arrived, he was coherent. A couple of friends agreed to monitor him that night at their apartment, and the police left.

The police continued to be slammed with calls involving Taylor's crew. In December 1984, another domestic quarrel involving Shelden and Taylor prompted a police response. Officers made sure Shelden hauled his clothes and personal belongings out of Taylor's apartment. As police stood nearby, tempers flared as the ex-lovers bickered over ten dollars he supposedly owed her. Shelden insisted he was broke. He promised Taylor he was leaving Beatrice for good. Nobody was arrested that day, according to reports.

As 1984 drew to a close, the twenty-one-year-old Taylor had a new younger boyfriend, Jon Darren "Jon D" Munstermann, age seventeen. His long brown hair dangled past his shoulders, and he had a beard and mustache. By now, Taylor shared a downtown apartment loft with a mentally disturbed woman named Charlotte Mendenhall-Bishop, age twenty-nine. Taylor's troublesome ex-boyfriend, Clifford Shelden, also was staying there.

On New Year's Eve, a fight erupted after a night of hard drinking. Shortly after midnight, Charlotte Mendenhall-Bishop wandered into the Beatrice police station sporting a swollen black eye. She claimed Taylor and another woman had beaten her up. Officers converged on the apartment and ordered Taylor and Shelden to leave. Despite suffering a black eye, Mendenhall-Bishop declined to press criminal charges. A week later, a woman alerted the police that Taylor had continued hanging around Bishop-Mendenhall's upstairs apartment unit and was threatening to beat up all redheads, reports show. Days later, the same woman called police again. Now, Taylor was blurting out derogatory names and warning the woman she'd better watch who she squeals on.

By the end of January 1985, the landlord requested that police officers be on standby as he evicted several people from his Ella Street rental property. There, Taylor and her new teenage boyfriend were told by police to leave the building at once. Taylor grew belligerent as the Beatrice cops gave her fifteen minutes to pack up her belongings.

"That's OK," she roared at police. "You guys quit fucking with me because I have a gun coming and next week I'm going to blow through everyone in town."

The police officers brushed off her threats and did not take her seriously. In any event, Taylor and Munstermann were evicted. Meanwhile, Charlotte Mendenhall-Bishop and her new freeloading boyfriend, Shelden, got to stay. However, the angry landlord warned Shelden he had one week to find a new place to live since he was not paying any rent.

Finally, on the morning of February 5, 1985, the landlord who already booted Taylor out of the apartment once before was ready to blow a gasket. He discovered she had sneaked back and was staying there against his orders. This time, the fed up landlord did not just remove Taylor. He also evicted Mendenhall-Bishop. Once Beatrice police officers arrived, both women begrudgingly left the Ella Street apartment rather than risk jail time.

Later that afternoon, a group of local troublemakers gathered outside the home of Kathy Bartak, who lived with her down-on-his-luck boyfriend, James Dean. There was yelling and commotion. People were taunting Taylor and her teenage lover, Munstermann, to step outside. By now, the couple was engaged, though the engagement would not last. Police cars arrived and defused tensions. Three young men and one woman left the area at once. No arrests were necessary.

That same night, Helen Wilson, age sixty-eight, was raped, sodomized and suffocated to death inside her second-floor apartment at 212 N. Sixth St.

CHAPTER 8
THE NON-SECRETOR

Following the Wilson homicide, the Beatrice police asked newspaper delivery carrier Earl Crome if he had spotted anyone suspicious wandering the downtown area that day. Crome usually began his downtown delivery route around 4:15 a.m.

"Earl stated he saw nobody, emphasizing nobody, out walking around when he was dropping off papers and that the only vehicle he did see was the one I was driving at the time .... This would be one of the new unmarked police cars which was operated on the morning of 2-6-1985 by Lieutenant (Bill) Fitzgerald," a police report stated.

Despite having little to go on, the city police detectives had noteworthy clues to narrow their focus at Helen Wilson's apartment. "The jamb next to the door appeared to be pried away from the door so something could be slipped through," Police Chief Luckeroth announced at a press conference.

The *Beatrice Daily Sun* newspaper also reported in its February 7, 1985, edition that Wilson's hands had been bound and there was an overturned footstool near her body. "But there was not a lot of damage to the apartment," the chief was quoted as saying. Obviously, the most critical lead came after the autopsy. Serology testing revealed the rapist-killer had a type B blood and was a non-secretor. "I guess the non-secretor part of it was the catch," remembered Stevens, the original lead detective. Stevens knew the rare blood type was an important distinction to track the killer's identity.

Within a month of the murder, the town's rumor mill was in full swing and the loons were out in force. There were all kinds of crazy stories suggesting who killed Wilson. On March 2, JoAnn Taylor's ex-boyfriend, Mark Goodson, wandered into the Beatrice police station. He demanded to speak with an officer. Officer Alan Baldwin, who later became a police chief in Cozad and Seward, Nebraska, interviewed him. The cops were well aware of Goodson and Taylor's volatile relationship. This time, Goodson claimed Taylor had just confessed over the phone to murdering Wilson. Around 3:30 p.m., Goodson said he used a pay phone at the local supermarket to call Taylor, who was now back in High Shoals, North Carolina, with a former husband. Officer Baldwin asked whether Taylor had implicated anybody else in the murder besides herself. "Her brother, Joseph Edgar White, otherwise known as Lobo," Goodson remarked.

Baldwin passed along the information to other lead detectives, including Sam Stevens. In turn, Stevens shrugged off the notion that Taylor killed Wilson. "I had really no reason to be looking at women for anything to do with this rape, other than for information," Stevens explained.

Besides, as a long-time local police detective, Stevens knew Taylor was unreliable. Hardly anything she ever said was true. She could never be trusted as a witness or a confidential informant. "You couldn't talk to JoAnn," Stevens remarked. "She would change her stories during the conversation. I just could never make heads or tails out of JoAnn."

***

In the months before the Wilson homicide, Joseph White, age twenty two, was trying to get his life in gear. The scruffy, brown-haired beanpole had been going with a woman named Linda who lived behind a grocery store in Beatrice. But the romance soured and White was kicked out of his girlfriend's apartment in December of 1984. With nowhere else to go, White approached Kathy Gonzalez. She was a mutual friend of White's and his former girlfriend, Linda. Gonzalez, a gentle, kind-hearted woman, felt sorry for White, court transcripts show. After all, it was dangerous for anyone to be homeless during the dead of winter in Nebraska. "He asked if he could stay with me a couple of days so he could get cleaned up and look for a job," Gonzalez said.

Gonzalez happened to live in the third-floor apartment directly above Helen Wilson's apartment, Unit 4. In January of 1985, the recently married woman agreed to let White stay at her apartment. "She wasn't living with her husband. They were in the process of getting a divorce," White told detective Stevens, court records show. "As I understood it, it was a situation of a marriage to keep an illegal alien in the country."

However, White didn't repay Gonzalez with the same graciousness she exhibited by taking him off the street. He turned into a loafer. His personal hygiene nose-dived. He went several days without taking a bath or shower. "I mean, he never took a bath, and when I saw him after Linda had kicked him out, he smelled pretty bad, and I kind of hinted around that he should take a bath and he wouldn't," Gonzalez said.

One day, she and White walked to the nearby supermarket to get White's food stamps. "And on the way back, he said something to the effect that he knew that I was pretty broke and would I like to make some money by helping him rip somebody off?" Gonzalez recalled. "And I said, 'No!'"

After a few more days, Gonzalez could not take it any longer. His body odor was the problem. White agreed to find somewhere else to stay, Gonzalez remembered. White was typical of her inner circle of friends: dirt poor, no automobile, and no savings account. He was just trying to skate by and keep his head above water in life. During those short few months she knew White, Gonzalez recalled he acted macho and carried a switchblade. "He used to say that he was black-balled by the Mafia," Gonzalez told authorities. "Now, I don't know any Mafia members, but I always heard they kind of put them in the bottom of the ocean or something when they didn't want them in the Mafia anymore."

Gonzalez ordered White to leave her apartment. "I don't remember seeing him after that," she said.

***

When the senseless murder of Helen Wilson rattled the town about six weeks later Beatrice residents gobbled up details in their local newspapers, the *Beatrice Daily Sun* and the *Lincoln Journal,* the state capital's former afternoon newspaper.

White's drinking tab continued to balloon. As White swigged his liquor, he listened as the regulars spouted out their cockamamie theories about the murder. Since White did not subscribe to a newspaper or follow the local news on the radio or TV, he was stunned upon learning of the horrendous crime and shocked as bar patrons recited their laundry list of people who might be the widow's notorious killer. Some of the drunkards mentioned White's name.

"I didn't even know anything about it except that I was told on the street that her son had found her," White later told authorities. "And it was the gossip at the R&S Bar."

The skinny Alabama native in his early twenties knew he had a military ID card in his jeans pocket. Perhaps the information on this item could disprove any suggestion he'd been involved in the violent rape and murder, White thought.

CHAPTER 9
JOSEPH'S TALE

Joseph Edgar White grew up around Cullman, Alabama, a coal-mining region in the Deep South settled during the 1870s by a German refugee who was a military colonel, according to city historical records. Summers in Cullman, a city of 13,000, were unbearably hot and humid. Cullman sits along Interstate 64, about fifty miles from Birmingham.

As a youth, White had a normal childhood, the second oldest of six siblings, court transcripts show. He was definitely an average Joe during his formative years at Holly Pond High School, the small school district he attended on the outskirts of Cullman. His academic transcripts show the word "average" was checked a lot regarding his reliability, courtesy, ability to get along with fellow pupils, behavior, and cooperativeness. As a senior, White earned C's in trigonometry, A's in government/economics, a D and a B-minus in chemistry. He also performed average to slightly below average in English and typing, classes that did not record letter grades. During his senior year, he earned one checkmark labeled "good" – for attendance. His main blemish on his final report card was a mark of "poor" for leadership.

On May 25, 1981, White was ranked thirty-first out of seventy-two graduating seniors. At age eighteen, he was tall though skinny as a wooden plank. After high school, White proudly served his country for three years in the U.S. Army, including a tour of overseas duty in Korea. According to court transcripts, Private First Class Joseph White received a special letter of appreciation in August of 1982 from his commanding officer, Ralph P. Steen Jr., while White was serving in Company A, 304th Signal Battalion (Corps.)

"Your hard work has not gone unnoticed and has played a critical role in the unit's successful completion of all major field training exercises and commitments ... It has been a privilege and pleasure to be your commander. Many thanks for a job well done."

White's stint in the U.S. Army was not all glowing, however. He was ousted from the Army as a result of alcohol-related problems, court transcripts show, but overall White still drew an honorable discharge from the service. From there, he decided to hitchhike his way across the country. He wound up in Los Angeles, on Hollywood Boulevard, where he worked as a nude model, court transcripts show. There he met JoAnn Taylor, formerly of Nebraska, and the two struck up a friendship.

His decision to follow Taylor back to Beatrice in the fall of 1984 changed the course of his life. While there, White was quite the lady's man. He had several different girlfriends and later insisted he only experimented in bisexuality on one occasion, with his former roommate, Tom Winslow. Any criminal offenses investigated by the Beatrice Police Department involving White were of a petty nature. One such crime occurred around 12:45 a.m. on December 22, 1984. An older woman who lived in the 700 block of South Third Street alerted police that a young man had tried to kick in her door. White, who was walking in the area, was arrested on suspicion of disorderly conduct and malicious mischief, a pair of misdemeanors, police records show.

***

About two months later, after hearing the wild suspicions of local bar patrons, White marched straight into the Beatrice police station on a cold February day. When he found Detective Stevens' office, he waltzed right inside.

"He heard that I was looking for him," Stevens recalled later. "And I said, well, we needed to talk about some blood, take some blood tests."

As the lead detective in the Wilson homicide, Stevens already knew the Nebraska State Patrol's crime lab had determined the elusive rapist-killer possessed type B blood and was a non-secretor. White's military ID card showed he had type O blood. "And to me that kind of almost eliminated him, not completely eliminated him," Stevens said.

During the short interview, White informed the Beatrice detective he was moving away – but not to go into hiding. "I think he said he was going to Alabama," Stevens remembered. "I know he was going to his mother's house. Now, whether he made it there or not at that time, I don't know."

A few years after the murder, Stevens and White crossed paths again. "I told you I was leaving town to go take a job with a traveling carnival, but after I got there, I found out that the place had done moved on," White explained, according to transcripts. "They didn't need a roustabout."

Back in 1985, Stevens moved past White as a potential murder suspect. The fact that nobody in active Nebraska law enforcement was pursuing White did not matter to former Beatrice police officer Burt Searcey. He was doggedly pursuing White as his prime suspect after learning of White's arrest for trying to kick in a woman's door early one December morning in 1984.

"After having obtained the information of a Joseph E. White having been involved in that incident I then proceeded to re-contact my confidential informants who advised me that Joseph White was an individual who was basically unemployed, ran the streets, was known to indulge in drugs and a large amount of alcohol," Searcey noted in one of his first official reports, dated February 27, 1989. "I was further advised that he was known to associate himself with a Thomas Winslow, JoAnn Taylor, Clifford Sheldon [sic], Mark Goodson, Beth Johnson, Debbie Brown (Shelden) and Charlette Mindenhall [sic]."

That White and Taylor both left Beatrice within a month of the widow's murder further cemented Searcey's belief that they were involved. Moreover, Searcey came up with other reasons to finger White for the murder: White stayed in Kathy Gonzalez's apartment unit directly above Wilson's apartment in the weeks before the slaying, White engaged in gay sex with former roommate Tom Winslow, and he previously worked in California's adult entertainment industry.

Searcey also took a leap of imagination and speculated that White was fond of performing magic tricks with money at parties or when otherwise drinking with an audience. Searcey remained preoccupied with the torn five-dollar bill discovered in the murder victim's kitchen.

Years later, Luckeroth testified the Beatrice Police Department never once received any leads or helpful information as a result of Searcey's investigation. "I think he wanted to make a name for himself. ... I never had any, you know, official notice that he was a private investigator."

***

In November of 1986, voters across rural Gage County elected a new sheriff, Jerry O. DeWitt. He had joined the

Nebraska State Patrol in 1963 and was assigned to Beatrice, where he became a familiar face around the community into the 1980s. DeWitt primarily handled road patrol duties, investigating crashes and busting drunken drivers. DeWitt had little on-the-job experience at solving murder cases, which were largely infrequent in this mostly farming region anyway.

When DeWitt took office in January of 1987, he hired Burt Searcey as a new deputy. Located across from the Gage County Courthouse, the Sheriff's Office on Lincoln Street was just a few blocks from the Beatrice Police Department, where Searcey had been employed from 1977 until 1982.

During the 1980s, the Gage County Sheriff's Office and the Beatrice Police Department, like many small-town law enforcement agencies, had their share of acrimony and contentious territorial turf battles. Previous sheriffs were often content with having their deputies patrol the county's roads and only investigate matters in the outlying communities. In the new sheriff's point of view, his deputies could theoretically investigate crimes in Beatrice since the city happened to be the county seat. Nearly half of the county's residents lived around Beatrice. The vast majority of towns scattered across Gage County had less than 1,000 people.

As for Searcey, he was glad to regain his stature in local law enforcement. He had a shiny badge, a professional uniform and a holster. Above all, he had arresting power to mess with people's freedom. But barely six months on the job as a sheriff's deputy, Searcey found himself embroiled in an off-duty assault allegation that warranted a Nebraska State Patrol investigation into the matter.

Trooper Dave Morris compiled a ten-page investigative memo based on his interview with Searcey at the Sheriff's Office shortly before noon on August 8, 1987. The night before, Searcey had gone out drinking with two friends who also lived in his apartment complex. Around 11:00 p.m., the three friends went to The Office Bar in downtown Beatrice and stayed about two hours. Searcey recalled that he sat with as many as six to eight friends at the table. He acknowledged he was drinking. "Approximately three beers, three bottles of beer," he told the Nebraska State Patrol. When he left around 1:00 a.m., he walked along Ella Street because his friend parked about a block away. Searcey said he saw a "full grown male subject laying in the seat, belly down, head facing north on the passenger side of the vehicle with only his underwear on and appeared to be in some type of movement," the State Patrol noted. "As I passed by, I really did not pay that much attention. I more or less wanted to ignore the situation," Searcey said. Then his two friends asked if he was going to ignore that man's behavior. "I then proceeded back to the car because I felt that the gentleman may be having sex in the car out in the open on a street."

Back at the parked car, Searcey noticed the driver's door was wide open and the man was lying on the seat wearing only underwear. "I opened my billfold up. I obtained my Sheriff's Department ID card," Searcey explained. Nobody else was in the car. Searcey accused the man of indecent exposure and warned him to get his clothes back on and leave. "He more or less just looked at me and he said, 'Well, let me see your ID,'" Searcey contended. "And I was holding it in my hand (for) him to observe it and it was at that point he jerked it out of my hand and tried to keep me from obtaining it back from him."

Searcey claimed he threatened to arrest the man for indecent exposure if the man did not return the sheriff's ID. But the man didn't comply. He supposedly extended his right hand toward the passenger seat. "I then proceeded to enter into his vehicle with the upper portion of my body and to reach his right arm and to pull his right arm toward me. ... I physically removed my ID card from his right hand," Searcey stated.

Searcey recalled seeing the man's blue jeans and shoes in the middle of the sidewalk near the parked vehicle. There was no shirt. Searcey claimed he asked why the man was wearing no clothes. "The only response I got from the individual was, 'I did it for you.'"

Trooper Morris pressed Searcey to explain why he chose to go back to the man's vehicle and engage in a confrontation after initially walking past the car. "Well, you know, I am a fellow officer," Searcey responded. "First of all, it was indecent exposure in my opinion. Second of all, I had two citizens who were with me that were just friends, and they felt very appalled by the situation. Felt that something ought to be done. Even though I was off duty, I felt that it was a duty of mine to respond to the citizens' request."

After lunging into the man's parked car and retrieving his sheriff's ID, Searcey tossed the pile of clothes back into the car, warning the man to get dressed and leave the area before more problems occurred.

At the end of the Nebraska State Patrol investigation surrounding the assault allegation, Trooper Dave Morris wrote: "I want to make note that Burdette L. Searcey is the suspect in this case."

No criminal charges arose from that incident. Searcey later testified he was not disciplined over that off-duty incident that occurred after a night of drinking.

***

As a sheriff's deputy, Searcey was not content with running radar and nabbing lead-footed speeders zooming through Gage County. The unsolved Helen Wilson murder from February 1985 remained on his mind. Searcey continued to pepper Sheriff Jerry DeWitt with suggestions that he be allowed to investigate the city Police Department's case. One day at work, Searcey assured Gage County jailer Kimberly Perkins he was going to "solve the case," court documents state. There was also another key public figure in Beatrice whom Searcey kept his eye on. As a road deputy, Searcey became familiar with not only the people around Beatrice, but the color, make and model of their vehicles, including that driven by Wayne Price. Price -- "Doc" as some called him -- was the clinical psychologist at the Blue Valley Mental Health Center who also moonlighted as a part-time sheriff's deputy. The county allowed Price to function as a police psychologist. Price organized numerous law enforcement training seminars and he often showed up at situations involving hostages or mentally deranged people who were threatening to harm themselves or others.

On a handful of occasions, Searcey flipped on his flashing red and blue lights when he saw Price driving casually through town. Price, unsure what traffic law he had broken, pulled off to the side of the road. Searcey left on his flashing lights as he approached Price's vehicle. But Price had not been speeding or violating any other traffic laws. Searcey just wanted to pick Doc's brain regarding the unsolved Wilson murder. "It reached the point where Price asked Searcey to stop pulling over his car. It was embarrassing to Price," court documents state.

***

As for the Beatrice Police Department, their investigation was beginning to feel hopeless. February 1988 marked the third anniversary of the unsolved murder, and there were no prime suspects on the police's radar anymore. It was definitely a cold case. With practically nowhere else to turn, Beatrice Police Capt. Elvin Waltke got in touch with Dar Emme – a self-professed psychic who lived near Denver, Colorado.

In turn, Detective Sam Stevens was asked to mail the following items of evidence from their murder case to the Denver psychic:

- A ring with seven colored stones that Wilson wore at the time of her murder.

- A photo of Wilson taken just weeks before her slaying.

- The pairs of garters, nylons, and foot booties Wilson wore.

- A copy of the police videotape of the crime scene.

- Four photos of Wilson at the scene of the crime.

- A map of Beatrice with an "X" marking where the murder happened.

More than seven months later, after back-and-forth phone tag, Stevens finally connected with Dar Emme to hear her revelations. She informed him that she was in the process of mailing back the package of evidentiary material. She also deduced that Wilson's murder was connected to someone within the family.

"It's very definitely family oriented," Emme proclaimed, "and we're just kind of having a little bit of suspicion as to whether it was, uh, the son-in-law, nephew or grandson, but uh, it's very definitely family-orientated and it seems to be motivated because of money and that thought that the person that killed her ... they deserved something from her."

Emme predicted the first name of one of the killers began with R and would be Richard or Robert. "This was a family member, but he was not by himself," Emme declared. "There's two people involved, uh, actually there's three. So with the two men involved, we've gotten the names that begin with an "R," Richard or Robert and the name Jimmy, um, perhaps Johnny, but it's Jimmy that's spelled with a Y. In other words, it's a grown man that's still being called Jimmy, Johnny, that type of thing, but the name that came through the strongest was somebody called Buddy or Bobby, but it's a nickname."

Emme also worked closely with her husband as part of her business of performing psychic readings. Her husband used to be a baker, and when he came home from work he often smelled like chocolate donuts. She said the smell of Wilson's clothes also gave her some insight into the murderer at large. "We've worked with several cases so we're getting used to a lot of this, but the smell, it's not the smell off of her clothes that was bothering us, the smell off of him," she relayed. "You know like when somebody works around chemicals or works around a feed lot or something like that you can smell? This guy had a very, very, strong smell about him and it was more than just a body odor smell," Emme told Stevens. "It seemed to be connected with either his work or the place that he lived."

At one point, Emme told the detective that she needed to ask him a few questions in order to help steer his agency in the right direction.

"Tell me the first name of your suspect," she implored.

"I honestly don't have a suspect," Stevens admitted. "Now, there have been a lot of family members that, like I say, that could very well be involved ... but I come up with some evidence that like it doesn't prove it was them."

The Denver psychic wanted to know if he had one person in his mind who could be the suspect.

"No," he admitted.

Finally, Stevens sought clarification on whether the psychic believed the homicide was related to jealousy over, perhaps an inheritance?

"Well, no it is a robbery, very definitely. They thought she had something and they went to get it, thinking that maybe she had some money."

According to the psychic, the killer was a hot-headed younger man who was convinced in his mind that Wilson had mistreated part of his family somehow.

"And that she had something that he felt he had a right to have and he was going to go over there and bully her to get it, thinking that she would never say anything, that she would be too afraid, too ashamed," Emme surmised. "She'd keep it to herself, only it went real screwed up and they ended up killing her."

The psychic also saw that the murderer's picture was within the victim's apartment living room. "There's a shelf unit that has the TV on it in the living room," Emme pointed out after reviewing the crime scene photos and video cassette tape. "The murderer's picture is in that living room."

All told, there were three main people responsible for the murder, the psychic declared.

"There's two men and a woman involved," Emme told Stevens.

Ultimately, Stevens did not give the well-intentioned out-of-state psychic's advice the time of day. Unbeknown to the Beatrice detective, others who were eager -- and perhaps desperate -- to solve the Wilson homicide at that stage might have had a different thought process in regards to the psychic's guidance.

***

In January 1989, Searcey reached his two-year anniversary with the Gage County Sheriff's Office. That month, he convinced his boss that his secret informants knew the killers' identities. With his first re-election campaign looming in 1990, Sheriff DeWitt was intrigued by the chance for his agency to bring the community's fears to rest. The murder investigation led by the Beatrice Police Department had lingered on for four long years, and no arrests were on the horizon.

When the sheriff turned his eager deputy loose, Searcey was literally starting from scratch. As of January 1989, he had not produced a single written police report regarding any of his personal investigative activities surrounding the Wilson slaying. He had no recorded interviews. In fact, he had nothing on paper to verify any of his supposed leads or past interviews with confidential informants when he had scurried around the Beatrice community, knocking on doors, identifying himself as a private investigator as far back as March of 1985. That was all inconsequential to Searcey. He would make up for nearly four years of lost time real fast.

CHAPTER 10
INFORMANT REVISITED

Around January 15, 1989, Lisa Podendorf was asked to come down to the Gage County Sheriff's Office for her first formal, tape-recorded interview. By this stage of her life, she had married her long-time boyfriend and went by her married name of Lisa Brown. Deputy Searcey began by asking the now twenty-one-year-old woman why she wanted to participate in that voluntary interview. "Because of some information I had took from JoAnn Taylor the morning after the death of Helen Wilson," Brown replied.

Brown confirmed she previously spoke with Searcey on two occasions – nearly four years earlier -- in April of 1985.

"Was I a law officer at the time?" he asked.

"No," she answered.

"How did I identify myself to you?"

"You said you were a private investigator investigating what happened," Brown said.

Searcey cut to the case. He asked Brown to recite a conversation that the two of them had back in 1985 when Taylor allegedly admitted her role in Wilson's homicide.

"I told you that she told me it up at the school about 7:30 in the morning on the morning after it happened."

Searcey pressed her to restate the time and date of her conversation with Taylor.

"Yes, about 7:30 that morning, the morning of February 6, 1985."

Searcey asked Brown a series of questions that seemed rather innocuous at the time.

"Have you ever discussed this information with anyone?"

"No."

"Did I ever give you any information and ask you if you were aware of any of those?"

"No."

"All the information which you are about to make known to me at this time is purely information which you were made aware of by JoAnn Taylor, is that correct?"

"Yes."

For emphasis, Searcey repeated the date and time at which Taylor supposedly had confessed committing the widow's murder. "You believe you stated that JoAnn spoke with you approximately 7:30 a.m. on February 6 while you were standing in the park by the Beatrice library?" he asked.

"Yes. When she started talking to me, we were alone. She came up to me and told me that or asked me if I knew why the police cars were over there."

Searcey interrupted, and asked where "there" was.

"Over at Helen Wilson's. Around her apartment building on Sixth Street. And I said, 'Well, I had heard that somebody had killed her.' And she said, 'Yeah, I know who did it.' And I said, 'Well, I think you're lying.' She goes, 'No, I'm not' … she turned her head and she had scratch marks on her head."

Searcey asked if anything else was revealed to her that morning outside the library.

"After I said that I didn't believe that she did it, she said, 'Well me and Lobo did it and if you tell the police or anybody,' she said, 'We'll kill ya.' And at that time I was scared, and then she said she knew that she could tell me how they found her, more or less, found Helen Wilson."

As Brown related their conversation from years earlier, Taylor had confessed "if they found her, she would have her hands tied behind her back and she would be laying on the living room floor by a footstool. And the footstool would be turned over."

As if the story could not get any stranger, Taylor then supposedly demanded Brown give her $500. "And I said, 'Why?'" Brown said during the recorded 1989 interview. "And she said, 'Cuz I have to get out of town before they find me,' meaning the police."

For the first time in the four-year-old murder case, Searcey had information for an official investigative report to share with his eager boss, Sheriff DeWitt. For investigatory purposes, Brown would be known as Confidential Informant No. 1.

The Brown interview was chalked up as a giant success. Searcey brimmed with confidence. His next goal was to secure someone else to bolster his murder theory. Charlotte Bishop filled that void as his Confidential Informant No. 2.

The young redhead was also known as Charlotte Mendenhall, Charlotte Krumm or Charlotte Watkins. Regardless of her last name, police records state that the five-foot-two, 170-pound woman was often delusional and known to hallucinate.

On February 25, 1989, Searcey arranged for a formal interview of Bishop in the presence of her lawyer in Lincoln. He was under the impression that Bishop had a riveting story to unload. He said he just didn't understand why she had kept silent for the past four years and three weeks.

"Well, see nobody asked me about it until now," she snapped.

During the interview, which was videotaped, Bishop was chain smoking. Again and again, she lit up a new cigarette as soon as she put her last butt out in the law office's ashtray. The interview would be revealing, but for the wrong reasons. When Searcey asked if she remembered when Wilson was murdered, Bishop wrongly guessed around October. Then she tried guessing August.

Bishop claimed she remembered Taylor had returned to their loft apartment the very next day after the murder and confessed. "She thought that she was involved in the murder," Bishop said. "Well, the statement she had made to me is, 'I think I killed somebody.'"

Bishop indicated that she never uttered a word about Taylor's confession even though Taylor had skipped town and moved far away, and Bishop later relocated to Lincoln. In Bishop's mind, she had good reason to zip her lips.

"She just told me to keep my mouth shut or something was going to happen to me."

Once, when they shared an apartment, Bishop said, Taylor filled their bathtub with scalding water and pushed Bishop into the tub with help of two others. "I had second-degree burns," Bishop professed. Searcey's informant said she went to the hospital but medical staff said her burns were not that bad.

Searcey's murder investigation now rested on a pair of tape-recorded statements, one from Lisa Brown and the other from Charlotte Bishop. He thought he was making terrific headway in lightning fashion.

For good measure, Gage County deputies made contact with a pair of local thugs being held in jail for an assault in Lincoln, in neighboring Lancaster County. A few months earlier, in October 1988, police said, Clifford Shelden and Tom Winslow used a tire iron to bash the skull of a man as part of a botched robbery. Court records show that Winslow served as the robbery decoy while Shelden clubbed the man, who miraculously survived.

Winslow, twenty-three, and Shelden, twenty-eight, were charged in Lancaster County with first-degree felony assault, felony robbery and use of a weapon to commit an assault. Without a doubt, both men faced decades in the Nebraska penal system.

The authorities at the Gage County Sheriff's Office smelled an opportunity. After all, Winslow and Shelden both ran around with the same rowdy acquaintances already under suspicion by Searcey in the Wilson murder. The tradeoff for implicating their old chums in that case could mean regaining their own freedom much sooner. Both Winslow and Clifford Shelden were eager and willing to take the bait.

As for Winslow, he knew he'd gotten off on the wrong foot with Searcey back in 1985, and Searcey never forgot it. Back then, Winslow told Searcey he was working at the Marshall's Truck Stop in Beatrice on the night of Wilson's murder. Searcey, through his network of contacts, found out otherwise. Winslow had phoned in sick on the night the elderly woman met her death. From that, Searcey locked into the belief that Winslow certainly was part of the deadly attack.

Without a doubt, Winslow had led a troubled life during the 1980s. He kept company with other misfits. He was unreliable. He lied constantly. He made terrible choices. He was caught up in a web of crime. Above all, he made a colossal, irreversible error in judgment by teaming up with Clifford Shelden to rob the Harvester Motel in Lincoln in October 1988, a crime that got out of hand and nearly turned into a homicide itself. Clearly, Winslow was a vulnerable inmate, desperate to avoid a long prison term for the brutal assault in Nebraska's capital city.

While he was jailed in the motel assault case, Winslow treaded on dangerous waters by letting Searcey visit the jail in Lincoln in early 1989 to interview him in regard to Helen Wilson's murder. The deputy started off reminding Winslow of their previous encounters.

Back in 1985, Tom Winslow denied any involvement in the killing of Beatrice widow Helen Wilson. Following his arrest in the October 1988 tire-iron beating of a Lincoln, Nebraska, motel clerk, Winslow agreed to implicate Joseph White and JoAnn Taylor in the 1985 rape and homicide of Helen Wilson.

"Thomas, can you advise me who I am at this time?"

"Deputy Searcey."

"Am I a deputy with the Gage County Sheriff's Department?"

"Yeah."

"Do you recall ever having spoke with me any time prior to this date?"

"A couple other times. You asked me about where I was supposedly when the incident took place and you asked me where my car was located at."

"Did I ask you where you were that specific evening before the homicide occurred?"

"I gave you an answer that I was at work, uh, Marshall's Truck Stop."

"Were you in fact at work the evening prior to the homicide occurring?"

"No, I wasn't. I called in sick I think because I had a cold or sore throat or something. I can't remember for sure."

"What did you do that particular evening?"

Winslow said he thought that he and his wife had bummed around in his 1973 Oldsmobile Cutlass from 6:30 to 7:30 p.m. This was the green car with a tan roof.

"Where was your '73 Oldsmobile that particular evening?" Searcey asked.

"I had loaned it out to …"

Before Winslow finished his answer, Searcey interrupted. "And who did you loan it out to?"

"I, uh, JoAnn Taylor and Lobo or Joseph White whatever you want to call him by, and Clifford Shelden had my vehicle that day."

Winslow was obviously lying. It would have been impossible for Shelden to borrow Winslow's car that day. On February 5 and 6, 1985, Shelden had been admitted to the Beatrice Community Hospital after contracting syphilis, a sexually transmitted disease, court records show.

Now four years after the Beatrice murder, Winslow patched together the following tale in an obvious effort to gain leniency and slash prison time off his own sorry predicament:

On Wednesday, February 6, 1985, Winslow said he heard the door slam at his apartment near one of the grocery stores in Beatrice. That morning two guests visited, JoAnn Taylor and Joseph White. Both were regular visitors to Winslow's abode. The commotion stirred Winslow out of bed. He fetched his pack of cigarettes from a living room end table. Meanwhile, White turned on the water faucets in the kitchen to wash his hands. Then White cooked himself eggs for breakfast. With the eggs on the stove, Winslow claimed Taylor uttered a cryptic comment.

"She said that they had to get the hell out of the state, and that the cops would be coming to question me about my car," Winslow assured Searcey.

However, neither spoke a word about any homicide, Winslow said, at least in his presence.

Searcey was not happy. He was sure Winslow knew far more than what he was letting on.

"Did you have an occasion to spend any time with them after that particular morning?" Searcey asked.

"No, because they left after they ate breakfast and said they'd be back later on that evening and they never showed back up."

Searcey found it hard to believe Winslow lost contact with his pair of tight-knit friends. After all, they were Winslow's ilk.

"You've never had contact with either one of them since?"

"No, I haven't."

Initially, Winslow had no misgivings about throwing White and Taylor under the bus in the murder investigation. He had not seen them in four years. He called White, his former roommate, moody and disturbed, a different personality.

"Just by a few conversations that we had together, he had a rough childhood and he drank a lot," Winslow said. "He was constantly going to R&S (Bar) drinking. And he'd roll in about one or two in the morning after the bar closed."

On many nights when they lived together, White returned home in a drunken stupor and passed out on Winslow's couch, Winslow said.

"You said you had a few talks with him. Did they ever get personal?"

Winslow picked up on the cues in Searcey's question and agreed that a couple of their talks became deeply personal when they shared an apartment.

"And he couldn't handle the thought of his mother being actually in his exact words, 'a whore,'" Winslow claimed.

Later on, White would vehemently deny he ever made such a ridiculous and false statement to Winslow about his own mother. It appeared Winslow had generated yet another lie, this time about White's mother.

At any rate, Winslow maintained to the sheriff's deputy eager to solve the Wilson murder that his conversations with White grew emotional at times.

"He'd cry, and he'd lean on my shoulder and cry and ask me how maybe he could of changed his life, and all I ever suggested to him was about his drinking and stuff. Maybe, if he treated women a little bit better ..."

Again, White later strenuously denied he ever cried on Winslow's shoulder, insisting he absolutely never did such a thing.

Winslow claimed that his former roommate often snapped at Taylor as she cooked White dinner.

"And if it wasn't cooked to his exact what he likes it, he'd blow off the handle or throw something at her. ... I don't know how many articles in my apartment I lost from being broke or thrown between the two of them at each other."

Usually, White wore Western garb reminiscent of cowboys. He preferred blue jeans and flannel shirts, lighter colors such as brown, blue and white, Winslow recalled.

"Anything else?" Searcey followed up.

"He never left home without his jean jacket. That man would wear it everywhere he went, and his cowboy boots."

White also had insulated stocking caps, Winslow helpfully recalled.

"He had one of the facial mask ones. Like it's the one you pull over your complete face and covers everything but your mouth and eyes," he said.

He also told Searcey that White also kept a knife strapped to the side of his belt.

"Did you ever hear or seen him threaten anybody with that or do anything with it?"

"Just when he was drinking he would get gutsy and pull it out."

Winslow's willingness to implicate his old friends was improving his own pathetic plight. Searcey reminded the young man that he had already caught Winslow lying to him once before, back in 1985, when Searcey showed up to question him about his whereabouts on the night of the murder.

"Well, one, it was about a murder episode," Winslow pointed out. "And I was scared, because I knew I did not have nothing to do with it ... and then you asked me automatically about my car, and it worried me because the car is registered in my dad's name, too, and I had an uncle that was on the police force at that time and I knew it would get back to my dad and everything and I lied because I think I was just scared because I didn't know what he was capable of doing."

Winslow denied knowing anything about the Wilson crime scene.

"Have you ever heard anybody talk about that?" Searcey asked.

"No."

"Is there anything else that you would like to add to this statement at this time?"

"No."

***

In March, the following month, the law enforcement hierarchy of Gage County became eager to strike an alliance with Winslow, who was sure go to prison for a long time for his role in the Harvester Motel beating. At the county jail in Lincoln, Winslow was escorted into a meeting room. There, he was joined by his lawyer, John Stevens Berry, who went on to become one of Nebraska's most famous criminal defense attorneys. The others present in the conference room were Gage County Sheriff Jerry DeWitt, Deputy Searcey and Gage County prosecutor Dick Smith. Another deputy ran the video camera. The camera was positioned so that only Searcey and Winslow's faces were shown.

That day, the Gage County prosecutor presented Winslow with a binding legal document known as a Use Immunity Agreement. Winslow presumed he would walk out of jail that evening -- provided he signed the form.

Of course, there were strings attached. First, the prosecution stipulated, Winslow needed to be "completely truthful" with regard to the Wilson homicide in Beatrice. If Winslow lived up to his end of the deal, his penalty for the tire-iron attack at Lincoln's Harvester Motel would be reduced a low-level felony by the Lincoln prosecutor. Secondly, Winslow would plead guilty to a Class IV felony back in Gage County related to Wilson's homicide. The sentences for both unrelated offenses would run simultaneously.

It seemed like Winslow was being offered the deal of a lifetime. If he signed the agreement, he would remain free until his sentencing. Without much hesitation, Winslow signed the paperwork. He was not overly concerned about the finer details in the agreement, which stipulated: "if Gage County authorities were able to bring forth evidence which would tie Mr. Winslow in the homicide case as a direct player, the Use Immunity Agreement between Mr. Winslow, Mr. Smith, and Mr. Berry would become nullified."

That night in Lincoln, Sheriff DeWitt overheard defense lawyer John Stevens Berry talking to Winslow as the deal was struck. The sheriff turned their comments into an investigative memo. "John S. Berry stated to his client that if he had lied about being a participant in the Helen Wilson Homicide that all bets were off and that he would be in a world of 'shit,'" DeWitt wrote.

Upon signing the pact, Winslow now claimed he and his wife, Beth Johnson, had gone bumming around Beatrice with White and Taylor in Winslow's green Oldsmobile. At some point, they parked near the old Lincoln Telephone & Telegraph Building where Wilson resided. However, Winslow was foggy on many details.

During the videotaped interview, Deputy Searcey asked all the questions, though it was clear on the video that other people in the room were handing him notebook sheets with other questions to bring up to Winslow.

"I don't remember how we entered the apartment, but after we got into the apartment ... Lobo and that lady was talking back and forth," Winslow told everyone. "There was a little argument and then the lady started for the phone and Lobo pushed her out of the way of the phone, pushed (her) into the bedroom. JoAnn followed and at that time I heard the lady scream and I exited."

Winslow denied he ever had attacked the older woman.

According to Winslow, he and his wife later talked with Taylor and White about the crime. "They just talked about how the lady fought with them and about the lady getting raped and Lobo raped her and JoAnn helped him, but that's all we ever talked about it. Then we all put it behind us."

Searcey expected Winslow to reveal more intimate details surrounding White's commission of the sexual assault.

"All he said is that in other words he fucked her, but that's all. I mean, he didn't tell me what positions or anything like that."

Searcey was not satisfied with Winslow's answer.

"He didn't tell you if he had sex with her by the normal vaginal area or by rectum?"

"I think he might of said something about rectum."

"No. You either know ..."

"I don't know. Honest."

According to Winslow's account, White and Taylor barged into his apartment the morning after the murder. "Lobo had some scratches on his back and Jo Ann had a few on her arms. Lobo showed his on his back and Jo Ann's were noticed. He said when he was raping her that she scratched him."

With his freedom at stake, Thomas Winslow said enough of the right things to be released from jail. After being locked up for five months, Winslow was happy to return to Wymore, in rural Gage County, where he lived.

By this stage, Searcey had netted a video-recorded statement from Lisa Brown implicating Taylor and White as the killers. A second video-recorded statement from Charlotte Bishop implicated Taylor in confessing to committing the murder. Now, there was a third recorded admission implicating Taylor and White thanks to inmate Winslow.

More than four long years had passed, and nobody had been held accountable for the dastardly killing of Helen Wilson in Beatrice. But that was about to change.

***

Within a matter of days, Searcey climbed aboard a small private aircraft. The pilot was Nebraska State Patrol Trooper Dave Morris, the same officer who previously investigated Searcey for jumping into the parked car of a man sitting in his underwear. Fewer than two years removed from that bizarre late night off-duty episode, Searcey was now Sheriff Jerry DeWitt's shining star.

On March 15, 1985, the aircraft's engine roared. The propellers sputtered. As the small plane rumbled down the municipal air strip, Searcey held onto his sacred possession – precious legal documents signed by Gage County Judge Steven Timm. The onetime hog farmer from Liberty, Nebraska, a tiny town of seventy-five people, had dusted off the cobwebs of his former police force's inactive murder investigation. He single-handedly put the murder mystery jigsaw puzzle together – all the while unbeknown to his former colleagues at the Beatrice Police Department. Searcey's murder probe was a closely guarded secret at the Gage County Sheriff's Office.

"I didn't think there was enough evidence to arrest anybody," Luckeroth would later say.

CHAPTER 11
ALABAMA, HERE WE COME

One of the most memorable phone calls of Sam Stevens' career happened while the Beatrice police detective was in St. Louis attending a police training seminar in March in 1989. His boss, Captain Elvin Waltke, notified him that a small plane was making a special landing in St. Louis to bring Stevens along on a mission.

A long-time Nebraska State Patrol Trooper, Jerry DeWitt was elected as the new sheriff of Gage County in November 1986. By January 1989, Sheriff's Deputy Burt Searcey had DeWitt's permission to investigate the Helen Wilson murder, even though it was the Beatrice Police Department's case. Photo courtesy of Beatrice Daily Sun

After stopping for Stevens, the aircraft eventually touched down at a small airport in Alabama. Besides the pilot, the entourage included first-term Gage County Sheriff DeWitt, Deputy Searcey, Stevens, Waltke and "Doc" Wayne Price.

Price may have held the oddest position in Nebraska law enforcement at that time. The clinical director of the Blue Valley Mental Health Center in Beatrice also held the job of police psychologist. Price heralded himself as having a rare specialized ability to psychoanalyze people under suspicion of various crimes. He dressed in professional attire. On some occasions, he interviewed criminals who had already undergone therapy sessions with him at Blue Valley. But when he entered a police station or jail to conduct an interview, Price wasn't doing therapy sessions. He was wearing his other hat as a tool of the sheriff and Gage County's prosecutor, County Attorney Richard T. "Dick" Smith.

In the air, Stevens was shocked as he learned that former Beatrice cast-offs Joseph White and JoAnn Taylor were being arrested in the Wilson murder. Stevens had known both of them during their brief time in Beatrice. "And I couldn't figure why in the world JoAnn would do this," Stevens remembered later.

During the flight, Stevens, with his doubts, was the odd man out. Sheriff DeWitt was gloating. "(DeWitt) told me on the plane, going and coming, that he wanted to make certain that they, the Sheriff's Office, was the one that solved the case," Stevens would later recall.

***

That year, White was twenty-six. He had moved beyond his wild and carefree days as "Lone Wolf Bronson," the nude male model trying to reach stardom in Hollywood. In fact, White was making something of his life back in his native Alabama. He displayed a strong work ethic at a sawmill in Garden City. He worked as a sawyer, earning five dollars per hour, which was above minimum wage at the time.

Mostly, White led a simple life. He still did not own a vehicle. He had about thirty dollars in his pocket, but no money in the bank, police reports indicate. White lived in a tiny community on the outskirts of Cullman. Four years removed from his time in Beatrice, Nebraska, White had long severed ties with his old partying pals including JoAnn Taylor, Tom Winslow, James Dean, and a host of other local characters.

So, on March 15, 1989, White couldn't have imagined that an Alabama SWAT team was rehearsing instructions to raid his home late that night. Raindrops pelted the ground as the team of gung-ho cops dressed in gear matching the dark sky staked out White's property. During the downpour, the Rambo-style officers stormed inside and snared White like a bear trap. Guns were drawn. White lifted his hands toward the sky. The lanky, young man with a beard was barefoot and bare-chested as he surrendered, insisting that he didn't know what crime he had committed.

The cops clutched their prisoner, who was clad only in his underwear and blue jeans. They whisked him outside and stuffed him into the back of an Alabama squad car. The rain gushed against the windows of the car running its flashing red and blue lights during the fifteen-minute drive back to the Cullman Police Department. There, the befuddled, rain-soaked prisoner was handed over to a trio of cops from Nebraska. White was placed in an interrogation room with Beatrice Police Detective Stevens, "Doc" Price, the police psychologist, and Sheriff's Deputy Searcey, the ringleader of the revived murder investigation from 900 miles away.

Sometime later, Stevens said he suspected Price's placement on the plane was part of a hidden agenda to determine his own willingness to help Gage County law officers implicate White and possibly others in the murder. After all, Stevens had been the original lead detective. And, unlike Searcey, Stevens had been involved in the investigation with the city's police since Day 1. Stevens had a deep understanding of the crime scene, unlike Searcey, who hadn't been on the scene at the time the murder and wasn't even a cop when he came up with his theory of the crime. Dating back to 1985, Stevens had conducted dozens and dozens of interviews of potential witnesses and suspects. He had experience dealing with White, including a prior interview. In contrast, Searcey had never met White face to face until now.

As he laid eyes on the prisoner, Searcey knew he had the upper hand. He glared at the sopping wet, bare-chested inmate sitting on a hard chair inside the Cullman Police Department interrogation room. Searcey had spent four long years bracing for this moment. He was convinced Joseph White was a predatory beast and, thanks to his own detective prowess, Searcey felt White was no longer a threat to other women in society.

As Stevens and Price sat nearby, Searcey took control of the interrogation. He began the midnight-hour interview by reading White the standard Miranda warnings and asked, "Do you have any questions as to why you been brought in?"

White looked at the form he'd been handed with astonishment.

"Yeah," he said. "Why am I a suspect in a case of Murder One?"

The egotistical deputy boasted how he had done a ton of legwork to reach this point. He had secured an arrest warrant signed off by a Nebraska judge showing probable cause that the young Alabama man was involved in the death of Helen Wilson.

"Helen Wilson?"

"Yes. An older lady in Beatrice, in February 5, 1985."

Searcey asked whether White remembered roaming the streets that night with a woman named JoAnn, as in JoAnn Taylor.

"JoAnn?"

"You're having a hard time remembering. Maybe it's because you don't want to remember, huh? Could that be, Joe?"

"No. It's just that all this has come down all of a sudden. You just hit me with a hell of a shock when you was telling me I was going for Murder One."

"Well, you're wanted for Murder One, Joe. I think you've got a lot of explaining to do. That's what I think."

White found himself in a giant mess. He tried to claw his way out. He remained defiant as he tried to answer the investigator's string of questions. First, White retold how he and Taylor had met while out West, where they hung around with a tall skinny blond guy, name of Mark Goodson.

"We all met in California. And we came back to Beatrice to see if we could get her kid back for her."

As for his nickname of Lobo, White was not embarrassed about its origin.

"I did some nude modeling out there under the name of Lone Wolf Bronson, and they started calling me Lobo."

Regarding Taylor, White said there was no denying she had an explosive temper. Once, Taylor got into a cat fight at White's regular watering hole, the R&S Bar. During that incident, Taylor clawed up a tall, short-haired blonde, White recalled. White lost contact with Taylor once he left Beatrice in February of 1985. He guessed she landed in Texas. They never had a sexual relationship, White professed.

Besides Taylor, the name of a second woman was dropped during the interrogation.

Searcey put forth his theory that a heavy-set woman named Kathy Gonzalez had hosted a beer party in her apartment directly above Helen Wilson's on the night of the sadistic attack.

"No, I never went to a party at Kathy's place."

Being truthful, White admitted he had stayed at Gonzalez's apartment weeks prior to the murder in that building, but that was after his break-up with his live-in girlfriend.

"I crashed out at her place because I didn't have a place to stay at the time."

Like Taylor, White also said he lost contact with Kathy Gonzalez. He had no idea where she lived nowadays. He had no reason to stay in contact.

By this stage, Searcey was agitated. He knew from watching multiple *Starsky and Hutch* episodes that the pivotal point in the police interrogation came when the suspect broke down and confessed his guilt. But Searcey had not broken White down. It was quite the opposite. White proclaimed his innocence rather forcefully. White gave no hint that he might confess.

Searcey tried to put White on the spot, imploring him to detail his whereabouts of the night of Wilson's murder from four years, one month and ten days earlier. White guessed he was probably hanging out at the R&S Bar that night.

"Could you verify that?"

"Not unless people there remember back that far and remember seeing me there. I was down there quite a bit."

"But what if you weren't at the R&S Bar? What if I know different?"

White backpedaled and guessed he would have spent the night at a friend's place, though he was unable to furnish any names. As it turns out, around the time of the Beatrice murder, White lived on the top floor of a house near the Gage County Sheriff's Office and Gage County Courthouse.

"So, you've never been in that apartment building, only when you went up to see the Gonzalez lady?" Searcey asked about the old Lincoln Telephone & Telegraph building.

"Yes."

"Never, ever, huh?"

"Never."

"You know Helen Wilson?"

"Who?"

"Helen Wilson?"

"No."

"Did JoAnn know her?"

"Not that I know of."

If this police interrogation was a boxing match, Searcey was not winning the bout with a knockout punch. As the clock ticked closer toward one o'clock in the morning, Searcey became exasperated. He was failing to make White buckle. His prisoner steadfastly denied ever setting foot inside Helen Wilson's apartment.

"What if I can put you in there?"

"I'd say you'd have to have some awful damn good proof."

"What if I have some awful damn good proof?"

"I'd like to see it."

"What if I showed it to you?"

"Show it."

Next, the testy interrogation turned to the names of the street corners in Beatrice. Searcey questioned whether White remembered Court Street, one of the busy thoroughfares in Beatrice, in close proximity to the three-story brick apartment where the murder happened.

"Really, all I remember about Beatrice … it's been a long time, I've been a lot of places … the only thing that I remember is R&S Bar, going there and the Brass Rail every once in a while, then working here and there."

Failing to make headway, Searcey tried to rile White. The Alabama man had no idea that Tom Winslow, his former bisexual roommate in Beatrice, had been caught up in his own wave of serious crime since White left Nebraska in 1985 and that Winslow might have become vulnerable to an investigator's tactics.

"Did you ever maybe break down and cry and tell Tom about some of your problems you had when [you] was a young man?"

"No. I'm not the kind to break down and cry and tell anybody nothing. Never have."

"Did you … tell him about how your mom was out running around with men all the time when you was a young man and it made you mad?"

"No."

"No? Never did tell him that?"

"No, because that'd been an outright lie."

"That ain't what I'd been told," Searcey said to White.

Searcey next said that JoAnn Taylor already had implicated him in the widow's death, and he claimed she was under arrest and singing like a canary.

"She's in custody, too, for Murder One. We've been talking to her. I got a feeling that somebody ain't telling something right. I don't know which one it is, but somebody is in a world of hurt."

"Yeah."

"So which one is it?"

"She's lying to you."

"I got other witnesses that can verify what she said is true, more than one. You were in that apartment that night."

"No."

"Only one thing, you lost something when you were in there, Joe," Searcey said, turning to address his colleague. "Mr. Stevens?"

At that point, Beatrice Detective Sam Stevens took his cue and spoke up. For the moment anyway, Stevens did his part to help his former subordinate run the murder investigation that Stevens previously led.

"The other part of a five-dollar bill," Stevens said.

"You lost it, Joe," Searcey said. "It's got fingerprints on it."

"What five-dollar bill?" White asked.

"It was lying on the floor," Stevens said.

"You forgot to take everything out with you," Searcey told the man who had been pulled from sleep into a real-life nightmare. "You made a mistake. It looked good for a while, but you made a mistake."

Searcey was stretching the truth, as the torn bill left on Wilson's floor did not have any identifiable fingerprints on it.

White was flabbergasted. He thought this talk of a five-dollar bill was utter nonsense.

"I don't know what you're talking about."

"That's not what JoAnn is telling us," Searcey said.

Next, Stevens said he needed to ask White a series of embarrassing questions. "The thing to do is to answer truthful."

"That's what I've been doing," White said.

At this point, Stevens went ahead and asked a number of questions about White's sexuality.

"Are you homosexual?" Stevens asked.

"No."

"Have you ever been homosexual?"

"No."

"Were you homosexual when you was in Beatrice, Nebraska?"

"No."

"Do you recall posing nude out in California?"

"Yes, I was bisexual for a while. I tried it that way. In fact, Tom (Winslow) did have me sleep with him one time. He asked me to and I did, other than that, no."

"But you did have sex with Tom Winslow?"

"One time."

Fielding more questions about his sexuality, White explained that he engaged in gay sex only at Winslow's prodding.

"He asked me to, and I was staying in his apartment at the time. Like I said, I had tried bisexuality at that time."

"And what do you classify Tom as?" Stevens asked White.

"Basically bisexual, because he was sleeping with Beth Johnson at the same time."

The Alabama man had endured enough deep-probing questions about his sexuality. Worse than that, he was taken aback by accusations he had raped and murdered a nearly seventy-year-old Nebraska widow. Sure, he had been involved in petty crime, but nothing like that. First-degree murder in Nebraska meant life in prison or the electric chair, one or the other, if convicted.

White grew agitated: "You come down here charging me with Murder One?"

Searcey: "You know why we did."

"Yeah, you've got reasonable suspicions."

"Yeah, but you know quite a bit."

"I'm telling you that somebody has been lying to you," White said. "And I know nothing of this Helen whatever her name is … except what I heard … on the streets."

As the interrogation persisted, White learned the Nebraska investigators intended to take a blood sample and hairs.

"We maybe even want some sperm," Searcey said.

"OK."

"You know that could positively identify you, right? You know that?"

"Yep," White said. "And it can also positively prove I wasn't there."

"Who was there if you wasn't, Joe?"

"I don't know. I have told you that five times in a row."

"Why would other people put themselves there and make themselves guilty and then say you was there with them if they weren't there?"

"Hell if I know."

"Huh? They're willing to take the rap."

"Well, I'm not because I'm not guilty of anything."

Finally, Searcey revealed that other people had confessed because it wore on their consciences, they could not live with themselves anymore.

"You didn't push the little old lady over?" Searcey said, pressing further.

"How could I? I wasn't there," White declared.

"You didn't take her into the bedroom?"

"I was not there."

"JoAnn Taylor said you both went in there."

"She lied."

"And wrestled with her on the bed."

"She lied."

Just like on the TV cop shows, Searcey decided to level with his murder suspect. It was time to boast about how he had pieced together his theory of Helen Wilson's murder. He speculated that White was one of four people inside Wilson's apartment during her last moments alive. He guessed the other three were JoAnn Taylor, Tom Winslow and Tom's wife, Beth Johnson.

"No doubt in my mind nobody meant to do what happened, but it happened. It happened. And it scared the hell out of everybody," Searcey declared.

At 1:09 a.m. on March 16, 1989, the tense interrogation halted. Despite his repeated denials of guilt, White was destined to return to Beatrice. The wheels of Nebraska's justice system were already turning, and it was chugging down the track with White. His arrest warrant for first-degree murder wasn't about to be torn up. After waiving extradition, White would be put on a plane bound for Beatrice.

CHAPTER 12
GLASS OF ICED TEA

After leaving Beatrice a few short weeks after Helen Wilson's death back in 1985, JoAnn Taylor had returned to High Shoals, North Carolina. She found work at a McDonald's restaurant but later abandoned plans to reunite with her first husband, whom she expected to be released from prison. Instead, she joined the Heart of America carnival shows, based in Augusta, Georgia. For most of that year, she traveled with the carnival, bouncing from town to town.

A native of North Carolina, Ada JoAnn Taylor battled severe psychiatric illnesses in addition to drug and alcohol abuse. By March 1989, Taylor emerged as one of Gage County Sheriff's Deputy Burt Searcey's prime suspects in the rape and murder of Helen Wilson.

In time, Taylor moved to Clyde, Texas, to resume a relationship with a former fiancé. While in the Lone Star State, Taylor rejoined a Jobs Corps program in San Marcus. She studied auto mechanics and nursing, court records show. By 1986, she fell in love with a seventeen-year-old student in the Job Corps, and they got married around Easter that year. She and her new husband moved to Palm Springs, California, where they lived with her new in-laws.

After two months in Palm Springs, she walked out on the marriage. She hitchhiked across the country and wound up in Tulsa, Oklahoma. She joined a carnival known as the James H. Drew Expositions, working in food stands and in the game booths. In Tulsa, she fell in love with a twenty-five-year-old man who worked at a gas station. The two eventually hitchhiked to York, Pennsylvania. Although they talked about marriage, wedding bells never panned out.

Next, she fell in love with another teenager, but that relationship flickered out and she went back to the carnival business. This time, she worked with a "human blockhead" and performed in illusions, court records show. She later talked of performing for the carnival as the girl from "The Exorcist" who could turn her head 360 degrees. For the circus, she also performed as "Ms. Electra," swallowing light bulbs and eating fire. "She also worked as the reptile girl with a sixteen-foot python," court documents state.

Apparently eating light bulbs, swallowing fire, and letting live pythons slither across her body got old. After being on the road for a while, Taylor returned to York, Pennsylvania. She fell in love with a former prisoner who was staying at a rescue mission. Despite that relationship, it was also around this same time that she met a man named Clint Wanker and, around May 1987, became pregnant with Wanker's child. "Clint had worked as a professional clown with the carnival and in the past had worked with underprivileged children. Therefore, (Taylor) believed he understood what she had been through in her life," court records state. However, over the next eighteen months, she remained in a steady relationship with the ex-convict from the rescue mission.

In late 1987, Taylor returned to Leicester, North Carolina, to see her mother for the first time in seven years. By this point, her parents had a dairy farm and her grandmother also lived there. When Taylor and the ex-con arrived together, she was already eight months pregnant and had a black eye as a result of domestic violence. Then, just before the birth of Taylor's third child, her boyfriend got into a spat with her grandmother and left her for good. On January 31, 1988, Taylor gave birth to a boy she named William Crisley Taylor Jr., in honor of her first husband. After the birth, she and her first husband reconnected briefly. He now had been out of prison for a couple of years. Their reunification didn't last, though, and one day he disappeared and drifted out of her life again. She chose to stick around her native North Carolina, living on public welfare to get by.

In 1988, she was on the move again. She brought her infant son back to York, hoping to reconcile with the violent ex-con who stayed at the rescue mission. It was a bad move. The domestic violence intensified. During the summer of 1988, Taylor was smacked in the right eye. The wound required ten stitches, court records show. When she refused to let her batterer see her baby boy, he grew livid. He "put a price on my head," Taylor later told a psychiatrist. Finally, the turbulent relationship ended for good in September 1988.

Three months later, in December, Taylor reached her breaking point. She lost patience with her nearly one-year-old son. Thoughts of suicide swirled inside her head. But she persevered, for the sake of her child. Over the Christmas holidays, she sought treatment in a hospital emergency room. The doctor prescribed Thorazine, an anti-psychotic medication. Shortly afterward, she became a meat slicer in York at J's Steak and Sub. But just in time for her son's first birthday, Taylor decided to leave Pennsylvania. She became convinced that her abusive ex-boyfriend would kill her son if she stayed there much longer.

She returned to her mother's dairy farm in unincorporated Leicester, North Carolina, about five miles from Asheville. She found herself in a serious romance with a man named Jim Phillips, whom she met when he worked at a McDonald's. They set a wedding date for April 18, 1989.

Unfortunately, their wedding plans came crashing down a month beforehand, thanks to Burt Searcey's investigative theory in an old murder case more than 1,000 miles away.

***

Late on the night on March 15, 1989, officers from the Buncombe County Sheriff's Office, armed with loaded guns, invaded the dairy farm outside Leicester. Taylor was rustled out of bed in her nightgown, marched outside and thrown into a squad car. She put her hands behind her back and offered no resistance. As the handcuffs were tightened, she learned she was being charged with first-degree murder, but that it wasn't a local crime.

After bringing her to Asheville, three local investigators questioned Taylor about her suspected involvement in a four-year-old murder halfway across the country in Beatrice, Nebraska. That initial interview was not recorded. However, Taylor was told that Nebraska cops could prove she committed the murder. She also heard that a name from her past, Joseph White, had implicated her -- clearly a lie fed by the cops as an investigative ploy.

Taylor was unaware that White had stubbornly denied any knowledge or involvement in the Beatrice homicide after being hauled into custody in Alabama. Pressured by the cops, and apparently believing she'd been implicated, she quickly confessed to participating in the murder, reports show. According to her version of events, she and White went to some woman's house to do yard work or trim the lady's trees.

"JoAnn's not real sure what time it was. She thinks it may have been dusk or maybe 5:30 or 6 in the afternoon," North Carolina investigators jotted down.

In any event, Taylor claimed White and another young man had joined her, though she failed to remember his name, reports state. Her official statement reflects that the murder of Helen Wilson happened this way:

When the lady answered her door, White requested a glass of iced tea. The woman went back inside to make White some tea. Meanwhile, Taylor asked permission to use the lady's bathroom. Then, when White and the other unidentified male entered her house, the lady grew upset. White turned berserk. He grabbed the lady's arm. "Let go," the woman hollered. White shoved the woman and smacked her into a table. White punched the older woman as his other helper held the lady against the floor. At that point, White indulged in raping the woman. Disgusted, Taylor said she turned her head away and tried not to watch. The idea of fleeing entered her mind, but the door was locked, she remembered. As the rape continued, White then threatened to harm Taylor. "Help me, bitch, or I will kill you then kill your daughter," Taylor said White had told her.

When White finished, he clutched Taylor and held her captive while the other guy got his turn to rape the old lady. During the second rape, the beaten woman stared into space. Her eyes were expressionless. Her screams were loud and frightful. Taylor said she saw the helpless victim's bare breasts. At this point, White dropped his trousers and positioned his knee onto his victim's left shoulder. He tightly gripped his knife. Then he stabbed the lady multiple times.

A trail of blood and stab wounds stretched across the body. Though the woman appeared lifeless, White and the other male continued raping her, according to Taylor.

Eventually, Taylor escaped the house and sat for at least ten minutes inside a small baby-blue colored car. She said she couldn't remember who owned that car. She thought they borrowed it. Anyway, when White emerged from the house he reached into the back seat where a plastic bag contained another set of clothes.

"Oh, you've got clothes?" she told police she remembered asking.

"Yeah, they're Lobo's clothes," she said the other man responded.

White grabbed the bag and ran back into the dead woman's home. There, he changed and returned to the parked car.

"That feels good," White said and grinned.

Then, the three sped off. Their first stop was at a filling station. Taylor figured White had stolen some money from the lady's house because he paid for gas with cash. After fueling up, the trio went out to eat, though Taylor admitted she was foggy on those details. Normally, White preferred McDonald's or the local truck stop restaurant. Later that night, Taylor recalled, she asked White why he raped and harmed the poor lady.

"She's a slut and a bitch. I just know," White reportedly said.

It was well after dark when the little blue car dropped off Taylor at her residence. She never saw or heard from White ever again, she said as she wrapped up her account for the arresting officers.

The North Carolina detectives noted in their reports that Taylor said she "can still shut her eyes and see the blood, the stab wounds and each of them taking turns raping this lady."

The North Carolina officials didn't know any of the actual details of the Beatrice murder so they didn't realize Taylor's confession pretty much got all the facts wrong.

After her arrest, Taylor looked catatonic. During one of her subsequent videotaped interviews with Nebraska police, she reiterated her paranoia that White would kidnap and kill her daughter, Rachel, even though the young girl was in the Nebraska foster care system and Taylor's parental rights had been revoked years ago. Regarding the murder of Wilson, "I tried to put it out of my mind," she remarked. "I tried to forget all about Nebraska completely. I tried to forget the people I knew here. When I leave a town, I leave it behind me, friends and everything is behind me. It's gone."

At the time of Taylor's arrest, Beatrice Detective Sam Stevens was not privy to Taylor's initial interview statement to the North Carolina cops. Many years later, when he was made aware of the statement, he noted he was flabbergasted by how distorted it was from reality. "She said here (Mrs. Wilson) was dead in her opinion, and then she goes down to the next line and says she was screaming," Stevens pointed out. "This don't make a bit of sense to me. (It) just makes me sick to read it."

A confession is nothing but garbage if the person's statement does not match the facts of the crime, Stevens would say later.

***

Following Taylor's arrest in Asheville by local authorities, some members of the Nebraska law enforcement entourage flew on from Alabama to North Carolina to apprehend her themselves.

On the flight back to Nebraska with prisoner Taylor, there was a hellacious storm – thunder, lightning and torrential rains. This was dangerous weather to fly a small aircraft cross-country. "JoAnn was really scared. She was crying. She was petrified," Stevens remembered.

At one point, Gage County Sheriff DeWitt insisted that the Nebraska State Patrol pilot fly through the storm anyway. "We probably should have landed and waited the storm out," Stevens reflected. "I'm not too sure about the state patrolman that was driving the airplane. Somewhere along the line, I think that he even said he was going to have to (land)."

But this small rickety plane was not about to land under any circumstances, not with gruff Sheriff DeWitt calling the shots. DeWitt even volunteered to take control of the wings. The small-town sheriff was a certified pilot and he had confidence in his aviation skills, court documents reflect. Stevens tried to stay calm. He sat in his seat and prayed silently, hoping they would not crash land into a cornfield. Initially, he failed to grasp why it was so vital to fly through the raging storm to rush back to Nebraska. Once the plane landed safely at the Beatrice Municipal Airport, the answer became apparent. "All of the reporters are there and the press was there and everybody's there waiting," Stevens said later.

Back on the ground, Stevens let DeWitt and the other cops on the plane enjoy their moment of newfound fame. "I wanted no part of it. I didn't talk to nobody," Stevens said.

Stevens scampered off the plane and avoided the media spotlight altogether. "I called the Police Department in Beatrice and told them to come pick me up," Stevens said.

***

The March 16, 1989, edition of the *Beatrice Daily Sun* carried a banner front-page headline: "Two arrested in 4-year-old Beatrice murder." A graphic showed maps of Alabama and North Carolina, the two states where the pair of co-defendants had been captured. The huge break in the crime was the talk of town and beyond. Nebraska television stations, local radio, the *Beatrice Daily Sun* and the *Lincoln Journal* dispatched journalists to gather up more details about the arrests that had caught everyone by surprise.

At the Gage County Courthouse, the county's top two elected officials, Sheriff DeWitt and prosecutor Dick Smith, afforded the Nebraska press the red carpet treatment. Smith's press conference lasted forty-five minutes. Reporters learned that White had appeared before a judge in Alabama and waived extradition. He was put on an American Airlines plane in Huntsville bound for Omaha. Beatrice Police Captain Elvin Waltke and Price, the police psychologist, accompanied him back. White was denied bail.

The Saturday, March 18, edition of the *Beatrice Daily Sun* published a large photo of co-defendant JoAnn Taylor stepping out of a sheriff's car at the Gage County Jail. Her wrists were bound by steel handcuffs. "In custody," the caption read. The Beatrice paper mentioned how the sheriff and his investigators had not gotten much sleep the past week. The sheriff told the hometown newspaper that Tom Winslow's information "played an important part" in the arrests of Taylor and White.

"Of course, our job is just now starting. We've got a long row to hoe yet," DeWitt told the newspaper. "I'm glad we're this far along. I know the community is well relieved."

For certain, the pair of arrests was well-received in southeast Nebraska. After all, the revolting murder of a Beatrice senior citizen had terrorized the town and gone unsolved for four long frustrating years. Now, there were two fewer empty beds at the Gage County Jail. Two former Beatrice vagabonds were being held in the jail facing first-degree murder charges.

"I'm glad they caught them," Bud Roberts of Wymore told the *Beatrice Daily Sun.*

"I assumed in my mind they'd never get caught," Phil Knowles of Beatrice told the newspaper.

Gage County Deputy Burt Searcey was credited in the newspaper for his tenacious investigative work. He made sure the Wilson killing was never forgotten.

Unbeknown to the public, Sheriff DeWitt was busy pulling strings behind the scenes. He tasked Deputy Mark Meints with obtaining a copy of the videotape recording of the Wilson crime scene, along with the recording of the autopsy. Those tapes were housed at the Beatrice Police Department, the original lead investigative agency. Without the sheriff gaining access to the crime scene videotape, it's highly doubtful any of the ensuing criminal prosecutions would succeed inside the halls of justice.

***

Of course, White and Taylor were not the only lost souls being charged in the Beatrice widow's murder. Now that they were in custody, the immunity deal with Tom Winslow was about to be torn to shreds after he'd had only a few days of freedom. Unbeknown to Winslow, Taylor was shown a police photo lineup inside the Gage County Jail. Authorities wanted her to implicate Winslow as the mystery man she spoke of during her initial statement back in North Carolina.

"I just recall making a photo lineup," Stevens later testified. "But there's tricks to doing photo lineups too because when you do a photo lineup, you put ... five, six pictures in there and probably eighty percent of the time, they pick number three, that's a known fact."

Before Taylor was furnished the photo lineup consisting of six male faces, she was told ahead of time that her one-time former boyfriend, Mark Goodson, had already been ruled out as a suspect. His photo was included in the photo lineup anyway. Another mugshot belonged to Winslow. Four additional mugshots came from guys Taylor didn't know. She picked out the mugshot of Winslow, just as the Gage County authorities wanted her to do. Years later, a trial lawyer representing one of the Beatrice 6 clients insinuated the photo lineup had been rigged.

***

Once in custody, Taylor changed her original story and claimed Winslow, now twenty-three, had also raped the widow and served as the getaway driver.

Around 7:00 p.m. on March 17, 1989, Sheriff's Deputies Gerald Lamkin and Mark Meints, and State Troopers Steven Gill and David Hanzelmann, converged on a trailer home on North Eighth Street in Wymore, Nebraska. When Winslow emerged on the porch, the four cops put him in cuffs, arresting him for first-degree murder.

Clearly, the powers of Gage County had suckered a desperate and gullible Tom Winslow into signing the Use Immunity Agreement that then catapulted their murder investigation with the issuance of arrest warrants for White and Taylor.

Then, just days later, that document was torn up under the pretext that Winslow had lied and minimized his true involvement in Wilson's rape-murder.

A day after Winslow's arrest in the murder, the Nebraska State Patrol plane flew Searcey to Dell City, Oklahoma, to interview Goodson, who was living there after joining the military. He acknowledged he had been in contact with the Beatrice Police Department within a few weeks of Wilson's murder claiming Taylor had confessed she and White had gotten away with the murder.

Searcey asked him, "In your own mind, after you hung up that telephone, when you got done talking to JoAnn Taylor, did you actually believe that she was involved in the murder?"

Goodson: "To a point, yes, it's just that I would not put anything past her because as I told you earlier, I woke up a couple times with her hands around my throat."

When Goodson insisted he had nothing to do with the widow's murder, Searcey believed him.

When White insisted he had nothing to do with the murder, Searcey refused to believe him.

***

After White was in custody, Deputy Meints ordered White to stand against the concrete block wall for his police mugshot. Beatrice Police Lieutenant Gary Wiebe came by to help obtain White's fingerprints. That night, White ate his first supper at the Gage County Jail. As he munched on his food, he struck up a conversation with a deputy.

"Joseph, in conversation, advised this deputy that he thought that he's only going to be in our facility for approximately one week as he returned to Nebraska to get this taken care of," Meints said in a written statement. "He stated he did not do the murder and wants to get this all taken care of and return back to his home."

CHAPTER 13
THE SNITCH

As the murder investigation continued, Sheriff DeWitt worked like a puppet master, pulling more behind-the-scenes strings. He notified the Lancaster County Jail in Lincoln that his agency wanted to interview inmate Clifford Shelden regarding his still developing murder probe.

Not surprisingly, Shelden responded favorably. Shelden saw a chance to shave many years off his eventual prison sentence for clubbing a man over the head with a tire iron during the Harvester Motel robbery attempt. Plus, it presented a golden opportunity to settle old scores with people who had wounded Shelden's heart and double-crossed him. During the 1980s, Shelden was a scoundrel and the kind of weasel who would squeal on his old friends because many of them no longer served his needs.

Deputy Searcey traveled to Lincoln to interview Shelden at the jail.

Now, more than four years after the fact, Clifford Shelden seemed to know practically everything about the Wilson murder, even though he had never been at the scene.

Hospital records confirmed Shelden had been treated for a venereal disease on the night of the murder. The sexually transmitted disease left him so ill he was unable to walk at that time, according to police reports. "I was in there because I have gonorrhea in my blood system," he told Searcey. While hospitalized, Shelden recalled that his future wife,

149

Debbie, often visited. They married about two months later. As for the murder, Shelden admitted he learned about it after he got out of the hospital.

With Searcey listening, Shelden made an unsubstantiated claim that JoAnn Taylor, the former girlfriend who broke his heart, had sent him a letter from Indiana within a few months of the killing. "She (asked) me a question why I married my wife, and then she asked to leave my wife and live down in Indiana with her," Shelden claimed, police reports show. "Specifically, she told me her, Tom Winslow and Joseph Edgar White was responsible for the death of Helen Wilson … (JoAnn), Tom and Joseph broke into her place, proceeded on taking her money and assaulting her sexually, assaulting her, murdering her."

"JoAnn Taylor actually wrote that in a letter to you?" Searcey asked.

"Yes."

"Did she tell you how much money may have been taken?"

"Somewhere between $800 or $1,800. She told me that it was either in her purse or some kind of container."

"And how did she find this money?"

"By, uh, rummaging through her apartment."

For unknown reasons, Searcey did not challenge the inmate's statements, which based on crime scene evidence seemed obviously false. More than $1,300 in cash and money market certificates had been left untouched in easy to find places in Wilson's apartment. Besides, both the Beatrice Police Department and esteemed FBI psychological profiler Pete Klismet already had ruled out robbery as the motive.

As the jail interview continued, Shelden declared that his former partner in crime, Tom Winslow, had confided in him about the murder. The two were no longer friends, he told Searcey.

"He told me that, um, they more or less dragged her into the living room, JoAnn Taylor and Joseph Edgar White. He told me that she was screaming and hollering and kicking her feet, fighting with them, so, uh, Joseph White grabbed a pillow and, uh, put it over her face to quiet her down. Then JoAnn, uh, held her wrists, and JoAnn called for Tom, and Tom came in and grabbed her legs to keep her, uh, feet from pounding on the floor because right underneath there was another apartment."

Then, savagery took over. In the words of Shelden, White told Tom Winslow, "Let's have a little fun with her."

"Joseph White tore off her clothes," Shelden said Winslow had told him.

"Did he have sexual intercourse with her?" Searcey asked.

"Yes, he did. And then JoAnn was caressing Mrs. Helen Wilson's body, uh, I believe she even got to kissing her or doing something else."

Searcey remained locked into the mindset that more than just the three people he arrested had been present.

"And who did Tom tell you was involved with the incident that night?"

Shelden sighed. "He said it was my wife, but I don't believe him whatsoever because I've known Tom too long, and I know he's a constant liar. He lies about everything."

Shelden said his wife, Debbie Shelden, supposedly smacked her head on Wilson's bedroom mirror, breaking the mirror and cutting her head. However, proving his story a fabrication, the crime scene showed no such chaos. Sheets had been yanked off the victim's bed, but no damage was done to any bedroom furniture. No mirrors were shattered, much less cracked.

Searcey: "I believe you stated she cut her head?"

Shelden: "Yeah, that's what Tom Winslow told me. That she just supposedly cut the back of her head and … blood was coming out of the back of her head."

Still, Shelden said he harbored serious doubts that his wife could have been involved. He did not see any clumps of missing hair or cuts to her head after being released from the hospital.

As Searcey wrapped up the interview, he asked Shelden whether, if he were called into court, he would testify to the very same statements he had given that day.

Shelden answered, "Yes, I would."

The cunning inmate had greased the wheels of justice against his ex-girlfriend Taylor, his former partner in crime Winslow and their mutual acquaintance White. Unfortunately for Clifford Shelden, by opening his mouth, he lost the woman he loved. He had implicated his own wife.

Something in Debbie Shelden's background convinced Searcey that she had an obvious link to the murder in apartment Unit 4.

CHAPTER 14
DEBBIE'S DILEMMA

Born in May of 1958, Debra (Brown) Shelden lived a meek and humble existence in her hometown of Beatrice. She came from a broken home and endured her share of hardships. She believed her father was a full-blooded Cherokee Indian and her mother was also part Cherokee, court transcripts reflect. Debbie was placed into the Nebraska foster care system when her mother gave her up for adoption. Fortunately, her foster mother was nice and there was never any abuse.

Debbie Shelden was a special education student while growing up in Beatrice. She was also a distant relative of murder victim Helen Wilson.

Debbie spent her formative years in the Beatrice Public Schools' special education program. Psychological testing put her into the borderline category for mild mental retardation, court transcripts show. She later claimed she skipped sixth grade when public school officials moved her from fifth to seventh grade as part of an apparent mix-up. At any rate, Debbie earned her diploma and graduated from Beatrice Community High School in 1976. Going to college was not an option, so Debbie took a low-paying job as an aide at the Beatrice State Developmental Center, the massive state-run institution that housed persons with profound and severe mental disabilities. But the job did not last long. In 1977, at age nineteen, she married after becoming pregnant and was then known as Debbie Hartman. When her child was born, Debbie wanted to return to work, but her foster mother cautioned her to stay home and care for her newborn. It soon became apparent Debbie lacked many necessary life skills to function in society and raise a child. Compounding her problems, Debbie's marriage collapsed. By 1978, at the age of twenty, Debbie was divorced and collecting public welfare, court records show. Around this time, child protective service officials intervened after child abuse allegations arose. Debbie's child was removed from her care. During this miserable time in her life, Debbie began to undergo therapy sessions with the clinical psychologists at Blue Valley in Beatrice – including clinical director Wayne Price.

"Debbie does seem to have a sincere concern for her child and the desire to care for the child and to meet its needs emotionally and physically ... At the present time, however, she does not appear to have learned how to do so."

-- Wayne R. Price from a memo to probation officials, October 24, 1978.

Ultimately, Debbie put her only child up for adoption on the advice of her court-appointed psychologists, child welfare agents and adult probation officials. Debbie was weak-willed and susceptible to outside influence. "She recognizes the need for a stable home and a two-parent family, which she feels she cannot give the child," another psychologist wrote the Gage County Court on February 2, 1979.

The 1980s were chaotic and unstable for Debbie Hartman. During that period, she mostly lived with her mother and stepfather. She relocated clear across the state, residing in North Platte, Ogallala and even Wyoming, court records state. Debbie gravitated toward other like-minded souls who battled their own personal demons and mental disorders. These were dreary folks, some of them homeless and living in a car. They would struggle to find jobs and were constantly on the move. At one point, Debbie visited the Indian Center in Lincoln and told them she thought she had Cherokee heritage. She was left with the impression that if she proved she was three-fourths American Indian, she could receive tribal money. However, Debbie was not an ambitious person. She didn't follow through.

In 1984, Debbie returned to her hometown of Beatrice. There, she fell madly in love with Clifford Shelden. Debbie later testified the blossoming romance made her stepfather livid. "He was jealous, and he kicked me out," she later testified.

Then, two months after the murder of Helen Wilson, the couple married in April of 1985. At first, they shared a trailer, but since Clifford had no job, they often found themselves behind on the rent.

One day, Debbie heard someone knocking on her trailer door. It was a nicely dressed man with a mustache and glasses who identified himself as a private investigator. After introducing himself, Burt Searcey told Debbie and the other trailer occupants that he was there investigating the Helen Wilson slaying. That day, Debbie Shelden denied knowing anything, but acknowledged Wilson was her great-aunt. Her new husband, Clifford Shelden, told Searcey he had been in the hospital, so he had a solid alibi. Tom Winslow and his wife, Beth Johnson, also denied knowing anything about the widow's rape and murder.

That following month, the Sheldens moved out of the trailer and into a vacant four-room unit at 212 N. Sixth St. -- *the same unit where Wilson had been raped and murdered!*

Debbie later testified how she experienced nightmares and had difficulty sleeping at the unit where her great-aunt suffered her excruciating death.

As an adult, Debbie Shelden battled severe obesity and wore thick eyeglasses. She had long straight dark hair and usually wore a frown on her face. She was impressionable and vulnerable.

From 1985 until 1989, Debbie stayed faithfully married to Clifford Shelden, the same Beatrice rascal who had been infatuated with JoAnn Taylor and had delusions of bringing Taylor to Montana, according to reports. By the late 1980s, Debbie lost contact with her first child, who had been placed in foster care. Thanks to her second marriage, Debbie was now a mother once again. She and Clifford named their child Fantasia and happily raised her without interference from the Nebraska court system. However, the marriage was on the rocks by late 1988 after Clifford went to jail for partnering up with Tom Winslow in the armed robbery and beating at the Harvester Motel in Lincoln. Still, Debbie persevered. She and her child moved to the Lamp Lighter trailer court in Lincoln.

In the spring of 1989, Debbie Shelden was unaware that she was about to become another target in the criminal investigation of the 1985 Wilson homicide.

***

This time, Beatrice Police Detective Stevens was with Sheriff's Deputy Searcey when they knocked on the door of Debbie's mobile home. Debbie denied she had any involvement or first-hand knowledge about the murder of her great-aunt. What she knew about the slaying came from the *Beatrice Daily Sun* or from television news, she explained.

Besides, she and her great-aunt had met on only a couple of occasions -- at extended family dinners during the holidays.

The two cops left the trailer park that afternoon in 1989 without making headway. But during the forty-mile drive back to Beatrice, Searcey pondered the young woman's demeanor. Then he thought about her reaction to his questions.

"I just felt that the way she acted and stuff, that she may have some knowledge of it," Searcey said later. "She was always kind of a suspect of mine because she was a niece of the lady that was killed."

On April 13, Searcey and Deputy Gerald Lamkin drove back to Debbie's home at the Lincoln trailer park. She agreed to let them interview her again, this time at the Lincoln Police Department. The interview lasted from about 4:00 to 7:00 p.m. The news wasn't good, she learned. Her jailed husband had just implicated her the day before as being present with Taylor, White, and Winslow during her great-aunt's murder. The mentally disabled woman's nerves were rattled. Her first child had already been taken away from her. Was she now about to lose her second child, her sweet daughter Fantasia, if she didn't play ball with these pesky sheriff's deputies? In Debbie's mind, perhaps the only way to keep her family intact was to confess, even if that meant going along with Deputy Searcey's far-fetched assertions.

Given her plight, she wilted under the pressure. That evening, Debbie Shelden was taken into custody and brought back to Beatrice, charged as an accomplice in the killing of her great-aunt. At the Gage County Jail, she swapped out her civilian clothes for orange prisoner garb. Even though she already had implicated herself in the Wilson murder, Debbie Shelden remained compliant, still wanting to please her captors. The following afternoon, on April 14, 1989, the new jailhouse prisoner sat down for another interview. But when she claimed under questioning to have been one of four people present, Searcey quickly corrected her, telling her that he knew there were at least five people involved.

"And did all five of you people get into Mr. Winslow's vehicle?"

"Yes."

"Who was in the vehicle?"

Debbie Shelden rattled off the names of her old acquaintances, Tom Winslow, JoAnn Taylor, Joseph White, James Dean, and herself.

"Are you sure of that?"

"Yes."

Of course, she already knew the first three names were people who already had been charged with the murder.

Shelden claimed she and James Dean rode together in the back seat.

"And he was a friend of yours?"

"Yes."

She was asked to describe James Dean.

"I would say he's five-ten, kind of heavy. He's got dark hair, brown eyes, kind of muscular to tall."

Searcey reminded Shelden that during her previous police interviews, she never once mentioned Dean's presence at the crime.

"And now you say James Dean was there. And yesterday you couldn't remember that. Is that what you were telling us? And why couldn't you remember that?"

The weak-willed woman did not have a strong response.

"I was blocking it, I guess. I wasn't thinking enough to get it all out."

Searcey turned up the heat.

"Are you lying to us?" he asked.

"No."

"Are you telling us the truth?"

"Yes."

Shelden said she guessed the rape lasted up to two hours long. She maintained that Winslow, White and Taylor had carried the screaming woman from her bedroom out to the living room where the rape became more violent and ultimately turned fatal.

"Why didn't you just run away and get some help?" Searcey asked.

"I was scared. I didn't know that they were even going to try anything."

She claimed the crime was all Taylor's idea. It was intended to be a robbery.

Afterward, she said, the five young adults regrouped back at Winslow's green Oldsmobile. Winslow, Taylor and White crowded into the front seat. Debbie Shelden and Dean again hopped in the back. Shelden said she thought she was let out back at her apartment.

"I stayed there and washed my hair."

"And why did you wash your hair?"

"The stuff that was in my hair, the wet puss stuff, the kind of like blood. And it was wet, gooey stuff. I washed it out."

Searcey asked about Dean's demeanor as the brutal attack unfolded.

"It was no big deal to him. According to his actions, he didn't act like he cared."

CHAPTER 15
THE POLYGRAPH TEST

He was born in 1964 with a famous name, but James Leroy Dean's life was nothing like a glamorous Hollywood movie. Dean came from Columbus, Nebraska, a blue-collar city similar in size to Beatrice during the 1960s.

Dean was physically abused as a boy by his father, court records reflect. By the time he was fifteen, Dean's father had deserted the family. As a teenager, Dean was hyperactive and a heavy smoker. After his family moved to Oklahoma, Dean was sent to a juvenile detention center. At age sixteen, he moved back to Nebraska, but chose to drop out high school in ninth grade. Dean ended up in Beatrice around 1981. In his twenties, Dean drank a lot and hung around the bars. He gravitated toward other disenfranchised lost souls.

James Leroy Dean had his share of problems – he grew up in a broken home and he was hyperactive -- but he never expected to find himself jailed as an accomplice in the rape and murder of Beatrice widow Helen Wilson.

In 1985, Dean traveled to Lincoln and to Fremont to spend time with his mother and his sister. He also settled down with a woman named Kathy Bartak and had two children with her. After working for a while in Beatrice as a bricklayer, Dean became a demolition contractor in Lincoln.

On April 15, 1989, Dean's twenty-fifth birthday, he parked his truck at the Hy-Vee grocery store on Lincoln's north side and got a ride to his work assignment. Hours later, his employer brought him back to the parking lot. As Dean went to his fetch his truck, a team of Nebraska police officers surrounded him with guns drawn -- ready to shoot, if necessary. Dean was astonished. He had no idea what crime he could have committed. To his surprise, Dean found himself the fifth co-defendant swept up in the four-year-old Beatrice murder case. Dean was stuffed into a squad car and driven to the Lancaster County Jail in Lincoln.

Eventually, Gage County Deputies Burdette Searcey and Gerald Lamkin made the forty-mile drive up Highway 77 to bring Dean back to the Gage County Jail. At the jail, Dean furnished saliva and blood samples, court documents show. The next day, April 16, Deputies Searcey and Lamkin interviewed their new prisoner for nearly three hours. Dean steadfastly maintained he was innocent.

At the jail, Dean was permitted to make one phone call. On April 17, he dialed up an attorney he knew in Lincoln named Richard Schmeling. Schmeling worked in general practice and had previously represented Dean on a number of misdemeanor traffic offenses. Dean's desperate phone calls were in vain. Schmeling opted to steer clear of Dean and chose not meet with the jailed prisoner until after the court made his formal appointment as defense counsel on April 19, 1989. A decade later, Schmeling was officially disbarred by the Nebraska Supreme Court based on unethical conduct involving a number of unrelated civil cases.

On April 17, 1989, another banner front-page headline appeared in the Beatrice paper: "Five in custody in Wilson murder." Dean sported a thick dark mustache and a sullen look in his jailhouse mugshot that ran in the *Beatrice Daily Sun*. At the Gage County Courthouse, Judge Steven Timm denied Dean the chance to post bail.

***

Back in 1985, Dean hadn't given much thought to Helen Wilson's murder, something that touched a deep nerve for many around Beatrice. Obviously, Dean was aware of the case because it was the talk of the town and the subject of several front-page newspaper articles. Like the others, Dean was clueless that he would later become sucked into Burdette Searcey's dragnet.

He was now one of a staggering five co-defendants all jailed and awaiting trial in the rape and murder of the elderly widow. White, twenty-six, of Cullman, Alabama; Taylor, twenty-five, of Asheville, North Carolina; and Winslow, twenty-three, of Wymore, Nebraska, were all facing first-degree murder charges. Dean, twenty-five, and Debbie Shelden, thirty, both of Lincoln, were being charged with aiding and abetting a first-degree murder. If Dean and Shelden took their cases to a jury trial and lost, they faced a maximum penalty of life in prison. Compounding their plight, Dean and Shelden were dirt poor, just like the others, so they had to rely on the appointments of public defenders for their legal representation.

Less than two weeks after being arrested, Debbie Shelden threw in the towel and gave up her fight to prove her innocence. In extraordinarily quick fashion, she admitted guilt in open court, in the presence of her public defender, the prosecutor and before the judge.

163

"I plead guilty because I was there at the scene, and I should be properly punished," Debbie Shelden told long-time Gage County District Judge William Rist, the local newspaper reported. A front-page headline with Debbie's depressing mugshot ran in the *Beatrice Daily Sun* on April 27, 1989, "Shelden pleads guilty to amended murder charge."

Decades later, Beatrice attorney Paul Korslund reflected on his representation of Debbie Shelden as her court-appointed counsel and the decision to let her plead guilty.

"I cared deeply about Debbie from the beginning of my representation. I believed she was innocent because she had no criminal intent, a key element the prosecution would have to prove to obtain a conviction. I never doubted, however, that the story she told me was not the truth … The job of a defense attorney is to get the best possible result for the client, and I tried hard to do that. I also worked to be sure she would not lose custody of her child. I thought long and hard about taking her case to trial and mounting a defense that she had no criminal intent. I consulted with my law partners. My partners and I concluded that it was an enormous risk to go to trial with a possible result of life imprisonment.

"A jury would have been revolted by the facts of the crime," Korslund explained. "The other option was to plead to the lower charge with the prosecutor recommending the most lenient prison sentence and showing the judge that she had cooperated fully."

Korslund also gleaned the victim's family probably would not oppose early parole for Shelden, given that she was a relative and the first defendant to enter a guilty plea.

"It was in her best interest, under all the attendant circumstances, to have her cooperate and plead to a lesser crime and drastically reduced possible sentence," Korslund said.

Days later, a second domino was about to topple thanks to the wheelers and dealers of the Gage County justice system. Prosecutor Dick Smith worked out another pact, this time with Dean's court-appointed counsel, Richard Schmeling. Dean would plead guilty in connection with Wilson's slaying if he failed an upcoming polygraph test at the office of Paul "Jake" Jacobson, a highly decorated retired Lincoln Police Department detective.

On Saturday, April 29, a pair of Gage County deputies removed the shackled prisoner from his jail cell. Years later, Dean recalled being tormented by the deputies during his transport that day, repeatedly being told how he was likely to die in Nebraska's electric chair if he failed to be truthful about the facts of the killing. Upon their arrival in Lincoln, Dean nonetheless strutted into Paul Jacobson's office full of exuberance and confidence. He remained his usual hyperactive self. After exchanging pleasantries, he smoked several cigarettes and drank a cup of coffee. Dean boasted how he couldn't wait to take his polygraph test. Dean presumed Gage County would dismiss the felony murder charges and release him from the jail, once he passed the test.

Jacobson had more than twenty years as a licensed polygraph examiner in Nebraska. However, in 1989 Jacobson's detective skills were in decline. He was in his early sixties, collecting a police pension after being retired from Lincoln police force for a number of years. From the outset, before asking the suspect any questions, Jacobson took Searcey at his word that Dean and his circle of deadbeat friends had perpetrated the rape and murder in Beatrice.

"There was no doubt in Deputy Searcey's mind that James Dean had at least been in the apartment on the night of the homicide from the previous investigation he had done," Jacobson wrote Gage County prosecutor Dick Smith in a memo.

On that Saturday in April 1989, Dean told the examiner he used to be a very good liar until a couple of years ago, when he realized he needed to change his ways, reports note. Jacobson made up his mind he wasn't impressed with Dean.

"He is hardly the epitome of truthfulness, yet in a lot of ways, he might be safer in jail at the present time," Jacobson wrote in his report.

According to the interview transcripts, Dean was not entirely sure he had an airtight alibi on the night of the murder some four years ago. His memory was fuzzy. He just knew he wouldn't have been living with his estranged girlfriend, Kathy Bartak, around that period. In early 1985, Dean explained, he mostly bounced back and forth between Lincoln and Beatrice. However, Dean insisted he was never at Wilson's apartment at any point during the murder.

Jacobson was skeptical. In fact, he leveled with Dean that Nebraska's prisons were loaded with people convicted of more severe crimes than the ones they actually committed. The fidgety young man refused to heed Jacobson's advice to confess, and Jacobson hooked up his polygraph machine to measure Dean's pulse and breathing.

Jacobson's polygraph test included the following critical questions and responses by Dean:

Did you deliberately lie when you said you were not in Helen Wilson's apartment the night she was murdered?

No.

Is there anything about this murder that you are trying to hide from me?

No.

Were you present when Helen Wilson was raped and murdered?

No.

Did you go inside of Helen Wilson's apartment the night she was murdered?

No.

Have you told me the complete and absolute truth about everything?

Yes.

Do you have knowledge about Helen Wilson's murder that you are trying to hide from me?

No.

Have you tried to lie to me at any time today?

No.

Once the test was finished, Dean remained chatty, asking Jacobson how he did. Jacobson told Dean that he already knew the answer. Dean nodded and bragged he had passed. Jacobson removed the apparatus from Dean's body and proceeded to show the hyperactive young man his charts from the polygraph machine. There were three possible outcomes: no deception, deception or inconclusive.

For Dean's scores, Jacobson circled the box "Deception Indicated." Dean's polygraph scores looked terrible, Jacobson assured him.

Dean was unfazed. At this stage, Jacobson tried to persuade Dean to consider pleading guilty to a lesser crime than first-degree murder. After all, Dean's very life was now at stake. He was on the verge of being convicted of murder. Until being told he failed the polygraph test, Dean hadn't given much thought to pleading guilty to anything.

"I am fully convinced that he has knowledge he is not sharing and will not change his story until he is backed into a corner," Jacobson stated in his report.

Jacobson ended his polygraph examination report of Dean by trying to drum up more taxpayer-funded business for himself. Reports show he offered to give Gage County a discount rate, if prosecutor Dick Smith retained Jacobson's polygraph services for the other co-defendants in the case, including Debbie Shelden:

"P.S. I should add that in the pre-test interview, I asked Jimmie [Dean] what kind of people that Winslow, White and Taylor were, which you may already know, as to sexual preference," Jacobson wrote Smith. "He said that Taylor was not very selective as she made it with both men and women as did Winslow, but as far as Lobo was concerned, he did not think he was a homosexual."

***

A deal's a deal especially when it involves the criminal justice system. James Dean was now obligated to plead guilty in the death of Helen Wilson thanks to the failed polygraph test results. But there remained a giant problem: Dean remained forceful in his claims of innocence – even after being told he flunked that dubious polygraph test. The prosecutor and sheriff reached the conclusion that Dean needed a friendly visit from "Doc" Wayne Price, the clinical director at the Blue Valley Mental Health Center. These men knew Price was their secret weapon. Perhaps Price, moonlighting as Sheriff's Deputy Price, could use his powers of persuasion to manipulate the vulnerable young man to come to terms with what the law enforcement professionals were sure was his guilt. Just three days after Dean supposedly flunked his polygraph test, the young man fraught with anxiety attacks and a troubled upbringing met with Price for a so-called emergency psychiatric evaluation. In turn, Price wrote a four-page memo to prosecutor Dick Smith based on his interpretation of his May 2, 1989, interview with inmate James Dean:

"The polygraph was positive indicating lying but Mr. Dean continued to persist in his assertion that he was not in the apartment or involved in the homicide," Price wrote.

As this so-called "emergency consultation" interview wore on, Price led Dean into believing that perhaps Dean was really involved in the heinous crime.

"He began to realize that the polygraph was revealing at least at the unconscious level his awareness that he was present in the apartment but could not reconcile his being present with the conscious belief that he was not there ... After a rather extended discussion with Mr. Dean as well as his attorney, he had developed to the scenario that it was likely that Mr. Dean was present in the apartment," Price wrote.

"Consequently it is my clinical impression that he was overwhelmed by the violence that he witnessed, was unable to aid Mrs. Wilson and was unable to flee due to the emotional trauma and may have been further traumatized by comments of the other persons in the apartment."

Several days later, the criminal justice heavyweights of Gage County assembled at the Sheriff's Office: Sheriff DeWitt, Deputy Searcey and prosecutor Smith. Public defender

Richard Schmeling was also there. Dean was led into the office. That afternoon, the sheriff popped a videocassette tape into a recorder and turned on the television. The tape showed the shocking crime scene in 1985, with Helen Wilson's lifeless body sprawled across the living room floor of her apartment in her light-blue nightgown. A feeling of revulsion settled in as Dean watched the video. He grew teary-eyed.

The viewing of the crime scene video was working like a brainwashing technique to imprint the gory details upon Dean's frazzled brain.

Court records reflect that Schmeling, Dean's public defender, had a vivid recollection of Dean's reaction. "I was present for this viewing and recall that Dean was very emotionally affected by this videotape," Schmeling stated. "Dean leaned his head onto my shoulder, and crying, exclaimed, 'Oh, that poor lady, that poor lady!'"

Shortly after, the binding plea agreement was presented. It stipulated Dean would waive his right to a preliminary hearing. Gage County would file an amended charge of aiding and abetting to the second-degree murder of Helen Wilson. Dean volunteered to plead guilty though more than just that was expected to gain leniency at sentencing time.

"The defendant agrees to testify truthfully in any and all cases and give total cooperation to the State of Nebraska regarding the homicide of Helen L. Wilson," county prosecutor Dick Smith wrote. Additionally, Dean would not be sentenced until all of the homicide cases went to trial. "The State will make no recommendation regarding sentencing if the defendant complies with all of the above."

Smith signed the document. Schmeling signed the form. At the bottom right-hand corner, where the type read "James

Dean, Defendant," Dean sealed his fate by signing his name on the dotted line. Sheriff DeWitt made a point to type up a crude investigative memo to stick into Dean's criminal file.

The sheriff's memo stated:

"When I took James Dean his supper, he confided in me that he felt better since he had told the truth about the Helen Wilson homicide. He stated that he had to get this off his mind as it was killing him to think about it in his cell. I asked him why he had held out so long; and he stated he was afraid someone would hurt him if he told the truth. I assured him that no one was going to hurt him and that as long as he was in my custody I would see to that. James became teary eyed when he was telling me that. He was relieved that he had finally admitted to being in the apartment when Helen Wilson was killed."

Back in his solitary jail cell, Dean also began experiencing nightmares. The videotape of the crime scene showing Helen Wilson's body had messed with his mind.

CHAPTER 16
DETECTIVE WANTS OUT

The extremely high-profile nature of the small-town murder case had tremendous potential to cement political and professional legacies around the Gage County Courthouse. But some leaders thought they recognized they had a rat on their ship. Beatrice Police Detective Sam Stevens appeared to be poking holes in their work, undermining their efforts.

After White and Taylor were detained and awaiting trial, Stevens began to assess the strengths and weaknesses of the sheriff's case. Once Stevens learned the confidential informants for Searcey's arrest warrants were really Lisa Brown and Charlotte Bishop, the Beatrice detective began to harbor grave doubts. After all, JoAnn Taylor's mental disorders and her delusional behavior were well-documented. She drifted in and out of reality. Stevens was skeptical that Taylor had confessed to a bitter enemy. He remembered Taylor nearly broke Brown's arm during that one memorable cat fight outside a downtown tavern. "JoAnn chased her out or something. And I think she ... wound the window up on her door and almost broke her wrist or something," Stevens noted.

As he dug deeper into the case, Stevens realized Brown was blabbing around town that Taylor and White had raped and suffocated the widow. "And that was, I think, in retaliation toward JoAnn Taylor," Stevens said.

Years later, Stevens erupted in laughter when asked under oath about Charlotte Bishop's credibility as a police informant. "She's about like a JoAnn only three times as bad," Stevens laughed. "She was just a liar. And she just lied. And I almost want to say a mental case. She was a very, very, unsanitary girl. She didn't take care of herself. I hate to say the words in reports, but maybe a retard?"

After the arrests of White and Taylor, Stevens was directed by the prosecutor to interview Lisa Brown's father-in-law. During the interview, Stevens made an off-the-cuff remark. "Anyway, for some reason later on or that day or something, Officer Searcey went back and questioned Wilber Brown," Stevens recalled. "And Wilber told him that I had a bunch of stuff that I had said that apparently wasn't true. I don't remember what it was ..."

Gage County leaders decided to steamroll Detective Stevens before his meddling in the Wilson murder case caused them irreparable harm. Still, a friendly co-worker tipped off Stevens to a top-secret meeting taking place at county offices. Even though Stevens remembered he was off that day, he stormed in anyway.

"It must have been my day off because I know I had drank a few beers," Stevens remembered. When Stevens showed up unannounced at the Sheriff's Office, he said a civilian employee asked, "What are you doing?"

"I hear they're talking about me," Stevens replied, and the confrontation intensified.

"You can't go in there!"

"I can go in there!"

"You can't go in there!"

"I can go in there!"

Finally, Stevens barged into the closed-door meeting.

"If this is a closed meeting," Stevens shouted, "I should be invited if it's about me."

His presence caused a ruckus. "Sheriff DeWitt throws everything on the floor, gets all upset and goes on a rampage," Stevens recalled later.

Besides noticing the sheriff, Stevens saw prosecutor Dick Smith, plus his own immediate supervisor, Beatrice Police Captain Elvin Waltke. Others included the Beatrice mayor and the Gage County Board of Supervisors chairman, Stevens later testified. Stevens said he begged the prosecutor to tell him what was being discussed behind those closed doors.

"Richard, I'm a Catholic, just the same as you are, why don't we be truthful?" Stevens recalled saying.

But Dick Smith and the rest of the room stayed mum. "Nobody would tell me what's going on," he said.

Stevens knew there was growing suspicion that he needed to be removed from the Wilson investigation, once and for all. "So I got a memo saying that I was to stay out of this case because I was muddying the waters, which I did," Stevens would explain.

From that moment forward, Stevens stayed out of the Wilson murder case.

Stevens figured that Price, the police psychologist, helped engineer his dismissal. Price had found his interview techniques counterproductive to the mission of finding Joseph White guilty of the widow's murder, Stevens would later testify. Looking back, Stevens was perplexed as to why

Price had been put on the plane to silently observe their interrogation of White in Alabama.

"I can't understand it to this day why he was there, especially when I got the idea he was trying to evaluate me," Stevens testified later. "He said I was interrogating in a fashion to be not guilty instead of guilty. I guess he didn't like that I wasn't pushing hard enough to get a statement."

While in Alabama, Stevens remembered that he met with White's mother at the jail in Cullman. That fateful day, her son waived extradition and agreed to return to Nebraska to face first-degree murder charges. "I told her that I would see that he got back safely in a few weeks. I think that's what I told her."

Why did the detective make such a remark to a murder defendant's relative?

"I could never believe that Joe White would have been involved. I wasn't one hundred percent sure about the other ones. How could he be arrested for rape and it wasn't the blood type we was looking for?"

After working alongside Searcey during the White and Taylor interviews, Stevens realized his former colleague's interview methods were incredibly poor.

"It's easy to lead somebody into getting the right answers you want," Stevens said. "I'll give you an example. (Like) did you see the footstool in the dining room? Well, naturally, JoAnn's going to answer yes. I could make JoAnn answer yes or no to any question I wanted, put it in any way, shape or form that I wanted JoAnn to answer. And that was my only problem working with Officer Searcey ... that it was just too many interrogating questions there. In other words, he almost give the person the answer before he asked the question."

By late spring 1989, Stevens was no longer a worry for the four rising stars of Gage County's justice team: Burt Searcey, Jerry DeWitt, Dick Smith, and Wayne Price. The divorce was mutual.

"I stayed out of it. I just kept away from it," Stevens said.

Shortly afterward, James Dean and Debbie Shelden had become Gage County's fourth and fifth co-defendants. Although their arrests were based on shaky second-hand hearsay testimony, both pleaded guilty in successive fashion. Their speedy plea agreements, plus Taylor's repeated admissions of guilt, made Stevens start to second-guess his original detective work.

"I was getting to where I was convinced that maybe they were involved all the time."

The prosecutorial team had known since February of 1985 that the bloodstains collected from Wilson's bedroom belonged to someone with type B blood. They also knew her rapist/semen depositor had type B blood and was a non-secretor. Lab tests showed Wilson belonged to the type O blood family.

Keeping that in mind, here's a rundown of the blood types of the first five incarcerated defendants as of late April 1989:

JoAnn Taylor had type O blood.

Joseph White had type O blood.

Tom Winslow had type A blood.

Debbie Shelden had type AB blood.

James Dean had type O blood.

In the words of prosecutor Dick Smith many years later: "At that time in the investigation, there was a pink elephant in the room. Male sperm, blood B, non-secretor. That's the pink elephant."

Not one of the five jailed co-defendants had type B blood. The Gage County Sheriff's Office needed to find someone with type B blood to tie back to the murder.

In late May 1989, Nebraska State Patrol pilot Dave Morris revved up his small aircraft once again. Four passengers climbed aboard: Sheriff DeWitt and three deputies, Searcey, Gerald Lamkin, and Mark Meints. Their latest out of state destination was the Mile High City of Denver, Colorado.

CHAPTER 17
CONVINCING KATHY

Kathy (Knehans) Gonzalez grew up in Superior, a dwindling Nebraska town of 2,500 residents only two miles from the Kansas state line. The community prides itself as being the Victorian Capital of Nebraska. But Gonzalez's life was far short of nobility. Life was a struggle and she was constantly on the move.

During the early 1980s, Gonzalez lived about eighty-five miles east of Superior, in an apartment building at 212 N. Sixth St. in Beatrice. However, she left town just a few weeks after Helen Wilson's murder in the unit directly below hers. She then worked in Omaha, the state's largest city, at a Duff's Smorgasbord restaurant, and a year later she moved a few hours west to Kearney, population 25,000, where she became bored. She hit the road again and hoped to leave Nebraska in her rear view mirror. "I was just

Kathy Gonzalez lived in the apartment unit above Helen Wilson on the night of February 5, 1985. By 1989, Gonzalez had moved out to Denver where she worked at an upscale restaurant inside the Oxford Hotel

hitchhiking, and Fort Worth seemed to be a nice place to be," Gonzalez remembered.

Initially, she ended up in River Oaks, Texas, a Fort Worth suburb. There, she baby-sat and cleaned houses to pay her bills. After six months in Texas, Gonzalez moved to Denver and acclimated to living amid the majestic beauty of the Rocky Mountains. Far removed from Nebraska, Gonzalez had no idea she was about to turn into the sixth person charged in the 1985 rape and murder of Helen Wilson.

On the afternoon of May 25, 1989, a team of determined cops descended on her Denver apartment on Sherman Street. But Gonzalez was not home. Next, they proceeded to the McCormick's Fish House on Seventeenth Street, where they had learned she worked. The restaurant was tucked in the basement of the Oxford Hotel. After traveling all the way from Beatrice, Searcey and Sheriff DeWitt stormed into McCormick's. Searcey looked over the diners and wait staff. Then he saw a large woman with coal-black hair busy in the kitchen cutting up squid, news media reports state.

"Hi, Kathy," Searcey exclaimed.

Gonzalez locked eyes on the stranger. What he said next mortified her. Searcey eagerly announced he had a warrant for her arrest. She was being accused of aiding and abetting in a murder.

"What?" she shouted.

An accompanying Denver cop slapped handcuffs on her. She was being charged in the death of Helen Wilson. "I've been worrying about this for five years," she said, reports reflect.

At the Denver jail, Searcey rattled off the names of the other folks he had taken down in the case: White, Winslow, Taylor, Shelden, and Dean.

"And I didn't know Joe White until they said that he went as Lobo," Gonzalez said. "Because when they said Joe White, I just kind of went, 'No,' and he said, 'Well, did you know him as Lobo?' And I kind of was surprised because I had heard he had died."

Obviously, White had not died, though Searcey suspected White was spreading false rumors to get away with murder. Gonzalez insisted the Nebraska investigators were making a colossal mistake. She proclaimed her innocence. Besides, the Beatrice Police Department already interviewed her during a building canvass way back in 1985, she said.

Unlike her co-defendants, Gonzalez had a vivid recollection of her whereabouts on the night of the homicide. Gonzalez knew she had gone to the local mall earlier that evening. She returned home by 8:00 p.m. and stayed in her apartment the rest of the night. She knew she watched a movie about the Corsican Brothers, a flick that featured one of her favorite actors, Trevor Eve. "He was the only one I wanted to watch it for," Gonzalez said. "It was about two brothers that were born Siamese twins and separated at birth and how they grew up on Corsica and it was like during early times, like Louis XV times, what have you, 1500, 1600, something like that, 1700s."

Gonzalez also knew she worked the next morning at Beatrice's Elks Country Club. There, she washed dishes and cooked. That day, over the lunch hour, a waitress overheard a table of customers talking about somebody being murdered in Beatrice. "I was shocked," Gonzalez said. "At first I thought she was kidding and then when she said she wasn't, she came back and she said that it happened in the apartment below mine. I was really shocked. … I mean, it's not every day somebody gets murdered below you."

Gonzalez had lived alone in the old Lincoln Telephone & Telegraph building starting around August of 1984. She was married briefly that same year to a man from Bolivia, but the marriage abruptly ended. Gonzalez had a relatively minor criminal history. She was arrested for shoplifting merchandise at a Beatrice supermarket around Christmas 1984. She also had a prior drunken driving arrest during her early twenties, records show. But she had never been in jail for any serious crime.

In 1985, the Beatrice cops never remotely considered her a suspect or an accomplice in Wilson's slaying. City police also did not think her bloodstained bra that was found in the trash bin behind the apartment complex had any connection whatsoever to the homicide. Even though the bra was initially put into the city's evidence storage room, officers later destroyed it, surmising it was irrelevant.

Deputy Searcey had a drastically different view. Once he re-read his former agency's reports, he solidified his belief that Kathy Gonzalez was hiding her involvement. Given that the blood in Wilson's apartment did not seem to belong to any of the first five co-defendants, Searcey presumed it must have come from Gonzalez.

Astoundingly, Searcey now had arrested six people -- three men and three women. All remained housed in the Gage County Jail, a small detention facility that rarely accommodated more than two dozen prisoners at a given time.

***

By late June 1989, Kathy Gonzalez was worn down mentally. She had now spent a month in jail in Beatrice facing murder charges. Since Gonzalez didn't have any money, the courts assigned her a public defender, Donald C. Sass, an attorney from Fairbury, about thirty miles away. She thought the only way to prove her innocence and clear her name was to submit to a polygraph test. Once again, Paul Jacobson, the well-known retired Lincoln police detective was retained by prosecutor Dick Smith to administer her polygraph test.

"She agreed with her attorney that she had nothing to lose," Jacobson stated. "Kathy told me that she was not nervous about the test for those reasons and that she had never been at the scene or in the apartment of Helen Wilson at any time. She actually did not show all those movements that you find in a lot of the guilty."

After her jailers delivered Gonzalez to the polygraph operator's office, she smoked five cigarettes before her test. She made three trips to the bathroom, Jacobson noted, a major sign of nervousness. Jacobson later remarked that unlike her fellow co-defendants, Gonzalez appeared bright. She had graduated from a small high school in Hebron, Nebraska, in 1978. She consistently maintained steady employment, working in hotels, food service and nursing care.

She talked in a straightforward manner. "Kathy really did not look 'guilty,'" Jacobson observed. "She told me more than once that she was not involved, but seemed to be more concerned with the fact that many of the news accounts were using her maiden name, which is Knehans. She did not seem to be that much concerned that she was in jail for a serious charge."

Here were the relevant questions that Jacobson used to administer the lie-detector test to Kathy Gonzalez:

Did you lie when you said you were not in the apartment of Helen Wilson that night?

No.

Did you ever see Helen Wilson that night in her apartment?

No.

Were you present when Joseph White, Tom Winslow, and JoAnn Taylor were demanding money from Helen Wilson?

No.

Did you get a nosebleed in the bedroom of Helen Wilson?

No.

Have you told me the complete and absolute truth about everything?

Yes.

Did you go in to the bedroom of Helen Wilson that night?

No.

Is there anything that you are trying to hide from me as to what happened that night?

No.

Have you tried to lie to any of the questions on this test?

No.

Afterward, Jacobson wrote in his reports that her exam was "a disaster." He scored her test "Deception indicated."

Jacobson's correspondence with prosecutor Dick Smith made it clear that he saw himself as a vital part of the prosecution's team, rather than an independent, unbiased examiner. He was clearly convinced Gonzalez was hiding her guilt.

"I think there are a few reasons she is hanging tight at this stage, the first being that she does not actually know that her blood has been identified," Jacobson informed Smith. "However, it also is noticeable that the blood questions cause the big response on the polygraph. Secondly, she does not feel as guilty because she probably was not present when the sexual assaults and death occurred and she no doubt feels that she is carrying less of a burden than the others, including Jim Dean and Deb Shelden, and definitely less than the other three."

In his letter to the prosecutor, Jacobson remarked that Kathy Gonzalez was not very vocal for someone claiming innocence. "The strange thing to me is that she does not make more of a protest as to her innocence as many do. But, of course, if you are not innocent, that is good cause," Jacobson wrote.

Jacobson ended by stating: "I have worked on a good many murder cases, both as a Lincoln police officer and since retiring, but I think you get credit for having one of the most difficult … You are probably playing a waiting game with Kathy. When she finds out about the blood test and that she is in the big leagues, it might be a whole different story."

True, Gonzalez had type B blood, the same type as Helen Wilson's rapist. However, Dr. Reena Roy, the Nebraska State Patrol lab serologist, ultimately determined that Gonzalez's blood type contained a different genetic marker from the blood collected in Helen Wilson's apartment. To overcome this obvious handicap, the prosecution concocted a theory that any blood found in the victim's apartment must be a mixed sample involving Gonzalez and at least one her co-defendants, perhaps Debbie Shelden's.

As the summer of 1989 wore on, members of Gage County's law and justice team had their work cut out for them. Someone still needed to program the mind of Kathy Gonzalez to fall in line with her other co-defendants who were pleading guilty.

After Gonzalez was told she had flunked her polygraph test, the Gage County Sheriff's Office again deployed the services of Wayne Price, their useful police psychologist. Price knew the drill. He needed to use his mastery of psychology to convince Gonzalez to come to grips with her own guilt. "Doc" Price was up to the task.

***

After a few months in jail, Gonzalez felt tremendous pressure to enter a plea bargain like the other defendants. With her public defender's blessing, Gonzalez met with Price for a psychotherapy session on September 12, 1989. Price asked his questions in a polite and friendly tone. As he sat with her, he asked why Joseph White wound up living at her third-floor apartment in the days leading up to the murder.

"It was in the winter time … He knew where I lived but he asked if he could stay for a week, and I said 'Sure, as long as you don't bug me because I hate to be bugged at my home,'" she explained. "Well, after a week, I kicked him out because he refused to take a bath. And I wasn't going to live somewhere where I was paying the rent and he wasn't even going to take a bath. That's sad. And I don't remember seeing him after that. I heard that he left town and he got killed later on a motorcycle or in a motorcycle accident."

"Good try on his part," Price snidely remarked.

Gonzalez did not understand the sarcasm.

"It's a way to disappear," he followed up. "Except he's here now."

Price asked how well Gonzalez knew Helen Wilson.

"I didn't. I don't know what she looks like," Gonzalez replied.

"Have you ever had any memory problems before?"

"No. Other then you know, school memorizing stuff like that, but no."

"Did Lobo come on to you?"

"No. I mean he was friendly enough ... He always says, 'Hi, how are you, what you been up to?' He never bugged me when he was staying there other than not taking a bath."

Price floated the idea that perhaps Gonzalez was present as the others raped and murdered Wilson but blacked out the awful event.

"I would like to find out if there's any way that could be," Gonzalez said. "I mean, why would I block this out? I mean, it had to be pretty bad."

"I've been involved in a lot of investigations and this one was bad," Price replied. "There's a lot more than just killing."

Wilson had been brutalized sexually in many ways, he told Gonzalez. "And it could have triggered enough stress in the past experiences just standing there watching it that it could have just overwhelmed you. As far as I know, no one has accused you of brutalizing her in any way."

"I was just there. That's what they're saying," Gonzalez echoed back to Price.

"Unfortunately, there was several people who was 'just there.' Too many."

Gonzalez remembered her old three-story apartment had roughly ten units, but only a couple of vacancies.

"Why didn't anybody else hear anything?" she asked. "That's a lot of people. And it's not like it was a loud building. You heard doors slam shut."

Price had an answer. "My guess is that people may have heard noises and didn't want to be involved. And now, there's no way they're going to come forward and say, 'I heard a murder take place and I could have done something but I'm going to tell you now that I didn't.'"

Gonzalez was terrified of a jury of Gage County strangers deciding her fate. Her trial date was drawing near. How could she testify that she left her third apartment around 10:30 p.m., came down a flight of stairs and joined the company of several loosely connected male and female acquaintances who brutalized and sodomized a friendly widow nearing her sixty-ninth birthday? Above all, Gonzalez had absolutely no memory of such a horrid event.

"And what if I wasn't there and they're just saying this? I mean, because they're saying I was fully dressed. I don't understand. If [it] was in the middle of the night, all I would have to do is go downstairs. Why would I be wearing shoes and socks?" Gonzalez said as she struggled to make sense of the story Price was spinning.

"You might not have been upstairs," Price suggested.

"I was upstairs because I remember going to bed after the movie. I remember the movie."

Because of the trauma she supposedly witnessed, Gonzalez's brain may be playing games with her, Price speculated.

"And I wouldn't remember leaving or coming back?" Gonzalez asked the psychologist.

"Not necessarily. And she was sexually brutalized. My guess is that they wanted an audience and they wanted scapegoats."

Gonzalez was a scapegoat all right, becoming one as she absorbed Price's version of events. "And I'm one of them.

Cause it's like ...," she said, starting to repeat the accepted version of events.

Price interrupted her.

"Kathy, if you're there and not participating, it's a very different situation (than) if you're there participating."

"There's no way I could have. There's no way. I know that in my heart."

Price asked whether White might have wanted her there in the bedroom while he raped and sodomized the elderly tenant.

"Maybe," Gonzalez replied to Price's speculation. "I don't presume to know how he thinks but he is a person that would implicate somebody else to get out of something. I saw him do it two or three different times with (his former girlfriend)."

At this point, Gonzalez was mortified about her future. Her life looked bleak. She might spend the rest of her life in a lonely prison cell. She would be cut off from society.

"I realize what kind of situation I'm in, and I don't know how to prove anything because I don't know what to say."

"It's frightening," Price assured her.

At that moment, Price steered their conversation to the bloody bra, the one fished out of the apartment trash bin shortly after the murder.

"Oh, well, that was so embarrassing," Gonzalez said. "A couple of days earlier ... I went out and I bought all new underwear, socks, underwear, you know, bras, the whole shebang. So I sat down and I even threw out a couple of nightgowns because I never wore them, and I just tossed them all in a bag and put them in a box, took them down to the Dumpster. I work in a restaurant for crying out loud. I'm a woman. I have my period. I do things."

At that instant, Price knew it was more important to listen than to talk.

"And when I cut myself," Gonzalez continued, "chances are I'm going to do this (she motioned with her hand) before I get to a sink because I don't like things dripping off my hand. And so evidently, one of the bras had blood on it and (Beatrice police) asked me about this. I mean, it was on the front page of the paper."

The *Beatrice Daily Sun* had published a front-page photo of an officer digging through the apartment's trash bin back in February of 1985.

Gonzalez also recalled how rumors were rampant around the small town.

"I know that she was raped and killed. That was what one newspaper said. And then they never gave details ... I heard they suffocated her with a pillow and I heard that she was stabbed. I heard her head got cut off and her arms got cut off and they just put a piece in each different room and, after a while, it's like I wasn't even thinking about that, you know?"

After the homicide, Gonzalez had been heckled by a few crude jokesters. Some of them knocked on her apartment door late at night and suggested they might be the apartment building killer, she told Price. As a single woman who lived alone, the ongoing episodes were unnerving. A few weeks after the slaying, a male friend convinced Gonzalez to move to Omaha, about a hundred miles away.

Finally, Price leveled with her. The odds were that she probably was present, but managed to block the violent crime from her memory.

Gonzalez sighed.

"We don't want you held responsible for anything you didn't do, and you know I have no idea what Lobo or JoAnn and Winslow are going to say about you," Price warned her.

Gonzalez insisted she didn't even know this Tom Winslow character.

"You apparently don't want to. He's in the penal complex now because he got convicted for an assault in Lincoln. He beat a guy senseless with a tire iron; again, a very brutal beating. He's apparently very violent in that crime."

Price tried to use words of comfort to convince Gonzalez to implicate herself. He told her she would be safe and treated well in the Gage County Jail. She would continue to remain isolated from her five co-defendants.

But Gonzalez did not find his words reassuring in the least. "OK, but in the meantime my life has just went down the tubes. No …"

For the first time, Gonzalez broke down and began sobbing. Tears poured down her cheeks.

"It's OK to cry," Price told her.

"I know. I've started over before. I'll do it again."

"Sometimes crying lets some of the pressure off too. You laugh. You can talk. You can cry."

"I'd rather laugh. That's about the only possibility left."

Kathy Gonzalez's spirits were broken. Her life was shattered. She wasn't returning to Denver. Hard prison life in Nebraska appeared inevitable.

Before sending her back to her cell, Price complimented Gonzalez on her behavior during their interview.

"I can tell you, you're fully sane. You know right from wrong. You're in good shape there. You're basically a healthy person."

The woman whose seemingly normal life in Colorado had been uprooted out of nowhere on May 25, 1989, wasn't so sure.

"Then why don't I remember? Am I ever going to find out?" Gonzalez asked the psychologist.

"I think it comes back."

"Do you think that will trigger anything?"

"I really don't think it would open up old wounds. I think it would just give you sense of relief where you can put pieces together and go forward then. But, we'll work with you. We're not out to railroad you in any way, OK?"

"OK," Gonzalez repeated.

But life was not OK. Even the public defender assigned by the courts to represent her, Donald C. Sass, did not believe in her innocence. She had every right to be terrified about her fate.

***

On October 5, 1989, Gonzalez, age twenty-nine, reluctantly turned her life over to the Nebraska Department of Corrections. The binding legal document stipulated that Kathy Gonzalez aka Kathy Knehans would plead no contest to a reduced charge of aiding and abetting in the second-degree murder of Helen Wilson. In exchange, Gonzalez "must testify truthfully to the best of her recollection in any and all cases and give total cooperation to the State of Nebraska" in the homicide. In turn, Gonzalez would be recommended for a ten-year prison sentence "if she complies with all of the above."

The form was signed by prosecutor Dick Smith, public defender Donald C. Sass and Gonzalez. She would be out of prison before she was an old maid, but her life would never be same, regardless.

CHAPTER 18
THE ALL-SEEING EYE

By the time the leaves changed colors in 1989, JoAnn Taylor had spent more than six months locked away in jail during an investigation of the sexual assault and murder of a woman she didn't even know. Now age twenty-six, Taylor grew acclimated to the rigid rules and orders of jail life. One day that autumn, she was led into an interview room of well-dressed lawyers. On hand were prosecutor Dick Smith, the defense attorneys for Tom Winslow and Joseph White, and her court-appointed counsel, Lyle J. Koenig.

Decades later, Koenig explained that he put forth a vigorous defense on behalf of his indigent client.

"We filed just about every motion known to the mind of man in defending Jo Taylor," Koenig explained. "The principal problem, however, was the specter of the electric chair. Had we not had the death penalty in Nebraska at the time, or if she would have been charged with second-degree murder, I would have tried this case in a heartbeat. However, when they took the death penalty off the table in exchange for a plea, I felt that we couldn't ignore it."

In fact, Taylor underwent a rigorous mental competency evaluation at Koenig's request after her extradition to Nebraska. During that interview, Taylor told Omaha psychiatrist Dr. Bruce Gutnik "in my head and in my heart I know I wasn't there."

"Ms. Taylor indicates that she does not know where she was on February 5th and 6th of 1985. She says that she confessed to the police after they said that Joe White told them she was there. ... She was quite firm in reconfirming to me that she was not present at the time of the crime. She did think ... she could have been there and not recall it." – Dr. Bruce Gutnik, psychological evaluation of JoAnn Taylor, dated May 30, 1989

Although Gutnik's detailed report for the court raised doubts about Taylor's guilt, her own attorney wasn't so sure. He contemplated her dilemma. If she took her chances at trial and lost, Koenig thought there was a great possibility the North Carolina native would become Nebraska's only woman housed on Death Row. "I do remember that the mood in the community was very adverse to all of the defendants," Koenig said. "Given the details of the homicide that appeared in the press, feeling in the community was running very strongly against these defendants."

***

Taylor pleaded guilty to the reduced charge of second-degree murder. In exchange, the prosecutor did not seek the death penalty. However, her cooperation against the other co-defendants was paramount. She promised "to testify truthfully" and give total cooperation in any and all cases involving Helen Wilson's death. Her sentencing would not take place until all of her co-defendants went to trial. "The state will make a recommendation of fifteen years imprisonment for a sentence in this case if the defendant complies with all of the above," prosecutor Dick Smith stated.

This was another slick move orchestrated by the prosecutor. The Wilson murder was vicious, evil and repulsive – the autopsy showed she was sodomized after death. There would be pandemonium if a local judge were to go easy on someone convicted of killing one of the community's most beloved older residents. Surely, Smith knew that the sentencing judge would give Taylor a much stiffer sentence that what the prosecutor would be "recommending."

So that fall, the room full of attorneys gathered to take Taylor's sworn deposition in preparation for White's murder trial, less than six weeks away. White scoffed at the idea of taking a plea deal even though four other co-defendants – JoAnn Taylor, Kathy Gonzalez, Debbie Shelden and James Dean – had all cut deals with the prosecutor and planned to line up against him at his scheduled trial. The only holdout was Tom Winslow. While in jail, he recanted his earlier statement implicating White and the others as being involved.

After six months in the Gage County Jail, Taylor had already broken off her engagement to Jim Phillips, formerly of Pennsylvania. "I am now engaged to someone else, Clint Wanker," she told the room of attorneys. While facing murder charges, Taylor got engaged to Wanker through written correspondence. "He works on tow boats that haul jet fuel and chemicals, very dangerous chemicals." Wanker and Taylor had been previously engaged in 1987, according to court transcripts. "We kind of lost touch until he wrote my mother and my mother forwarded the letter to me and he said he ain't letting me get lost again."

White's astute public defender, Toney Redman, reminded Taylor how her life in North Carolina had been uprooted over a four-year-old murder case halfway across the country. "I can handle it," Taylor responded. "I am like my daddy, I am tough. I am a survivor."

At the time of the sworn deposition on September 28, 1989, Redman asked Taylor whether she really thought she had been involved in the murder.

"I know I was, but I was forced to be," Taylor replied.

Taylor said she learned from prosecutor Smith and her public defender Lyle Koenig that White refused to confess to the gruesome crime. "I figured that when he found out I made my deal he would roll over. He would be smart in my opinion. It would save his ass in the long run because if he took a deal now he would be a lot better off than facing the death penalty."

Regarding her other co-defendants, Taylor admitted she barely knew Kathy Gonzalez, and she didn't really like Tom Winslow. "I wouldn't go to bed with him," Taylor declared.

When White's lawyer, Redman, brought up the name Clint Wanker, Taylor gushed. "We are just … we are soul mates. That's the easiest way to explain it without making you all think I'm crazy. He's a clairvoyant. He has clairvoyant abilities."

Redman was intrigued. He sought to learn more details.

"He is a seventh-level psychic. He's a white warlock," Taylor revealed to the roomful of attorneys.

Taylor said they originally met sometime around 1984 at a carnival in Sioux City, Iowa. "I was a ride jock, and he was a professional clown. His abilities, he didn't let known to me until back in 1987 when I had his son. But I was not quite two months pregnant when he looked at me and he woke me up one night, and he said the baby was crying. And I said, 'What baby?' because I didn't know I was pregnant at the time. And, he looked at me said, 'You are pregnant. You are going to have a little boy and he is going to weigh twelve pounds' if I go to term. And he was right. I had a little boy and he weighed seven pounds, one ounce."

Redman was puzzled. "And that's what convinced you he was psychic?"

"Yes. And, a couple other things he had foreseen. He had foreseen a death of a man, and we could not pinpoint the person, and come to find out it was his father's death."

Wanker, who lived in Leland, Mississippi, apparently did not foresee things in dreams. "He has visions that come to him. While he is awake as well as when he is busy doing something," Taylor said.

Redman remarked he had always been interested in psychics and clairvoyance. "But I have never heard of a seventh-level psychic. What does that mean?"

Taylor explained that Wanker was somewhere between a beginning psychic and a high priest. He also had out of body experiences. She said she, too, was slowly learning this ability, known as astral projection.

"See, back when I was younger, I saw a best friend of mine killed in a car wreck and she was seventeen miles out in the country on a country road and I was at home. I saw it right as it happened and come to find out, if I had told somebody to go and check in the area, I could have saved her life. She was there for seventeen hours and she had bled to death from internal injuries and everything," Taylor said. "Now that I have been with Clint, I am learning to understand."

As for astral projection, the person's soul can remove itself from the body, Taylor informed the curious lawyers. "And you can send your soul to a place or another person."

Taylor still considered herself a beginning-level psychic, but said she communicated telepathically with Wanker from her jail cell. "We can communicate thoughts. I can hear his voice." In fact, she said, Wanker helped her decide accepting the plea bargain in her murder case was best for her.

"Well, when he first found out about my case, he had a vision of me being released, but we could not foresee a date. He could see me coming home. Since my plea bargain, he has had a vision of his mother calling the ship, calling the boat and having him call home and me being on the other end of the phone. But neither time he could pinpoint a date."

So far, Taylor had yet to master from Wanker the art of casting spells. She said he strictly practiced good magic to protect her from evil forces. "He has given me a chant which goes to my protection shield."

Redman sought to know more. "Tell me about your chant and your protection shield. I'm curious. I might need one myself."

Taylor revealed she had a witch's star in the shape of a pentagram. "It just keeps me from being harmed. I hold it facing away from me close to my heart when I do my chant. I keep it either in my pocket or in my bra at all times." Back in her jail cell, Taylor said she also had "an all-seeing eye."

"Well, it's for protection as well, keeps evil from coming into my cell." About a century ago, Taylor claimed, someone had died on the public property where the jail was later built. "But there is another spirit in my cell. She is a spirit that has committed suicide, so she is earthbound."

The spirit hovering inside her cell at the Gage County Jail could never enter heaven or hell. "She is bound to the earth because she killed herself ... Before I got my seeing eye she bothered me quite a bit. She would wake me up in the middle of the night."

Taylor explained her all-seeing sign was drawn on a picture Wanker mailed her. "No evil can touch me basically, if say, there was an evil spirit or if say for that matter my old cellmate had gotten hyper and she wanted to throw punches, she would not have been able to touch me because there is a protection shield around, protection aura in my cell. That's the easiest way to explain it."

Once, she said, the all-seeing eye stopped Taylor from committing suicide in her jail cell while facing the murder charge. She told the lawyers she tried to strangle herself with a piece of elastic she pulled out of her jail-issued garments. "I had tied it around my neck and everything, and that's as far as I had gotten because I have Clint's picture on my desk and I have a picture of our son on my desk and right then is when I heard his voice saying, 'Baby, I love you. You can't do this. I am going to be here no matter what.' And just hearing him tell me he loves me helps. And I have not been depressed at all. I have not had any anxiety problems since I have had the eye."

As far as details about the ghost who haunted her cell, she revealed the specter wore Victorian-era clothes. "She is blonde and very young. She died probably on the ground the building is built on."

When White's attorney steered the conversation to the subject of karma, Taylor declared she had lived five past lives.

"You have had five?"

"Yes. Clint has noticed them. I haven't. When Clint and I had planned to get married … when I tried the dress on, when I looked back in the mirror, I saw me as a blond with my hair up in the way the Victorian women used to wear it. And I walked out and Clint was there and a friend of ours was there that did not know anything of our abilities or anything. He looked at me and he said, 'When did you become a blonde and style your hair like that?' I said, 'My hair is hanging down and it's brown.' He said, 'You looked like a blonde for a minute.'

"So we know that one of my lives has been during the Victorian ages, but we cannot pinpoint anything further than that."

Redman wondered how Taylor knew she'd had other lives. "Clint has picked it up through the tarot cards. We feel that my purpose on this world is not finished."

Taylor thought her present-day dilemma as a prisoner traced back to her biological father and to karma. "He was in prison when I was born. And he has thirty-five tattoos. I had never wanted a tattoo in my life until all of a sudden I just decided I wanted them, and now I have eight, and I had never met my dad until last year. And Mom and everybody kept telling me, 'You look just like your daddy.' But my father and my life are following the same footsteps right now."

Redman asked how.

"He was in prison for murder. And he served six years."

Now that Taylor had brought up the subject of murder, White's lawyer pulled together the wild strands of Taylor's spiritual beliefs and the official version of the Beatrice murder, asking whether pre-destiny and karma had something to do with Helen Wilson's death.

Taylor said she sensed she had a big burden to pay for her own mother's mistakes. "Because my mother, see, she died when she was fifteen. She had a heart attack. I was not here.

I was not thought of. I did not come along until she was eighteen. She was pronounced dead due to a heart attack. For some reason she was not, her body was not ready to let her go. She is still pushing."

Redman listened intently as the court reporter recorded Taylor's statements word for word. "I still don't understand," he professed. "Because she didn't die at fifteen when she was supposed to?"

Taylor nodded affirmatively. "I am paying for the same hell she should have been through in her life. I am her only daughter. And the only way to explain it is that with her not going when she should have died, it has placed me in jeopardy, and it will place the rest of our female generations in jeopardy until the debt is paid."

Redman asked to whom the debt must be paid.

"We don't know. We just know that's why I am going through the hell that I am going through all of these years."

Switching gears, Redman asked why Wilson was involved. "I take it you agree that what happened to her was predestined?"

"I can't say yes or no on that," Taylor said. She conceded that she had contemplated using her psychic powers to contact Wilson from beyond the grave, but ultimately nixed the idea. "It could cause me bodily and physical harm," she said.

Redman told Taylor that, given her powers, she could always go back and apologize to the murder victim.

"I have thought about it many a time, because I know that I was there by force, when it happened and I know it was not my doing," Taylor said. "Her death was not meant to happen."

CHAPTER 19
JOANN'S CONFESSION

As the deposition continued, Taylor insisted she never once thought about the night of the rape and murder until North Carolina authorities stormed her house and arrested her more than six months ago.

"You had blocked it out for four years? And never once thought about it?" Redman questioned.

"Nope, well, I was a carny all that time. I was on the road. I would not settle down anywhere. I was very quiet. I was closed into my own shell of not letting anybody get close to me, and Clint broke me through that shell when I met him."

Taylor admitted that when she first lived in Beatrice during the early 1980s, she underwent numerous psychotherapy sessions with Wayne Price, who was then the clinical director for Blue Valley who moonlighted as a sheriff's deputy. She saw him as an understanding therapist. "I was under his care for quite a while. He was OK. I could get along with him. He let me open myself up at my own pace."

She remembered how she had been anxious to meet with him after flying back to Beatrice from North Carolina after her arrest in March. "I freaked on the plane is the only way to explain it. Sam Stevens and Officer Searcey both said that I just froze. They don't know if it was because I saw ice on the wings of the plane, but it was within the last thirty minutes of the flight that I just totally went into shock. They said they shook me. They waved their hands in the front of me, hollered at me, tried to get me to blink, and I wouldn't blink. And it scared me, so when I got here, I asked for Dr. Price."

Rather quickly, Price responded to the jail, eager to see his former client now ensnared in a hideous murder case. She did not distinguish "Doc" as being a police officer. Redman asked if Taylor even knew what a police psychologist did.

"No, not really."

As far as her initial police interviews, Taylor recalled being asked if she knew a guy named Joe. She only knew him by his nickname of Lobo. "They asked me if I could remember the scene of the crime. I remembered a light-colored house."

She did remember Searcey and Stevens corrected her time and time again. "Then it dawned on me that it wasn't a house."

"You realized it wasn't a house after Stevens and other law enforcement told you it was an apartment, is that correct?" White's lawyer asked.

"Yeah."

"They took you by the building, didn't they?"

"Just recently, yes, but before that I realized it was an apartment building."

At first, Taylor had confessed there were only two others present during the murder. "Just me and the two guys; that's all I could remember at the time."

Redman mentioned the name of co-defendant James Dean, who wasn't arrested until a full month after Taylor. "When did you first remember James Dean being there?"

"God, couple months ago, about that."

"Who brought his name up?"

"I don't remember."

"Somebody supplied that information to you?"

"Yeah."

Redman reminded Taylor that she had never mentioned the presence of the sixth co-defendant, either.

"Do you remember Kathy Gonzalez being there?"

"I do now, yes."

Initially, Taylor also failed to mention the presence of the fifth co-defendant.

"Who helped you remember Deb Shelden being there?"

"I think it was through discussions with my attorney."

"Did you have a lot of the facts wrong at first, JoAnn?"

"Quite a few of them, yes."

Taylor admitted she was unable to reveal what events she had actually seen the night of the widow's murder.

"Is there anything?"

"Not that I can remember offhand."

"Did you ever have any dreams about this?"

"No, I don't dream."

Despite her terrible ordeal, Taylor chose not to tap into her fiance Clint Wanker's psychic powers to help her remember more facts about the murder. "Because with him being so many miles away it's really rough on us to try because it puts a strain on his strength."

As for White, Taylor maintained they once got along. "We shared an apartment, but we did not live together. We were not intimate."

Redman wondered if she had any fear of his client, White.

"Yes, I still have fear of the man. He has dislocated my jaw before, and we have had some pretty violent fistfights."

White's lawyer wanted to know if Taylor was even sure she had been in Wilson's apartment during the attack.

"Well, not completely one hundred percent sure, because, like I say, nobody can be one hundred percent but very close to it."

Taylor said she had never seen anybody tying a scarf around the victim's face – a crucial crime scene detail that, astonishingly, had turned into an irrelevant fact for the Gage County criminal justice team. Instead, a different narrative emerged: Helen Wilson was smothered with a couch pillow.

When White's lawyer asked how Wilson had died, Taylor confessed, "From my pillow being over her face."

"Who caused her death, JoAnn?"

"I don't know."

"Was it you?"

"I could never intentionally take someone's life."

In Taylor's words, five of them regrouped back outside at Winslow's Oldsmobile after the attack. Debbie Shelden was dropped off at her mother's residence. Then, Taylor and the three guys drove to the Marshall's Truck Stop for breakfast. As far as Gonzalez, Taylor didn't mention whether the co-defendant simply retreated back upstairs to her third-level apartment.

"Do you think it's kind of bizarre that you would have breakfast after killing a woman, after watching her being raped and sodomized?"

"Yeah."

Still, White's lawyer remained baffled by the fact that Taylor's confession didn't mesh with the crime scene report. Taylor said she never saw a thick afghan scarf tied around the victim's face.

"The only thing that was over her face when I left was the pink towel."

The towel came from a living room chair or the couch, she suggested.

"After I moved the pillow, Lobo had tossed the towel to me, and that's his thing with his lovers is to cover their face. I think it has to stem back with his nude modeling in L.A."

Taylor said that action could be traced back to their days of living in Los Angeles. "My roommate Coco had given her spare key to him, and one day I walked in on him and his lover and he had a pillow case over her head."

The pillow case, however, was not tied over her head, she clarified. "Pardon the expression, but like fucking her for glory. That's what it put me in mind of."

Redman admitted he never heard that expression. "I have heard of the paper sack expression."

"No, I have always heard, 'Put a flag over her face, and fuck her for glory,'" Taylor explained.

Redman reminded Taylor of a statement given by co-defendant James Dean. "While Lobo was having intercourse with her, they say that you were kissing and caressing her chest."

That was absolutely untrue, Taylor insisted. "I know it was said, but I have never been gay. I have never thought about being and I wouldn't do such a thing."

Redman also noted how the others blame her for hatching the idea of targeting Wilson's apartment. "Yeah, I have been told that it was supposedly my idea, but the funny thing is, I didn't know the woman, for one. For another, if it had been my idea, I would have had it planned out a hell of a lot better. I would have had the place cased out. I would have known the time and place that people went and came; and for another, I am going to tell you, I damn sure ain't built right to fuck her, now am I?"

Redman denied he ever accused her of such a thing.

Taylor was riled up. "No, but leave it to the rest of you fucking attorneys, and you will try to turn it around that way."

"I am not trying to say that at all."

"Yeah, right."

Lastly, Redman honed in on one of the oddest stories Taylor had told folks around Beatrice: that Joseph White was her father.

"I just thought he was because I had never met my real dad. I didn't realize that we were as close as we were in age either. I just thought it. I don't know what made me think it."

On the verge of his trial, White was twenty-six years old, just like she was. "It would be pretty tough for him to be your father, wouldn't it?" Redman asked.

"Yeah, I finally realized that. I figured that out after we came back here."

Redman turned and asked whether Taylor thought her lawyer, Lyle Koenig, who sat alongside her for the sworn deposition, could be her father.

"No. I know my daddy now, met him in 1987. Me and my dad get along great. We are two peas in a pod."

Redman asked Taylor to reveal the terms of her plea agreement with the prosecutor.

"That I help the county as much as possible."

"OK. And I take it part of the agreement is that you would testify at trial, if need be?"

"Yeah."

In what should have been a telling part of the deposition, Taylor revealed that she, too, had been shown a video of the horrific crime scene by the sheriff after her arrest, just as James Dean had. "I have seen the video, and I have seen pictures of the crime scene since," she said.

It was an example of the behind-the-scenes shenanigans of law enforcement officials at play, in this case Gage County Sheriff Jerry DeWitt. How far would any the murder cases against the six co-defendants have gone if DeWitt hadn't tasked his deputies with making a copy of the original crime scene videotape, a recording that was in the possession of the Beatrice Police Department?

CHAPTER 20
NO PLEA DEALS

Dating back to the 1980 Gas 'N Stop abduction and murder of Joyce Wiles, County Attorney Dick Smith had a longstanding track record of pushing for plea bargains instead of arguing cases before a jury. The Wilson murder case would be no exception. By October of 1989, Smith had secured plea agreements with four of the six co-defendants.

Joseph White grew up near Cullman, Alabama, and served in the U.S. Army after high school. In 1989, White proclaimed his innocence after being arrested in the rape and murder of Helen Wilson in Beatrice, Nebraska, where White previously lived.

The last remaining holdouts were Tom Winslow and Joseph White, the two men accused of committing a tag team rape upon the frail woman old enough to be their grandmother.

The persistent prosecutor nudged White to plead guilty, too, but White adamantly refused. The slender, bearded man from Alabama insisted he was being set up by liars and a rigged small-town Nebraska justice system. He wanted to go home. His lawyers, Toney Redman and Alan Stoler, went along with White's wishes to take his chances at trial, even if it meant that death by electrocution was very much on the table if the jury found White guilty.

On October 6, 1989, Gage County Deputies Doug Klaus and Richard Monfelt removed White from his cell and took him on a forty-mile drive. In Lincoln, they pulled in at a nicely manicured office building surrounded tall trees and shrubbery. It was the Calvert Street office suite of Paul Jacobson, the polygraph examiner. Fearing White was a dangerous prisoner, Jacobson gave the deputies instructions about his building's security.

That morning, White talked about his upbringing, his stint in the U.S. Army, his time in California as both a nude model and a denizen of the streets. He explained he got his nickname "Lone Wolf" in California as a result of being a loner. During that period, White was "working the streets," Jacobson's reports of the discussion reflect.

Jacobson was convinced of White's guilt in the widow's rape and murder. Therefore, the purpose of giving him a lie-detector test was not to gauge the truth, but to destroy his spirits by telling him that he had flunked the test. The prosecution still very much preferred to avoid a prolonged and tedious jury trial and perhaps White would throw in the towel and sign a plea deal after being demoralized by a flunked lie-detector exam. With Dick Smith's preference for plea deals as a fast and easy method of delivering Gage County justice, there was ample time to settle White's murder case up until the moment a jury was seated.

During his one-on-one session with Jacobson, White opened up during the pre-test interview, including admitting that his problems with alcohol began at eighteen. Then he answered questions about the homicide in a way that should have been a red flag.

"Joe told me that he could not remember anything and that actually all he knew about the case was what he had read, been told, or whatever," Jacobson wrote.

During the past six months, White noted he had access to a radio and television at the Gage County Jail. He also told Jacobson he read more than a hundred books since being incarcerated. On that particular morning, Jacobson happened to have a copy of the old *Lincoln Star* newspaper at his office. The newspaper contained a photo of White's co-defendant Kathy Gonzalez and a story about her pleading no contest in Helen Wilson's murder. Jacobson handed White the newspaper article to look over, and White said he was dumbfounded as to why the others continued to implicate him in the Beatrice murder.

"Alcoholics are very good liars, and I asked Joe if he had been drinking so much in Beatrice that he would not remember at times what went on," Jacobson stated in his report. "He said that was not the case because he usually did not have more than a couple of dollars at a time to buy beer or booze and that there was not supposed to have been drinking involved in this crime or case."

White acknowledged the murder case was the first time he ever faced serious trouble with the law.

Jacobson had devised the polygraph questions before the exam, and, in his follow-up letter to the prosecutor, Jacobson admitted he intentionally slipped in a test question aimed at rattling the accused killer.

"Some of these people can almost sit around long enough and think themselves innocent, and I expected that Joe might think he could beat the test," Jacobson advised. "So I had to put something in the test that he might not be looking for such as the bit about the tearing bill which supposedly was some kind of trademark for him or whatever."

Before the actual lie-detector test started, White acknowledged he had learned that a torn five-dollar bill was found at the crime scene. But he strongly denied the idea that he walked around Beatrice tearing up cash.

White also showed Jacobson how he used to give people his so-called "wolf sign." White held his hand upright. He put his thumb to the side and raised his first and fourth fingers. This hand gesture meant "I love you," Jacobson noted in his report. "I don't know much wolf talk unless he bared his fangs and I would know what that meant."

Here were the relevant questions and answers from White's polygraph test:

Did you deliberately lie when you said you were not present when Helen Wilson was being assaulted and robbed?

No.

Did you tear a five-dollar bill in half in Helen Wilson's apartment?

No.

Were you present in the living room when Taylor was smothering Helen Wilson with a pillow?

No.

Did you help rob Helen Wilson?

No.

Have you told me the complete and absolute truth about everything?

Yes.

Did you rape Helen Wilson?

No.

Did you help control Helen Wilson while Tom Winslow had his quote "fun"?

No.

Have you tried to lie to any of the questions on this test?

No.

Obviously, it doesn't take a brain surgeon to figure out what the results of the lie-detector test would be. Jacobson checked the box "Deception indicated."

"In my opinion, this man did everything but tell me the truth on this polygraph test, and I knew it was fruitless at this stage to expect him to change his story from not being able to remember. He remembers," Jacobson wrote the prosecutor.

Despite being told he miserably flunked the polygraph exam, White insisted there was no way he assaulted a sixty-eight-year-old lady.

He bragged that finding a young woman who wanted to sleep with him was as easy as snapping his fingers. White went into great detail about three different women he slept with in Beatrice, none of them Taylor or Gonzalez, his co-defendants. "He told me that he had no trouble getting a woman and had a reputation of being a gigolo and told me of conquests since arriving in Beatrice," Jacobson stated.

During their conversation, White opened up about his interest in penning a novel. "He is thinking of writing a book and does not know where to center his interest, but has done some thinking on a book on adventure, possibly a Western, and considerable thought on a book with a title he has not quite settled on, but it might be *"How to Be a Successful Gigolo,"* Jacobson stated.

In spite of being told he had flunked a polygraph test, White still refused to sign a typed-out plea agreement already prepared by the prosecutor. That document, dated September 28, 1989, gave White a chance to plead guilty to second-degree murder. By doing so, White could avoid a life prison sentence or the death penalty. White adamantly refused to sign the document anyway. He wanted a courtroom showdown against prosecutor Dick Smith and those he saw as the ringleaders at the Gage County Sheriff's Office who made him public enemy No. 1 all around southeastern Nebraska.

Smith did not wince. White would get his trial just as he desired.

CHAPTER 21
THE OLD WEST COURTHOUSE

Joseph White's murder trial was moved thirty miles down U.S. Highway 136 into neighboring Jefferson County because of enormous pretrial publicity around Beatrice.

Beginning on November 3, 1989, the old courthouse in Fairbury, the county seat, took center stage for an anticipated two-week-long trial. Fairbury, with a population of less than 4,400, had a rich history and the community was proud of its ties to the Old West. Local historical accounts fondly note that "Wild Bill" Hickok once shot a man over a money dispute on the outskirts of present-day Fairbury. Without a doubt, the most impressive building was the Jefferson County Courthouse, a limestone structure built around 1891 smack in the middle of the downtown square. A dome and large clock were added by 1910. According to Fairbury's website, the clock bell known as "Little Ben" tolls every hour.

That first week of November 1989, Fairbury's downtown was buzzing for a change. The jury trial was the talk of town and it meant an influx of out-of-town media attention. Murder trials in Jefferson County's distinctive courtroom with wooden floors and several rows of spectator chairs were few and far between.

The two prosecutors for Gage County, Dick Smith and his chief deputy, Jerry Shelton, had worked together for a decade. At the other table in the courtroom sat White and his pair of court-appointed attorneys Toney Redman of Lincoln and Alan Stoler of Omaha. They faced the daunting task of persuading twelve small-town Nebraskans to acquit their Alabama client in the murder of a dignified elderly widow who volunteered on Sundays at her Methodist church and was deeply loved and greatly missed by her extended family and all who knew her. Compounding matters for the defense team, at least four of White's co-defendants were on the prosecution's witness list and a fifth co-defendant, Tom Winslow, had also implicated White in an earlier videotaped interview with Searcey.

"We always questioned the credibility of the other people because they were so screwy," Redman would later explain. "But when you get five different people lined up against your client, the odds aren't very good. We had no idea how bad Joe was being set up."

Helen Wilson's relatives became a show of force throughout the trial. Their body language made it abundantly clear they weren't part of White's cheering section. They demanded justice.

***

Born in 1916, in rural Pickrell, Helen Loretta Jones was one of five children born to George and Ida Belle Jones. Besides her sister, Florence, she had three brothers, Art, Roy and Melvin. In 1934, at eighteen, she married Raymon Lathel Wilson and they lived in Beatrice, raising their three children, Janet (Jan), Darrell and Lawrence (Larry). They were married more than thirty-two years when Raymon died of a heart attack in 1966. The sudden death of her husband was a difficult cross to bear. At age fifty, she moved into an apartment and took a job at a local nursing home caring for the frail and elderly. Shortly thereafter, Helen Wilson suffered a mental breakdown. Luckily, her family was there for her. She moved into one of the units of an apartment house owned by her son Larry and daughter-in-law Edith (Edie). From that moment on, her frame of mind improved. She became more active in her community and became involved with various groups including the AARP. Since Wilson did not drive, the AARP became her way to hit the road and explore the country. She became a regular presence on some of the bus trips organized by the AARP, and she had a wonderful time. Her daughter-in-law Edie Wilson fondly recalls how the other travelers began calling her "Little Miss Sunshine."

"She would stand in the front of the bus and play games and entertain the passengers," her daughter-in-law said. "She also always had her camera ready. She loved taking pictures."

A conscientious photographer, Wilson often took a while before snapping a photo. When she took photos of her relatives, she was quite fond of saying, "Look natural now."

In the 1980s, Wilson was one of the most familiar faces around the church bingo halls in Beatrice. And she was quite good at it. She won several bingo games. The chance to strike the lucky jackpot at the bingo games hosted by St. Joseph Catholic Church drew all sorts of people. There were retirees, widows, blue-collar workers, and ... some of the town's disenfranchised lost souls. Among those who often showed up for bingo games were JoAnn Taylor, Clifford and Debbie Shelden, and Tom Winslow and his wife, Beth.

This was the same group of friends who were later targeted for Wilson's murder.

***

At the time of White's jury trial, prosecutor Dick Smith was well-rehearsed. He and his chief deputy county attorney, Jerry Shelton, had assembled an army of witnesses to parade into the courtroom. A lot was at stake, including White's life. A conviction for first-degree felony murder meant White faced being sentenced to die in Nebraska's electric chair.

The judge presiding over the murder trial was William Rist (pronounced Ryest), a longtime jurist in his mid-sixties. Rist had a reputation for holding lawyers accountable for being on time and well prepared when they arrived in his court.

The following twelve residents from around Fairbury were selected for the jury to determine the guilt or innocence of Joseph White:

- Georgene Arner, a lifelong local resident who was a homemaker and mother of four.

- David Beetley, an emergency medical technician in Fairbury who knew Sheriff DeWitt.

- Marilyn Endorf, a local furniture store employee whose farmer husband raised livestock.

- William J. Henry, a lumberyard employee, lifelong resident and Eagles Club member.

- Martin Jordening, a farmer and lifelong local resident.

- Catherine Kleine, a homemaker who was remodeling her husband's house.

- Donald Krause, a retired teacher and coach who had a cattle farm about ten miles from Fairbury.

- Betty Kujath, a Fairbury Public Schools food service worker of twenty-two years.

- Donna Leonard, who helped her husband run a family farm outside Fairbury.

- RoJane Meyer, who worked in accounting handling payroll and whose husband farmed.

- Janice Pfingsten, a local hardware store employee and lifelong local resident.

- Lynne Scheuler, a first-grade teacher in Hebron whose husband farmed near Fairbury.

The Nebraska residents chosen for the jury knew what was expected. They had a special civic duty. Though none of the jurors knew Helen Wilson, they easily related to her. Absolutely no woman nearing her sixty-ninth birthday deserved to be murdered under such distasteful and appalling circumstances, in of all places, the sanctity of her own apartment, a place she felt most comfortable and safe. Worst of all, Helen Wilson died in agony and her body was violated even after her horrific death.

During opening statements, prosecutor Smith foreshadowed the trial testimony over the coming days. "Ladies and gentlemen, the three eyewitnesses to this that we will call to testify, Ada JoAnn Taylor, James Dean, and Debra Shelden, are convicted murderers," Smith pronounced. "If the State could bring in a priest or a rabbi or a nun or minister that was there and put them on the stand for you, we would. But these are the people that were there."

The jury heard that JoAnn Taylor brewed a pot of coffee inside Wilson's kitchen after the elderly woman's rape and murder. "Then they looked around for money," Smith told the jury. "Money was found. Money was taken."

Actually, Smith's courtroom yarn about the money was untrue and misleading, but it wouldn't matter because nobody was there to correct him. In reality, in excess of $1,000 dollars had been left behind by the killer in the top drawer of Wilson's bedroom. The initial agency on the scene, the Beatrice Police Department, documented the recovery of at least nine twenty-dollar bills, three hundred-dollar bills, two fifty-dollar bills, another set of thirty twenty-dollar bills, plus several checks and money market accounts that brought the total to more than $1,300 – a lot of money for a half-dozen hoodlums intent on robbery to overlook in a tiny apartment dwelling.

***

From the defense's vantage point, the trial boiled down to the question of the killer's identity. During his opening statement, Toney Redman put forth an impassioned plea, stressing his belief in his client's staunch claims of innocence.

"Now, what I want you to look at, specifically, is the credibility of the state's witnesses, and I'm speaking specifically of Ada JoAnn Taylor, James Dean, and Deb Shelden. These are three people which the evidence will show have allowed the court to find them guilty of second-degree murder, and it's these people who the state claims to be eyewitnesses that were there that will relate to you that Joseph White was one of the individuals. So when they're explaining their part of the scenario to you, I want you to be judging them on their credibility," Redman said.

"Now it's interesting that Mr. Smith didn't mention a fourth person who I anticipate will testify," he continued. "That person is Kathleen Gonzalez. Kathy Gonzalez is the fourth person who has allowed the court to find her guilty of second-degree murder. I anticipate Kathy Gonzalez is going to take that chair right there and tell you she pled guilty to second-degree murder but she doesn't think she was there. She doesn't know what happened, but yet, she pled to second-degree murder."

The first agency on the crime scene, the Beatrice Police Department, tried to solve the murder by collecting evidence and analyzing the clues left behind in Unit 4, the defense attorney told jurors. "There is not one fingerprint that they can show belonged to Joe White," Redman argued. "There is no sperm sample that they can show belonged to Joe White. There is not one hair follicle that they can show belonged to Joe White. There is nothing that they can show that puts Joe White on the premises with the exception of these three incredible witnesses."

Some trial evidence would be gruesome, he warned the jury.

"This is a horrible case," Redman said. "You're going to see photographs of the deceased. You're going to see a crime scene video of the apartment. But remember that four people have already admitted to that crime. ... Listen closely to all of the evidence, not only the evidence of the state but the evidence of the defendant before you enter the jury room to make your deliberations. Thank you."

***

Before the heart of the trial got underway, White's lawyers asked Judge Rist to restrict the prosecution from introducing testimony regarding the defendant's so-called money tricks. These legal arguments were heard outside the presence of the seated jury. Co-counsel Alan Stoler predicted that prosecutors planned to call witnesses Lisa Brown and Taylor on this topic.

"Through their depositions, each of these two witnesses have seen Joseph White do something with a five-dollar bill and causing the bill to be ripped," Stoler said. "If they are allowed to testify as to those observations, the prejudicial value in this case would far outweigh any probative effect to aiding the fact ... We move to restrict the State from inquiring of the past observations of Joseph White in that specific trick."

Prosecutor Smith reminded the judge that a torn five-dollar bill was found at the scene of the murder. "There will be testimony elicited from the witness, JoAnn Taylor, that she heard a rip and she asked about it and she and the defendant had a conversation about it," Smith promised. "This does coincide with the trick with the five-dollar bill. Lisa Brown will back it up by saying she has seen him do this trick. That's his mark. That's what her conversation and statement will indicate. It was left. It was physical evidence at the scene of the crime. The witness heard it being ripped ..."

Judge Rist rejected the defense's motion. "I believe under the circumstances, Mr. Stoler, that I could not grant the motion at this time. The court does not have a sufficient context to know whether or not it's material or not. It could go either way. I'm going to overrule this motion. We'll simply have to deal with it at the time it arises."

***

Ivan "Red" Arnst was the prosecution's first witness. The seventy-four-year-old man was now a widower. His wife, Florence, who was Helen Wilson's sister, died in December 1987. Back on February 6, 1985, the Arnsts' lived in the next door apartment. Around 9:30 a.m. on that frigid Wednesday, Arnst realized that something terrible had happened to his sister in law. "Well, when I went in she was laying spread out on the living room floor," he told the jury. "Her nightgown was up over her head. She was sprawled out on the floor. I noticed her hand being bound, scarf over her face."

Arnst said he knew right away his sister-in-law was dead.

"As I was walking out, I noticed a bill, money laying on the kitchen floor, and I noticed her purse sitting right there."

The night before, he said he had taken out his hearing aids before he retired to bed around 11:30 p.m.

"Did you ever have an occasion to hear any loud noises through the walls there?" Smith asked.

"Not through the walls, no sir. The walls were thick. They were soundproofed, and you could hear nothing between the walls in the apartment."

"I have no further questions."

During cross examination, Redman inquired about the fact that the hallway was in total darkness on the morning Wilson's body was found. Arnst, who helped out as the building's handyman, explained what he learned. "I got a flashlight and went to the basement to where the switch fuse box was and turned the lights back on," Arnst testified. Downstairs, he found electrical wiring had been jerked out of the furnace, causing some tenants to lose their heat overnight. A stepstool was near where the wires were dislodged.

That same morning, as Arnst went into his sister-in-law's apartment, he said that he noticed her doorjamb was out of place. "There was a loose board on the jamb on the door. It was just the trim on the outside of the door. It was pried loose. It was away from the door."

The next witness, Billy Walker, was one of two emergency medical technicians whose ambulance responded to 212 N. Sixth St. that somber morning. He and John Jones arrived within two to three minutes of the call. "It was a lady laying on the floor. Her face was partially covered with a towel, rag," Walker testified. "We tried, Jones examined her, said he found no pulse, no heartbeat no respirations, and she was cold."

That first day of the trial, the jury watched the videotape recording of the crime scene that showed Wilson's dead body.

The final witness that day was Beatrice Police Lieutenant Gary Wiebe. The twenty-four-year police veteran described various crime scene photos he had taken including the bedroom wall where bloodstains were found. "What I observed about the body was it had a scarf tied over the face. The hands were bound. The feet were partially spread. The nightgown was pulled up exposing the crotch area of a female."

In Wilson's bedroom, Wiebe found her bedding pushed to the floor. Some pillows were strewn on the floor. "There was blood on the bed to the north end of the bed on the west wall."

In the kitchen, Wiebe said he spotted a torn five-dollar bill near the doorway.

During cross-examination by the defense, Wiebe acknowledged that the doorjamb was examined for signs of forced entry. "We remarked that the jamb was like away from the door a little bit. I think the remark was made that a credit card or knife could be put between the door and the side of the door."

As the trial rolled along, Beatrice Police Lieutenant Joe Hawkins, a twenty-year veteran, testified that he and fellow officers spent more than a dozen hours gathering clues inside the victim's apartment on the first day. In the back bedroom, a knife was found underneath a toppled Kmart brand tissue box. A photo of the kitchen showed a coffeepot.

"Did you touch that coffeepot?" Smith asked Hawkins.

"Yes, I did. Found that it was cold coffee in it. It was not warm."

Hawkins snapped photographs of the doorjamb. He thought it might signify forced entry.

"Did you ever develop any other evidence that there was forced entry?" Smith followed up.

"No, we did not."

This was an important point. The prosecutor wanted the jury to believe this broken doorjamb was not germane to the rape-murder. The primary reason was that it contradicted parts of the prosecution's narrative that the jury had yet to hear. Smith wanted everyone to believe that the victim heard loud knocking coming from her apartment door and, when she opened it, the group of six young men and women overpowered her and muscled their way inside.

As questioning continued, Smith brought up the name of a former Beatrice police officer named Burdette Searcey. "Was he a police officer on February 5, 1985, to your knowledge?"

"No, he was not," Hawkins testified.

Over time, Hawkins said, he had spoken with Searcey about the homicide. "He came in and talked to me."

Smith was setting the stage for the grand entrance into the courtroom of Deputy Searcey, but his appearance had to wait.

As the trial proceeded, Dr. John Porterfield testified that he had specialized in pathology since 1959, conducting so many autopsies he'd lost count. Surely, he had conducted thousands, the jury heard. During Wilson's autopsy, he found severe pneumonia had settled into her left lung. However, the pneumonia did not cause her death. On the contrary, the scarf knotted around the victim's head left a distinctive waffle pattern on the right side of her face. Deputy prosecutor Shelton asked how Porterfield concluded that homicide was the cause of death.

"Well, really, it's almost a lack of findings that you base it on. Remember, when I defined manner of death, it's either accident or suicide or homicide. ... And there was no findings that there were any cords around her neck that would cause her to accidently smother. She was on her right side, whether she died on her side or not, I can't say. To accidently smother that way, I can't imagine. To try to commit suicide by holding something over your face, it simply can't be done. I don't know if you know or not, but if you try to hold your breath or something over your face, eventually you're deprived of enough oxygen that you become unconscious and you'll start breathing again. So you can't commit suicide that way. So I'm left with homicide. ... All I know is the scarf was wrapped around her head."

Porterfield testified that the widow's left arm fracture "would hurt plenty." He further testified that her vagina and rectum both had been penetrated. The pathologist found plenty of sperm in her body. "I believe the time of death was somewhere around 10:00 p.m. on February 5, 1985, give or take a few hours."

***

The next witness, Darrell Wilson, was one of Helen Wilson's three grown children. His siblings were Janet Houseman of Beatrice and Larry Wilson of Scottsbluff. Darrell, a welder at the Hoover plant in town, recounted his final visit to his mother's apartment on the night of February 5, 1985. He got there about 6:45 p.m. While he was there, a local pharmacist from Poling Drug Store stopped by to deliver some cold medicine. His mother paid with a check, her son remembered. Around 9:00 p.m., Darrell Wilson's wife, Katie, stopped over after her bowling league finished. That night, Helen Wilson wore slacks and either a beige turtleneck or a wide-necked sweater as they mingled in her living room. While there, her son cracked open a couple cans of beer and kept his mother company. "I couldn't tell you the color of the slacks," he testified.

"Did your mother ever mention the name of Joseph White?" Smith asked.

"No, sir."

"Did she ever mention the name Ada JoAnn Taylor?"

"No, sir."

"Did she ever mention the name of Thomas Winslow?"

"No, sir."

"Did she ever mention the name of James Dean?"

"No, sir."

"Did she ever mention the name of Kathy Gonzalez?"

"No, sir."

"Did she ever mention the name of Debra Shelden?"

"A long time ago."

Debra Shelden, one of the convicted co-defendants, was related to the family. She was the daughter of one of Darrell Wilson's cousins, he testified.

When his wife took the stand, Katie Wilson told the jury how she always would stop at her mother-in-law's apartment on Tuesday nights after bowling to chit-chat and drink coffee. Heading into trial, Smith had decided to make the coffeepot a key focus of his questioning. On the night of February 5, 1985, Katie Wilson said she went into her mother in law's kitchen. That night no coffee was made. "She wasn't feeling well and she told me that. She said, 'Sorry, Katie, I didn't make any coffee.'"

Katie Wilson settled for a glass of water from the faucet instead.

"Was there any coffee in the coffeemaker?" the prosecutor inquired.

"No, sir."

"Was it clean?"

"Yes, sir."

Toward 10:00 p.m., Katie Wilson said she walked out into the second-floor hallway, the last time she saw her mother-in-law alive. "I told her to be sure to lock the door. So she shut the door, and I waited, and she locked the door. I heard the click."

Katie Wilson testified that she told her ailing mother-in-law that she would call around midnight, to remind her to take her regular dose of medicine. The jury heard how Katie Wilson had tried calling three times. First, at 11:50 p.m., she let the phone ring six times. She figured Helen Wilson was asleep. "I thought I'd call her exactly at midnight like I told her I would." At midnight, the phone rang three more times. Katie Wilson said she made a third and final attempt at 12:10 a.m.

"I let it ring six or seven times."

The jury was left to infer that Helen Wilson did not answer her phone because she was already dead.

So far, Smith had done a masterful job of setting the scene for the entrance of his shining star, Burt Searcey. The majority of his legwork on the case had occurred while he worked as a hog farmer, not a police officer. In most Nebraska small towns, police officers were exalted. In Fairbury, Searcey was certainly a witness the jury could easily relate to. The jury heard how he worked from 1977 until 1982 at the Beatrice Police Department. Then he sought another career path, the one that best defines Nebraska. "I resigned. I went into farming," Searcey testified.

"Deputy Searcey, calling your attention to the date of February 5 or the dates of February 5 and 6 of 1985. Were you a sworn officer on those dates?" Smith inquired.

"No, sir."

"Did you have any type of certificate to do investigation on those dates?"

"Yes, I did. I was a licensed private detective."

Years later, Searcey's claim on the witness stand that he was a licensed P.I. would be challenged. At any rate, he testified about starting to investigate Wilson's homicide within a month of her murder. "I initiated my own investigation due to the fact I knew the parties of the family that was involved. I also knew Mrs. Jan Houseman, and I had the need to investigate. It was something I loved to do."

Fast-forwarding four years in the testimony, the prosecutor noted that on March 15, 1989, Searcey had interviewed Joseph White at the Cullman Police Department in Alabama.

"You asked the defendant where he was on February 5, 1985, is that correct?"

"That's correct. He indicated he was in Beatrice, Nebraska, on that date."

"And did he give you any names of individuals that he was acquainted with back on February 5, 1985?"

"Yes, he did. Kathy Gonzalez, James Dean and another female that he knew as JoAnn."

Furthermore, Searcey said that White knew the brick complex where the murder occurred. "He also indicated to myself that he had been in that building on a few occasions."

The prosecutor asked if White knew somebody who lived there.

"He indicated that he knew a Kathy Gonzalez."

Lastly, Smith asked the star of the investigation if the same man he interviewed in Alabama was sitting in the Fairbury courtroom. "The individual would be the male subject sitting to the far west at the table just south of you, sir," Searcey answered.

"Let the record reflect, your honor, that he's identified the defendant," Smith announced.

"The record will so reflect," Judge Rist noted.

Next up, the prosecutor began the parade of pitiful co-defendants to testify before the jury.

CHAPTER 22
APARTMENT UNIT 4

Courthouse security escorted the plump woman wearing jail garb and handcuffs into the Fairbury courtroom. It was Debbie Shelden, the victim's great-niece. The jury wasn't told that Shelden was learning disabled. They just heard that she had pleaded guilty in connection with her own relative's murder.

Shelden had a giant incentive to testify to prosecutor Smith's liking. She had already lost her first child to the foster care system. She could not bear the thought of losing her little girl, Fantasia, whom she adored. For Shelden, the prospect of prison was not all bad. It offered an avenue to improve her education and job skills. At the time of her arrest, she had worked for a cleaning service in Lincoln. While she had been held in jail, she, too, was taken to the Lincoln office of polygraph examiner Paul Jacobson. In turn, he advised the prosecutor: "Nothing would please Debra more than seeing a long hitch for JoAnn as she has no love for her," Jacobson had predicted in a memo to the prosecutor. "I think you have a credible witness here who could do a good job on the stand." In the Fairbury courtroom, Smith called Shelden to the witness stand. "Can you give me your residence, please, your address?"

"612 Lincoln St., Gage County Jail."

The jury learned Shelden had lived in the jail for more than six months.

"Mrs. Shelden, why are you in the Gage County Jail?"

"Because I'm guilty of second-degree murder, aiding and abetting."

"Who are you guilty of aiding and abetting the second-degree murder of?"

"Mrs. Wilson."

Shelden testified that she awoke around 11:00 a.m. on the day of the murder. Jurors were told she had lived in a second-floor apartment with JoAnn Taylor, Charlotte Bishop, Debbie's future husband, Clifford Shelden, and JoAnn's then-boyfriend, Jon D. Munstermann. Late that night, she testified, she rode around in co-defendant Tom Winslow's green Oldsmobile. The car, loaded with five people, eventually stopped at 212 N. Sixth St. Everyone piled out and went up the stairs. They stood in front of Unit 4.

"JoAnn, after she knocked, Mrs. Wilson spoke to me," Shelden testified. "She said, 'Hello.' I said, 'Hello.'"

All of a sudden, everyone stampeded into the apartment. The prosecutor asked who shut the door.

"I did."

Minutes later, Shelden said she had been knocked unconscious after White manhandled her in the bedroom. When she regained her senses, she told the jury, she saw Tom Winslow taking a turn raping Wilson after White had finished his act of perversion upon the helpless widow.

Afterward, Shelden said, she, Dean and Taylor raced back to Winslow's car. She said that they sat there without the engine running for between fifteen minutes and a half-hour.

However, the jury was not told that temperatures had plunged well below zero that night, which would cast doubt on the notion that she and the others would sit waiting in an unheated parked car.

In any event, Shelden told the jury that eventually the carload of five misfits pulled away and sped down a nearby alleyway. She testified that she got mad at White in the car. "I yelled at him and asked him why he did it and everything, and he got mouthy and said to dump her. He dumped me out. I ended up at the apartment on Fifth and Ella."

Shelden testified that she never called the Beatrice police about the slaying. "I was told if I ever told anybody or anything that they would do the same to me."

Eventually, White's lawyer asked her to reveal the terms of her plea bargain.

"They're just going to give me ten years, request for ten years."

Reluctantly, Debbie had to admit in open court how she had given multiple statements to Deputy Searcey during the past year.

"Would you agree with me that you've changed your testimony a number of times?" Redman asked her.

"Yes. Nobody told me anything. I just did it."

Shelden conceded that at first, she had denied ever being involved in her great-aunt's homicide, and that when she finally implicated herself, she for some reason did not mention either James Dean or Kathy Gonzalez as co-conspirators.

"Do you remember in the statement that you gave Officer Searcey on April 13, that you weren't even aware that Dean or Gonzalez were there?" Redman asked.

"Yes."

"And Dr. Price has been working with you?"

"Yes."

"Working with you on your memory?"

"Yes."

"Because you couldn't remember anything?"

"Yes."

The jury was told that "Doc" Price served as a police psychologist at the Sheriff's Office in Beatrice. As Shelden continued, the twelve citizens deciding White's fate also gleaned that much of her testimony came as a result of interpretations of her dreams.

"In fact, your dreams helped you remember James Dean and Kathy Gonzalez, did they not?" Redman asked her.

"Yes."

The jury heard that Shelden and her husband, Clifford, had moved into the murder victim's apartment that May but only stayed about four weeks. The landlord evicted them because they had two dogs, which were illegal to keep in that building.

"And how often were you dreaming while you lived there?" Redman asked her.

"I had quite a few dreams. I had them every other day."

"And in those dreams you first recalled James Dean, did you not?" the defense attorney asked.

"Yes."

"And some while later, you later dream about Kathy Gonzalez, didn't you?"

"Yes."

"Did you dream about Joe White in those dreams?"

"He was in them also, yes."

"And all the facts about this case that you have told us today, you dreamed, did you not?"

"Yes."

Redman told the developmentally slow thirty-one-year-old that he wondered whether she could differentiate her dreams from the actual crime scene.

"They are identical," Shelden testified. "I saw the night of the homicide. I saw what I saw. I also saw most of it in my dreams."

About two weeks before White's trial, Shelden had been removed from her jail cell and put into Sheriff Jerry DeWitt's vehicle. He was behind the wheel, prosecutor Smith and Paul Korslund, Shelden's public defender, were the other passengers. The four went for a short ride in town, over past the old Lincoln Telephone & Telegraph building on Sixth Street. There, she pointed out the spot where she claimed Winslow had parked their getaway car.

After Shelden got off the witness stand, the sheriff was summoned to briefly explain the circumstances of the ride-along. "I believe it was County Attorney Mr. Smith's idea and her attorney," DeWitt testified.

"And your job was basically to drive around, is that correct?" asked White's defense co-counsel Alan Stoler during cross-examination.

"Yes."

"Was there any discussion taking place in the car other than directions given by Mrs. Shelden?"

"No, there wasn't."

"But prior to that there was some discussion to your recollection?"

"There may have been in my office, yes."

* * *

Like Debbie Shelden, the next trial witness' story also underwent an incredible transformation while inside the Gage County Jail. Between April and May, twenty-five-year-old James Dean strenuously denied having any involvement in the widow's death. Dating back to 1984, Dean and the murder defendant had been on friendly terms. They even worked together at the same company in Beatrice, laying bricks. Now, five years later, in November 1989, Dean was eagerly helping prosecutor Smith lay the building blocks to send White to the Nebraska electric chair.

For the most part, Dean regurgitated Debbie Shelden's testimony except he spiced up some details. "Well, there was a knock on the door. Helen Wilson came to the door. She said, 'Hello.' Boom! Joseph Lobo and JoAnn Taylor pushed their way in, and then everybody just kind of followed."

For a brief moment, Dean said he darted back outside. "And then something stopped me, and I come back in. I was afraid they were going to blame this whole thing on me, this whole incident, this robbery-murder."

Dean's sensational testimony caught White's lawyers by surprise, especially when Dean stated that he was privy to four separate conversations with White to plan out the crime. He said one occurred in the kitchen of Dean's girlfriend, and another occurred about a week before the murder as Dean and White walked downtown.

"The topic of the conversation it was about a robbery and just taking some money," Dean testified.

"Were any names mentioned?" Smith asked.

"There was one name mentioned, which was Mrs. Wilson's," Dean said in court. "Lobo said it. He said, 'I've been thinking about a sexual assault,' but he had been talking like that in the past."

On the night of the murder, Dean testified, he had watched as co-defendant Debbie Shelden entered Wilson's bedroom. "And I heard this thud, and this crack and it sounded like a bone breaking. It was like when I broke my ankle. I heard the crack first."

"Who was doing what?" the prosecutor asked.

"Tom Winslow was still controlling the neck area. Taylor had a hold of the hands. White had the feet."

Dean told the jury he blanked out into a hazy fog for a few minutes. "I just froze. I didn't know what to do. I wasn't watching ... I turned back towards Mrs. Wilson, and I seen White laying on top of the body. He's going up and down."

The prosecutor asked Dean to describe the living room furniture. This was easy because the sheriff showed Dean the crime scene video back in May.

"There was a stool laying there and a couch, and I can't describe colors or what."

Dean said that he also saw co-defendant Tom Winslow's bare backside in the living room.

"What was JoAnn Taylor doing?" Smith asked.

"She was holding the hands and licking the upper area of the body of Mrs. Wilson."

In preparation for White's jury trial, Dean was pulled out of his jail cell on May 17, May 24, June 7, June 23, July 16 and on September 13 for interviews with Sheriff's Office personnel. These interviews helped Dean cobble together more lurid and incriminating details surrounding Wilson's murder. In fact, upon closer scrutiny, much of Dean's testimony appears suspiciously identical to the conversations Searcey had with Lancaster County inmate Clifford Shelden, who, interestingly, was never called to the witness stand for the trial.

Dean went on to testify that, as the murder victim lay motionless on her living room floor, Taylor wandered into the kitchen. She poured water, scooped up the grounds and brewed a fresh pot of steaming coffee. "I seen one person with a coffee cup, and that was Mr. White."

Before the band of outcasts darted out the door of Wilson's apartment and into the darkness, Dean said he caught a glimpse of the supposed sixth co-conspirator. "Kathy Gonzalez had a brown rag, kind of up to her face area. She was in the bathroom."

Afterward, he testified, everyone else headed to the Marshall's Truck Stop to fill up their bellies with breakfast. "Oh, there was general conversation about how nice it was to do it," Dean told the jury. "They would do it again. It was fun. That was the conversation between JoAnn Taylor and Lobo."

Dean maintained that he never spoke a word about the brutal acts of savagery over the next four years. "No, I sure didn't."

Dean told the jury how he was arrested nearly seven months ago back on his twenty-fifth birthday. "I was arrested at the Hy-Vee parking lot in Lincoln, Nebraska."

"And did you admit this incident to them at that time?" the prosecutor asked.

"No, sir, I didn't.

Dean said he decided to admit involvement the following month in May. "I discussed it with my attorney. I told it to Burdette Searcey, and I do believe it was the sheriff."

That same month, Dean said he had been removed from his jail cell to watch the crime scene videotape.

"Was that before or after you entered your plea?" Smith asked.

"That was before."

"Do you remember who was present when you saw that video?"

Dean remembered the others included his lawyer, prosecutor Smith, Searcey and the sheriff.

"I saw it in Jerry DeWitt's office at the Gage County Jail."

The prosecutor asked how Dean responded upon seeing the video.

"I broke down and cried. I seen the video, I didn't even see it all. I seen the part where Mrs. Wilson was laying on the floor."

"Did you have remembrances at that time?"

"Yes, I did."

"Are you sure that the defendant, Joseph White, was in that apartment on February 5, 1985?"

"Yes, I am."

"Are you sure you saw him on top of Mrs. Wilson on February 5, 1985?"

"Yes, I am."

"How far away from him were you when you saw this?"

"Three to four feet."

Once Dean stepped away from the witness stand, the prosecutor summoned the case's most delusional witness to the stand. It was her turn to implicate the tall skinny man she first met on Hollywood Boulevard during the early 1980s.

CHAPTER 23
THE PILLOW

When JoAnn Taylor entered the Jefferson County courtroom in jail garb and handcuffs, there was no telling what would come out of her mouth. The jury was told that she had visited with five different psychologists during her turbulent life. Back in 1984 and 1985, she explained, she became acquainted with the murder defendant, White. The two saw each other often, but were never lovers.

Taylor told the jury that she went bumming around in a car during the evening hours of February 5, 1985. During the ride, she grew scared because White started talking about a scheme to get money. "And I was going to go along with it or else there would be bodily harm to me or my daughter," she told the jury.

"You had a daughter at the time? Was she in the area of Beatrice?" Smith interjected.

"As far as I know, yes, sir."

Taylor testified they drove around for ninety minutes to two hours. They cruised along Beatrice's main circuits, Court and Sixth Streets, over and over. "We were going up Ella (Street) and we were coming to a stoplight and Mr. Dean spotted Kathy Gonzalez waving at the car. She was in the back of the building. She was waving."

Seeing Gonzalez prompted Winslow to jerk his steering wheel. His green Olds made a sharp turn into an alley near the old telephone building. There, the five spilled out of his car. They went straight up one flight of stairs and stood directly in front of Unit 4. "I kind of got stuck in front of the door, and I knocked on the door," Taylor testified. "She, Mrs. Wilson, came to the door."

The courtroom hushed in silence as Smith handed the prisoner a professional portrait. This photo was labeled as trial exhibit No. 1.

"Can you tell me what that is, if you know?"

"Yes, sir, that's a picture of Mrs. Wilson."

"Is that the same individual that answered the door?"

"Yes, sir."

Taylor testified that White grew boisterous. He ordered the widow to give him all her money. But Wilson refused to budge. Then Taylor said she thought she heard a loud whack.

"He slapped her."

"What was Mrs. Wilson saying?"

"That she was not giving it and for him to go away."

In the words of Taylor, Wilson was tossed to the floor. Then out of nowhere, Gonzalez, arrived from her upstairs apartment like a phantom and came into the widow's bedroom. More chaos ensued in the small confined area.

The jury heard that White grew so enraged that he shoved Debbie Shelden. "Debra got elbowed backwards. She hit the wall I believe," Taylor testified.

Shelden remained on the bedroom floor for at least fifteen minutes, Taylor estimated. "I don't remember if she was knocked out, but she was woozy."

Meanwhile, Dean stood around in the living room and Gonzalez suddenly vanished. "I believe she was in the bathroom though because I could still hear her voice."

As violence intensified, Wilson begged White for mercy. "At this time, I had also told him to leave her alone, that he needed to respect his elders, and I ended up getting hit for it in the jaw."

The jury heard how White and Tom Winslow carried the widow into her living room. They pinned her on the floor. They savagely raped her and caused excruciating pain.

"What was Mrs. Wilson doing?" Smith asked Taylor.

"Struggling, arguing."

Taylor said she positioned herself by the widow's head. "Was there anything near you at that time?"

Bingo. Taylor heard her cue. She knew just what to say.

"There was a smaller green footstool at the time. I shifted my foot and kicked it over."

Smith handed her exhibit No. 2. It was gruesome.

"It's a picture of Mrs. Wilson's body," Taylor responded.

"Did you see him rape her?"

"Yes, sir."

Nearby, Taylor said she saw a pillow on the couch, so she grabbed it.

"I had placed a pillow over her face because I didn't want her to see the face that would haunt her."

The prosecutor tried to act befuddled.

"Why would the face haunt her?"

243

Taylor told the courtroom that she was speaking from experience. "When you're raped, the face can haunt you."

Once the defendant finished having his way with Wilson, he and Winslow switched spots, the courtroom heard. At that point, Taylor continued to apply the couch pillow against the elderly woman's face.

"Was Mrs. Wilson moving anymore?"

"No, sir."

Wilson's lifeless body was left on the floor. Then, Taylor said, she and the others canvassed the apartment for money. She told the jury how she stole a single twenty-dollar bill from on top of the bedroom dresser. Then she ventured into the kitchen and turned on the coffeepot.

"Why did you make it?" Smith inquired.

"I don't know, to be totally honest with you."

"What happened after you found the twenty-dollar bill?"

"I said I had it. Let's go."

"Was any other money found?"

"Not to my knowledge."

Finally, Taylor said, she darted out the door with the stolen twenty-dollar bill in her pants pocket. According to her testimony, the second-floor hallway suddenly went dark. "We got as far as the staircase and the lights went out. I tripped and Jim Dean caught me before I fell. We made our way to the back door before the lights came back on."

Taylor said that once they were back at the car she asked White about a loud ripping sound she'd heard in the kitchen.

"What did he say?"

"He said just his five."

"Did you know what he was talking about when he said just his five?"

It was time for the prosecution to introduce the jury to the crude magic tricks of Joseph White – his apparent signature left after carrying out the murder, according to Burt Searcey.

"I've never really understood it," Taylor admitted. "I know he pulls a five-dollar bill out and he does something with it and he ends up with a ripped five-dollar bill. And he usually tosses part of it away."

Later on, at Marshall's Truck Stop, White bought everyone breakfast, Taylor testified. This was to celebrate the success of the robbery, rape and murder, the jury was led to infer.

On cross examination, White's lawyer Redman tried to portray Taylor as a brainless dolt. After all, she had experienced extensive periods of reported severe psychotic behavior and delusions throughout her life.

But who would the jury believe? A murder defendant's defense lawyer or a seemingly believable witness who claimed she was not only there but also a key participant in the murder herself?

Like the others, Taylor also watched the police videotape of the crime scene, she testified.

"And that helped you for your testimony today, is that correct, for your memory?" Redman asked.

"Yes, sir."

***

By early November 1989, Lisa (Podendorf) Brown was married with two children. She worked as a cashier in

Beatrice at the Price Chopper Food Center. If prosecutor Smith had any holes and weak links in his case, Brown shored them up in amazing fashion. She became the only witness in Beatrice ever produced by the prosecution who claimed she saw co-defendants White and Taylor arriving at the apartment building in Winslow's car on the night of Wilson's killing.

That night, Brown testified, she and her future husband had visited her mother around 9:00 p.m. Brown claimed they left around 10:00 p.m. As they bummed around their hometown under nightfall, they turned onto Sixth Street, which was U.S. Highway 77, the main drag through Beatrice. Brown told the jury she distinctly remembered spotting a familiar car.

"It was a green Oldsmobile with a brown top."

Brown recognized the car as belonging to Winslow, one of her former high school classmates. Eventually, they turned opposite directions.

"So you lost sight of the car at that point?" Smith inquired.

"Yes."

From there, Brown and her boyfriend cruised through the McDonald's parking lot. Then, they headed south back along Sixth Street.

"Did you ever see that car again that evening?"

"Yes, approximately 10:18 p.m."

The prosecutor wondered why Brown precisely remembered the time.

"Because there's a bank that sits on the corner of Court Street, and it was the time on it."

"Did you look at that?"

"I always do."

"And what did you see?"

"10:18 p.m."

Then in a flash, she saw the familiar green Oldsmobile again, so she said.

"Well, I was curious, being nosey and I watched and I saw the car turn into the alley."

She said the green Oldsmobile pulled into a lot on the east side of the brick three-story building where the deadly rape had yet to unfold.

According to Brown, she urged her boyfriend to hit the brakes in the middle of the street even though their traffic light showed green. Brown testified with amazing precision that she watched as everyone piled out of Winslow's car – under the cloak of darkness -- as she peered out the rear passenger side window.

"I saw people get out."

And one of those faces in the shadows, way off in the distance, she said, was murder defendant Joseph White. Besides him, Brown testified that she also saw Winslow behind the wheel.

"Did you recognize anyone else?" Smith asked.

"Yes. JoAnn Taylor."

Brown testified that she also saw a fourth person get out of the car. However, the prosecutor decided not to ask her to identify that person she supposedly saw. That would have posed an embarrassment to the prosecution and drawn her credibility into serious question because, initially, Brown had claimed she positively saw Winslow's wife, Beth

Johnson, exit the car. Being gullible, Searcey took that information as gospel and used that information as part of his original arrest warrants for White and Taylor, which the press then reported. Later, though, Searcey was forced to walk back part of his information. In taking Brown's statement at her word, Searcey overlooked the fact that Beth Johnson had already given an earlier statement to police to account for her whereabouts on the night of the murder.

Switching gears, Brown was asked by the prosecutor whether she ever had spoken with Taylor in connection with the murder probe.

"Yes. It was the sixth or seventh of February. I'm not sure."

Brown claimed their conversation happened near the public library.

"I saw scratch marks on the side of her neck."

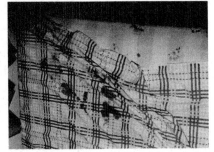

At the time of Joseph White's November 1989 jury trial, prosecutor Dick Smith convinced White's lawyers to agree to a stipulation that much of the human blood found at the crime scene was similar to that of White's co-defendant Kathy Gonzalez. Photo/ Beatrice Police Department

Though she had been only seventeen years old in 1985, Brown testified that she knew White fairly well and often saw him at beer parties in Beatrice where illicit drugs were present.

"Did you ever see him do any tricks with money?" Smith asked her.

It was time for Brown to connect the dots to sew up the Gage County murder case.

"Yes. He'd ask you for a bill and he'd ask you to point out a president, a dairy product and the name of a movie. And then the president happened to be on the bill, the dairy product, which is half and half -- at that time, he'd rip the bill in half -- and then the name of the movie, *Gone With the Wind*. He'd throw one half in the air and stick the other half in his pocket."

Brown was asked if White ever told her about any intimate relationship between himself and Taylor.

"Yes. He said that he was her stepfather."

As questioning wound down, Smith asked whether Brown had spoken with anyone prior to 1989 about the green Oldsmobile parked outside the murder victim's building.

"Yes. Burdette Searcey. He was a private investigator."

Smith asked if she had contacted the Beatrice Police Department with her information regarding the murder.

"No, because I was scared of what they'd do, JoAnn Taylor and Joseph White."

Her courtroom testimony made absolutely no sense, when you think about it. Why would Brown be willing to rat out Taylor two months after the slaying to an unlicensed private eye but be deathly afraid to speak with legitimate detectives at the Beatrice Police Department during any point during the next four years as Helen Wilson's murder went unsolved?

Something was not right with Lisa Brown's testimony, but whether the jury from around Fairbury picked up on that was yet to be determined.

***

Before the prosecution finished, prisoner Kathy Gonzalez was paraded into the courtroom. The jury heard that White had stayed in her apartment during the weeks prior to the murder.

Depending on how the jury interpreted her testimony, Gonzalez's comments could be the bow to wrap up the prosecution's package. The jury heard that Gonzalez had lost her dignity. She testified that she currently resided inside the Gage County Jail, having lived there for six months. "They arrested me for aiding and abetting the murder of Mrs. Helen Wilson."

Of the four already convicted defendants, Gonzalez was seemingly the only one with all her marbles. Debbie Shelden was developmentally disabled. JoAnn Taylor was psychotic and delusional. James Dean came from a terribly troubled home life and had severe emotional problems, court records show. Despite all the heartache she endured, Gonzalez remained firm in her belief that she did not participate in any violent crime in the apartment unit below hers. But, unfortunately, she did not have a lawyer who believed in her innocence. Her lawyer, Donald Sass, was pathetically bad.

By this stage in the trial, Dick Smith had produced three co-defendants who testified they saw Gonzalez being bloodied inside the victim's bedroom or serving as a lookout outside the apartment. Supposedly, Gonzalez also waved the carload of miscreants into the adjacent parking lot near the three-story apartment building.

And yet, suspiciously, the prosecutor chose not ask Gonzalez any direct questions in front of the jury regarding those events where her name had been mentioned by other co-defendants. Instead, Smith asked whether she had been convicted of aiding and abetting the second-degree murder of Helen Wilson.

"Yes."

"Did you plead to that charge?"

"Yes."

Next, Smith posed a narrowly focused question intended to let the jurors' imaginations run wild. He asked Gonzalez whether she ever had spoken with the defendant in 1985 about committing a crime.

"Yes, sir. We were walking home from the grocery store. Me and Lobo, or Joe White. He said something to the effect that, because I was broke, he asked me if I would be interested in helping him commit a burglary, sort of."

Keep in mind, the theme of the murder trial was that Wilson's apartment had been the target of a planned robbery. The jury was told that White went berserk after Wilson refused to hand over her money, and then that White enlisted Taylor and Winslow to pin down the woman down, indulge in a brutal gang rape and ultimately smother her to death.

The trial testimony was heartbreaking and gut-wrenching for the gallery of spectators to stomach, notably Helen Wilson's relatives. They heard testimony about broken bones, suffocation and their loved one being violently raped before and after her death. The Wilsons were not sophisticated people. They were everyday Nebraskans, good people who worked factory jobs, minded their business, and respected their police officers. The woman who was their mother, grandmother, and great-grandmother did not deserve such an awful death. At the courthouse in Fairbury, they had to bottle up their outrage toward the likes of James Dean, JoAnn Taylor, Debbie Shelden, and most of all, the tall slender man with the dark beard still professing his innocence, Joseph White, a native Alabaman.

***

On the afternoon of November 8, 1989, Sheriff DeWitt briefly took the stand again. He informed the jury that all six murder defendants remained segregated in his jail facility that held less than thirty prisoners. The sheriff assured the jury that the six co-defendants had not mingled to discuss the case at any time since their arrests.

"None of them have been together since they were in my custody."

At that point, the prosecution rested.

It was now up to White's public defense lawyers Toney Redman and Alan Stoler to present testimony, if they so desired.

CHAPTER 24
'THAT OLD WOMAN'

During the trial, lawyer Toney Redman would meander over to the downtown cafes and restaurants in Fairbury to grab a bite to eat during the noon hour break. It seemed like everyone in town knew Redman was defending the evil man on trial for Wilson's rape and murder. The locals around Jefferson County viewed Redman as a scumbag.

"I remember when we had to have lunch, everyone in the restaurant was just staring at me, like, 'How could you represent any of these people?'" Redman later recalled. "It seemed like from everybody we got the stink eye. It was the most difficult case I ever handled, emotionally and professionally. It was such a heinous crime."

Inside Fairbury's old courthouse, White sat through a parade of horrors. Witness after witness portrayed him as a despicable creep who deserved to burn in the fires of hell for the atrocities he committed against Wilson. The jury heard how White was a sadistic rapist, a human parasite, a premeditated robber, a mastermind murderer who robbed Beatrice of a tenderhearted and soft-spoken lady. How could any woman, particularly a kindly elderly woman be subjected to such a cruel rape and agonizing death?

So far within the trial, Judge William Rist had done a marvelous job as an impartial arbiter. The judge let the trial ebb and flow. And now that the prosecution was done clawing up the defendant, the judge needed to know whether the defense team would let White take the stand. Theoretically, the defense could send the case off to the jury and hope for the best.

"Now, Mr. White ... We are now at the point in the trial where you may offer evidence in your defense," Judge Rist advised. "One of your rights in that regard is to testify yourself. Another right you have is that you do not have to testify. And if you do not testify, no one can compel you or make you testify. Do you understand that right, sir?"

"Yes, sir."

The smooth veteran judge from Beatrice asked White's lead attorney, Redman, if the defense had made a decision.

"Yes, sir."

"And what would that decision be, Mr. White?"

"Yes, sir, I am ready to testify."

The judge reacted with surprise.

"You will testify?"

"Yes, sir," White repeated.

The tall defendant with long dark hair and brown eyes positioned himself at the witness chair. Defense co-counsel Alan Stoler handled the questions. The jury was reminded that White was not a native Nebraskan, a fact that certainly did not work in his favor. White was born and raised in Cullman County, Alabama, a foreign land in coal-mining country to this Nebraska jury consisting of mostly farmers or spouses of farmers. In fact, practically all of the twelve seated in judgment had lived their entire lives around Fairbury, a dwindling farming town of less than 4,400, with an entire county population of fewer than 8,800 people.

White came from a two-parent household, and his parents were both alive. He testified he had one older sister, plus two younger brothers and two younger sisters. White proudly graduated from Alabama's Holly Pond High School. He never had been married. At the time of his arrest, he worked as a sawyer and did part-time maintenance work for the Wright Brothers Corp. And White had a colorful nickname, the jury learned. For the past five years or so, many people did not refer to him as Joe or Joseph, rather as "Lobo." For a while, White was an aimless drifter. He moved to Beatrice in September 1984 only to skip town in roughly six months -- the same month Helen Wilson was slain. It was not an incredible leap for the jury to infer that White's vanishing act was no coincidence.

The jury also learned that White spent a lot of time drinking at the R&S Bar on Court Street.

"How often would you estimate you were at the R&S Bar?" Stoler asked.

"Well, just about every day."

When the weather allowed, White worked as a bricklayer for Estate Construction. He did not have a vehicle in Nebraska. Most everywhere he went in Beatrice he walked.

During the friendly line of questioning from his defense counsel, White was asked about James Dean and JoAnn Taylor, the co-defendants who had fingered him as a loathsome rapist. White remembered Dean helped him get the job as a bricklayer, but White's work ethic impressed the bosses so much that they paid White a higher wage than Dean.

"He seemed a bit jealous of the fact that he had got me the job, and I was making more money than he was and, in fact, more or less his supervisor," White told the jury.

As for Taylor, White chose to downplay his connection to her. "I met her in California, and we came out here together. More or less she was an acquaintance."

"Was she ever a girlfriend of yours?" Stoler asked.

"No."

White denied ever knowing co-defendant Debbie Shelden.

"Never met her during the time you were in Beatrice?"

"No."

White was asked if he knew Jon Darren Munstermann, the tall, brown-bearded teenager who dated Taylor in January of 1985. "Well JoAnn had claimed that I was her father, and he wanted to ask me for her hand in marriage."

"Were you the father of JoAnn Taylor?" Stoler asked.

"No."

"Did you ever tell her that you were her father?"

"No."

White testified that he had last seen Taylor about a month before the murder. He had not seen Tom Winslow, his former roommate, since December 1984. White confirmed that he stayed at Gonzalez's apartment about a month before the murder, but there was nothing sinister about his stay there.

"Did you ever talk about doing a burglary with her?" Stoler asked.

"No."

"Anything like that?"

"No."

At the time of the murder, White was renting an apartment across from the Gage County Sheriff's Office. But by the middle of February, White packed his bags and hopped on a bus. "I had gone home to Alabama and lived with my parents. I had gotten homesick and called my mother for a bus ticket to come home."

During a bus station transfer, White testified, he used a pay phone to call someone with a traveling carnival in New Mexico. "But when I called, the phone had been disconnected."

White's lawyer asked if he ever had known Helen Wilson.

"No, I didn't."

"Did you participate in her apartment on the fifth of February, 1985?"

"No."

"And your knowledge of the incident of the circumstances happening to Helen Wilson came from the newspaper and gossip?"

"Yes, sir."

After White left Beatrice, he said, he lost contact with his old acquaintances from around the town including Taylor.

"Are you scared right now, Mr. White?" Stoler asked.

"Yes, sir, because my life is in the hands of twelve people I don't know."

During cross examination, prosecutor Dick Smith eagerly hammered home his belief that the torn five-dollar bill was not left on the victim's floor by accident.

"You were asked about a five-dollar trick on direct examination," Smith pointed out. "Do you remember that?"

"Yes, sir."

"Did you ever perform that trick?"

"No, I didn't."

The prosecutor reacted with profound amazement.

"Never in your life?"

"Never."

"You never performed it in front of Lisa Brown?"

"No."

The prosecutor approached the defendant. He handed White a trial exhibit showing the crime scene photo of the ripped five-dollar bill.

"Do you know where that was found?"

"No, sir."

The prosecutor was flabbergasted.

"You sat in the courtroom and listened to the testimony, and you don't know where that was found?"

"As far as what has been said in the courtroom, yes, I do. That was found in Helen Wilson's apartment."

Now that the prosecutor had riled up White, Smith set the stage for a dramatic courtroom exchange. It was a moment in the jury trial that the lawyers would remember for decades.

Smith handed the defendant trial exhibit No. 1. It was the professional portrait of the dignified Helen Wilson. White clutched the item in his hands. Then, he looked up at his examiner, who was trying to drill him.

"Can you tell me what this is?" Smith asked.

"It's a picture of an old woman," White snapped.

White's reaction sent a shivering chill through the Jefferson County District Courtroom. Even White's defense attorneys winced. Deep down, they knew their client could not have given a more disrespectful answer. The prosecutor pounced on White's cold-hearted reaction. He repeated White's answer aloud to make sure everyone on the jury heard it again.

"Have you ever seen that *old woman* before?" Smith bellowed.

"No, sir," White answered.

Common sense made Smith realize he need not go on. White's insensitive reaction to the murder victim's portrait spoke volumes. It was wise to stop while the prosecutor was way ahead.

"I have no more questions," Smith abruptly announced.

Later, during a 2016 interview, Redman distinctly remembered White's damaging cross-examination testimony as if it happened yesterday.

"Joe White was being very honest," Redman reflected. "But he came across as a very cold and calculating person. I pretty much figured we were done at that point. It was certainly the most damning moment of that trial. By the end of the trial, it was pretty much a given how the verdict was going to go."

***

One interesting footnote about the trial of Joseph White is that at no point did the jury ever hear directly from any scientists or scientific expert witnesses surrounding the blood and semen found at the crime scene. Instead, Smith presented the judge and jury with a stipulation about the evidence that would allow the prosecution to avoid putting Dr. Reena Roy, the lab serologist for the Nebraska State Patrol crime lab in Lincoln, on the witness stand. If she were to testify, her answers to some questions might expose a number of flaws in the prosecution's case.

Judge Rist asked White's lawyers about the serology stipulation.

"Any objection?"

"No, your honor," Redman answered.

"Stipulation is received."

So shortly before noon, the twelve fair-minded and responsible jurors from around Fairbury retreated behind closed doors to hash out the Alabama man's guilt or innocence. First, they were fed lunch by the court. The jury's foreman, William J. Henry, and the others were advised that if deliberations reached 9:00 p.m., they would be sequestered for the night at an area hotel on the court's dime and resume deliberations the following morning.

That afternoon, after the jury was sent to deliberate, several members of the Wilson family met inside one of the downtown cafes across from the courthouse. They were disgusted by White's reaction on the witness stand when he was shown the portrait of Helen Wilson. "He stated it was some old lady," remembered Edie Wilson, the victim's daughter-in-law, who lives in Scottsbluff. "Gramma was a very young-acting and -looking lady. This upset the family and the jury."

By 3:40 p.m., the jury of twelve was back in its box. All told, the jurors needed less than three hours to deliberate.

Speaking to the jury members, Judge Rist inquired if they had reached a unanimous verdict.

"Yes, we have," Henry proclaimed.

The judge asked Henry to hand over the formal paperwork. The clerk of the District Court read the verdict aloud for everyone in the crowded courtroom.

"In the District Court of Jefferson County, Nebraska, the State of Nebraska, plaintiff, versus Joseph Edgar White, defendant, verdict of the jury: We the jury, duly impaneled and sworn to well and truly try and true deliverance make between the State of Nebraska and Joseph Edgar White, prisoner at the bar, do find the said defendant guilty."

The document, dated November 9, 1989, was signed by the jury's foreman. One by one, the judge called upon each juror by name. Each of them answered affirmatively. They all endorsed the verdict. As a consequence, White was now convicted of first-degree felony murder, meaning he caused the death of Wilson while in the commission of another crime, in this case, robbery and rape, the jury concluded.

"The court finds that the verdict is unanimous," Judge Rist pronounced. "The defendant is remanded to the custody of the sheriff."

Lastly, the judge complimented the jury for its dedication and public service. "Ladies and gentlemen of the jury, it's been a long hard case. You have been diligent and attentive during the trial. The court thanks you for that attention. You are discharged now from further service in this case."

Several members of the Wilson family packed the courtroom when the verdict was read. White was guilty just as they thought.

"I remember standing at the bottom of some cement steps outside of the courthouse with all of the family hugging each other and celebrating," said Edie Wilson, Helen's daughter-in-law. "I looked up and there stood Burt Searcey. I told the rest of the family, 'There stands our hero.' He came down the stairs and received congratulations from all of us."

Redman said his client took the verdict in stride. "Joe was a good guy. He was very cooperative and a decent guy. He adamantly insisted that he was not guilty."

With the jury's duty done, next up was the sentencing phase. Prosecutor Smith thought a death sentence in Nebraska's electric chair was appropriate. But one man would decide White's punishment: Gage County District Judge William B. Rist. He could sentence White to die by electrocution, which was Nebraska's sanctioned method of capital punishment in 1989, or sentence White to spend the rest of his life in a Nebraska state penitentiary. Neither option was good for the defendant.

Nobody knew what the judge would do.

***

In the wake of White's humiliating defeat at trial, co-defendant Tom Winslow saw the inevitable writing on the wall. After conferring with his attorney, John Stevens Berry, Winslow pleaded no contest on December 8, 1989, to second-degree murder, thus avoiding a trial by not admitting to but not contesting his guilt. The prosecutor promised not to make any recommendation at sentencing. Winslow would lose many years of his life to the Nebraska Department of Corrections, but at least his life was spared. At least in his case, Nebraska's electric chair was off the table.

As for the others convicted of lesser roles, Debbie Shelden, Kathy Gonzalez and James Dean, all received ten-year prison terms.

At Winslow's sentencing on January 29, 1990, his lawyer John Stevens Berry told the courtroom that his client called him at home, after being charged with murder in the four-year-old Wilson investigation. "I instructed him that I'd see him the next day. I couldn't talk to him that night. I told him, 'Don't talk to anybody until I see you.' Tom Winslow would not follow my advice, insisted on talking to the officers, and so this story began."

Believing his client was guilty, Berry also asked the court to recognize how "Tom Winslow was always a cooperative witness. He did not put the State through a trial, did not put the victim's family through the agony of going through a second trial," the Lincoln defense lawyer explained.

Lastly, Berry touched on Winslow's past, which included a history of psychiatric treatment, including suicidal behavior and depressed mood swings. Winslow, he said, is easily influenced, who wants to please, is depressed and beset by many psychological problems.

"He was brutally beat upon at a young age. The details are in the pre-sentence investigation. I will not discuss it further," Berry said. "The Correctional Services says in the past he has had problems with friends and has been a follower in the past because he has wanted to be accepted. Again, generally, Mr. Winslow seems passive-dependent."

Indeed, Winslow had already been convicted of felony assault for his role in the tire-iron beating in Lincoln, a vicious attack that left a motel clerk in a wheelchair. "Tom Winslow was the decoy or setup or whatever it was," Berry declared. "It was Clifford Shelden that struck (the victim) with the tire iron. Mr. Winslow is a follower. He's ill, but he's a man who has undergone a great deal of trauma of in his lifetime including participation in this brutal and terrible tragedy."

His lawyer reiterated that Winslow had no memory of the rape and murder, court records show. Incidentally, Winslow went down as the only one of the co-defendants who refused to testify against White, his former roommate, at the jury trial in Fairbury. Winslow's reasoning was simple: He refused to commit perjury.

The court, however, was convinced of his guilt. Judge Rist referred back to one of the court-ordered psychiatric evaluations indicating there was no reason why Winslow could not remember the events on the night of Wilson's murder. "I think I can read that together with the diagnosis of possible malingering," Rist declared. "It says to me that Mr. Winslow knows what happened the night of the Wilson murder. He is simply unwilling to say. That's his choice, but I think that's what he record indicates."

The judge sentenced Winslow to fifty years in prison. Winslow committed "unspeakable deviant sexual assaults" on Helen Wilson, Rist declared.

Theoretically, Winslow needed to serve at least twenty-five years for any chance at parole. Even at that time, convicts sentenced for raping and killing elderly widows wouldn't be prime candidates for early release from Nebraska's tough-as-nails criminal justice system.

CHAPTER 25
LIFE OR DEATH

Before Joseph White could be strapped into the Nebraska electric chair and fed thousands of volts of electricity, the state required a special court hearing to weigh arguments for or against the imposition of capital punishment. But first, on January 18, 1990, White's lawyers Redman and Stoler put up a last-ditch, desperate effort to indefinitely delay the sentencing of their client.

In 1990, DNA testing was a relatively new and unfamiliar phenomenon and old-school court officials greeted it with incredible skepticism. White's lawyers asked the judge to postpone sentencing until the court administered DNA testing on some of the key items of evidence recovered from the February 5, 1985, crime scene and presented at the jury trial.

Prosecutor Dick Smith vehemently opposed the prospect of DNA testing. White's trial was already over. "We would advise the court that the defense has had knowledge of the substances that I presume they want to test, which would be sperm, for probably a good four to five months prior to the trial date," Smith argued.

Smith also contended the forensic evidence being sought for DNA testing was too old for such testing. "The (Federal) Bureau of Investigation will not do DNA testing on DNA topics unless the substance was obtained subsequent to December of 1988. These substances were obtained in

March of 1985. They won't even testify to them. Their experts won't even get on the stand ... If we could have done this, the state would have had it done."

Judge Rist found the defense motions baseless. "And they are overruled," he declared.

It was now time for the lawyers to spar over the death penalty.

Smith argued that sending White to the electric chair was warranted. His research showed that other courts across Nebraska had relied upon the following criteria in capital murder cases: relishing of the murder by the killer, infliction of gratuitous violence upon the victim, needless mutilation, senselessness of crime and the victim's helplessness. Without a doubt, this crime was senseless and painful. "Her arm was broken. She had severe injuries to the other arm. She had cracked ribs. The description of the defendant having his way with her on her ribs could very easily explain that," Smith argued.

She was also rendered helpless.

"A sixty-eight-year-old woman being held by two twenty-year-old men, one of them being the defendant," Smith argued.

The judge was reminded that co-defendant James Dean testified he had heard Wilson's bones snapping inside her bedroom. "She was still alive when she was brought out into the living room and sexually assaulted by the defendant. We feel this is not even beyond a reasonable doubt on this one issue that this defendant could be sentenced to death in the state of Nebraska. ... I think it would only be repetitive to continually go over how senseless this killing was, how depraved it was and how helpless the victim was."

However, based on prior case law involving death-penalty cases, even Smith realized that his fight to give White a death sentence was probably unrealistic. After all, none of White's five co-defendants received a prison term exceeding life.

"Unfortunately in this case there are co-defendants, and those co-defendants, the state, unfortunately had to make plea agreements with," Smith argued. "When one's heart says the death penalty should be imposed, one's mind knows, that under the law, it can't done ... As much as I'm sure everyone's heart would like, at least on this side, a death sentence, we understand that it is not possible."

An elder statesman on the bench, Rist was regarded as a good judge. He was not swayed by emotion or public outcry. He took the capital punishment arguments under advisement and set the sentencing for February 16, 1990.

On that memorable day inside the Gage County Courthouse, Dick Smith and Jerry Shelton stood for the prosecution. White, the convicted murderer, was led into court in shackles and handcuffs. He greeted his public defenders Toney Redman and Alan Stoler for one final time.

"Mr. White, you've been previously convicted in this court of the crime of murder in the first degree," Rist declared. "I advise you again of that judgment of conviction. I also advise you at this time of the duty of the court to pass sentence against you upon that conviction and I ask if you have anything to say as to why the judgment of the court ought not be passed."

"Yes, sir, I do," White declared. "I was convicted under perjurous testimony."

With his life at stake, White blurted out his strong objections to the proceedings. White spoke with vigor. The gritty Southern man's remarks were brief and to the point.

"I am not guilty of this crime," he vowed. "I have never been guilty of this crime, and even if the sentence is getting out due to parole, then I will take that opportunity to prove my innocence."

The courtroom in Beatrice fell silent.

"Anything else you wish to say?" Rist asked.

"No, sir."

Rist brushed off White's fervent denials of guilt. "What you have said does not constitute reason why sentence ought not be passed."

Rist said he took a number of factors into consideration as he weighed the death penalty.

The judge recognized Taylor had received a forty-year sentence after pleading guilty to second-degree murder and co-conspirator Tom Winslow got a fifty-year prison term.

Based on the trial testimony, White's actions inside the apartment did not appear to have caused Wilson's death, the judge concluded.

"At most he was an aider and abettor with respect to the murder. Given the seriousness of the nature of the death penalty, the court finds that such considerations mitigate against the imposition of such penalty in this case."

The judge had only one other sentencing option left.

"For the offense of murder in the first degree [for] which the defendant has been convicted, he be and is hereby sentenced to life imprisonment in an institution under the jurisdiction of the Department of Corrections of Nebraska," Rist pronounced.

Obviously, White's family and friends in Alabama were floored by the devastating outcome of his case. For White, the separation from his family would be like a death sentence in its own right. While White was incarcerated in Nebraska during the murder investigation, his son had been born back in Alabama. But the joy of being a father was tempered by the fact that their separation would be permanent. He would lose out on the chance to watch his baby boy crawl, walk, or talk. Moreover, heading into the trial, White had assured his father he was innocent, White's hometown newspaper reported. The Whites remained in his corner, but they were powerless. They could not undo the murder conviction on his record. A jury of twelve ordinary small-town Nebraskans had been convinced of White's guilt, and that's what mattered most.

White was sent to live out his days at the Nebraska State Penitentiary in Lincoln. His family had to move on with their lives without him, and they hated it.

Just a few days before White's sentencing, an international news story began circulating across American newspapers, big and small: the story of Nelson Mandela, who got a life prison sentence in South Africa in the 1960s during the rise of apartheid, convicted of sabotage and conspiring to overthrow the South African government. The same week that Mandela was freed after serving more than twenty-seven years of unjust imprisonment, twenty-seven-year-old Joseph White was given a life sentence for a small-town murder in rural Nebraska, a conviction he declared was unjust. Those following the Wilson murder case were generally satisfied that the punishment fit the crime.

***

In time, White adapted to life on the inside, though the adjustment was not easy. The Nebraska Department of Corrections assigned White prison inmate No. 40645. He had an eternity to sit around his prison cell and mope. Maybe he could hope for a tornado, earthquake or raging fire to engulf the prison. A natural disaster seemed White's best hope to break free from the shackles of spending infinity in prison. White had never seen his life shaping up this way. He never had any dreams or great plans to spend significant time in Nebraska.

After leaving the Army in 1981, White had been a vagabond. He traveled with a carnival. He hitchhiked. He dabbled in Hollywood's adult pornography industry. He bounced from town to town. He came to Beatrice with no intentions of staying long, and within five or six months, he was gone. Then, four years later, he was back in Nebraska, obviously not by choice.

Now in 1990, the worst years of White's life remained ahead of him. He was one of the condemned. In prison, he learned to obey the rules and follow orders rather than rebel or mouth off as many convicts often choose. "In prison, they called me Alabama or 'Bama or Al," White later told the *Lincoln Journal Star.*

Because of the incredible distance and financial hardships, White's relatives in Alabama were only able to visit him once a year. At the Nebraska State Penitentiary, prison officials gave White one of the lowliest jobs, being a janitor. The job paid about $1.20 per day. Eventually, through perseverance, White was moved into a wood shop, making 38 cents per hour, the Lincoln newspaper reported.

White was a miser. He pinched every penny he could. He needed it for one purpose: to hire a skilled lawyer.

***

Overall, the citizens of Beatrice and notably the Wilson relatives were grateful to shut the book on this horrible case. More than anything, the community preferred to be known as a warm and safe place to raise a family or to live out one's retirement. Nobody wanted the stinging notoriety of being associated with one of rural Nebraska's most repulsive murders of the 1980s. For some, resolution of the murder case marked a time of great adulation. The two local political shining stars became Gage County Attorney Dick Smith and Sheriff Jerry DeWitt. Both went on to win re-election in 1990, 1994, 1998 and 2002. The prosecutor and sheriff would savor their press clippings.

DeWitt later told the Beatrice newspaper that the Wilson case was one of the highlights of his tenure as sheriff. In fact, back in 1990, the county lawman with a rugged persona even used the enormously high-profile murder case to stir the pot and smear his crosstown rivals over at the Beatrice Police Department.

***

In a 1990 article published in the *Lincoln Journal*, Sheriff DeWitt blamed the city's police department for Wilson's murder remaining unsolved as long as it had. "In twenty-seven years, I've never seen anything as atrocious as what they did," DeWitt told the newspaper.

In the unflattering article, the Beatrice police were lambasted for destroying the blood-stained bra belonging to Kathy Gonzalez long before White's case went to trial. This was

271

the bra found in the trash outside after the murder was discovered in Wilson's apartment.

"They make mention about the bra, this missing bra that supposedly had blood that was never analyzed," Donald Luckeroth, the long-time Beatrice chief, would later explain. "That seemed to be a big focus of everybody. The officer that took care of the evidence said that thing started to mold and so he threw it away. But it was found in a Dumpster. And I don't know that it had anything to do with this case."

Luckeroth spent his entire career as a cop in Beatrice dating back to the 1950s. He distinctly remembered his agency handled nine murder cases during his eighteen-year administration as chief, before retiring in 1992. The Wilson murder was the only case under his leadership he did not get solved, Luckeroth pointed out later.

That same *Lincoln Journal* article that glorified the Gage County Sheriff's Office included comments from Luckeroth saying that the murder probe "was screwed up."

Many years later, Luckeroth still remembered how reporters were hounding him back in 1990 about why the rape-murder was not solved under his watch as Beatrice police chief.

"Well, the media just kept on us and kept on us and kept on us," Luckeroth said in 2010. "And I said, well, it's better to get them off our back so we'll say maybe we did screw up. I thought it was screwed up. But I didn't necessarily think we screwed it up."

CHAPTER 26
TRIALS REMAIN

After the convictions, Burdette "Burt" Searcey relished his newfound celebrity status around southeast Nebraska. Most of all, he was endeared by the victim's family. Many around Beatrice revered him for cracking the Wilson murder. Thanks to his investigative prowess, he took the credit for putting three men and three women in prison for a terrifying murder. "I think I probably done most of what I needed to have done myself," Searcey pointed out.

He had been promoted to lieutenant, a key supervisory position, in the Sheriff's Office. He recalled receiving a heap of praise for securing the six murder convictions. "I wouldn't say it was an exuberant high-five thing, but I think, you know, people were saying, 'Hey, good job,' you know, 'hard work.'"

On March 2, 1990, about a week after White was sentenced to life in prison, Lincoln polygraph examiner Paul Jacobson sent a warm letter of congratulations to Sheriff DeWitt. Jacobson made sure the sheriff recognized how his ace detective had changed the dynamics of the previously stalled murder investigation handled by Beatrice police.

"I would imagine that the County Attorney feels a bit relieved, too, to have this past year over with and to have such satisfactory results," Jacobson wrote. "You and your people deserve a world of praise and especially Burdette for having picked up that fumbled ball and to have scored. That is difficult as all hell after such a long period of time, but you got the job done."

In closing, Jacobson predicted the citizens of Gage County "can sleep easier now."

That same year, Gage County nominated Searcey for the prestigious VFW J. Edgar Hoover Award given to the national law enforcement officer of the year.

"During his tenure with the Sheriff's Department, he has made the rank of lieutenant. He also was instrumental in solving a major homicide case which was four years old and included six arrests connected to this case, covering a five-state area: Nebraska, Oklahoma, Colorado, Alabama and North Carolina," Searcey's nomination paperwork stated. "His dedication to solving this case even while not in the law enforcement field for a period of time demands respect from his fellow officers."

Over the next couple of years, Searcey was not shy about discussing his starring role in bringing the killers of Wilson to justice. One such presentation took place before a criminology class at the Southeast Community College campus in Beatrice. Afterward, one of the instructors sent him a letter.

"Dear Lt. Searcey: Thank you for sharing your knowledge and expertise with my Criminology students. It was apparent from the myriad of questions that they were very interested in hearing what you had to say."

Searcey enjoyed the prestige his community had bestowed upon him. Then, on April 21, 1993, an off-duty bar scuffle blemished his record. When asked about the ugly episode years later, Searcey gave this account under oath:

"Well, I was involved in an altercation. I was at our country club, the bar of the country club or the golf course/country club. And a gentleman that had been a bartender there or was bartending hit me, a guy by the name of Garcia."

The bar scuffle happened around 6:30 or 7:00 at night.

"He quit tending bar. I had ordered a drink, and I was drinking my drink. ... Anyway, the young man that was tending bar, who knew me quite well, honestly, I can tell you today probably didn't like me. And so when he got done tending bar, he came around and sat from me to the end of the table. And he started making derogatory statements about law enforcement deputies and everything. And I just turned like this. And I said, 'What would be wrong with deputies?' And he stood up and he came toward me. So I stood up and he hit me. And he knocked me clear down."

Searcey said he got off the floor. "And I said why did you do that? And he hit me again, knocked me clear down again."

According to Searcey's version, someone else in the country club then began hollering at the bartender. "And I then was trying to pursue him to talk to him. And he run out of the building from where I could see. And the next thing I know, I hear somebody screaming and hollering, and it's in the foyer, some ways away from where I was. Obviously, someone had beat this young man up after he run away from me. I see the man and it's apparent that he's bleeding."

In the spring of 1993, Searcey was a forty-four-year-old sheriff's lieutenant who supposedly just got punched right in the face twice – both times unprovoked. Amazingly, he did not even recommend criminal charges be brought against the bartender. "That wasn't for me to determine," Searcey maintained. "It was investigated by the Beatrice Police Department."

Searcey believed they each initially received a county court summons accusing them of assault. "I can't remember what degree of assault," Searcey testified. "But it was for assault, mutual."

However, both of the tickets were ultimately dismissed. "The only thing I know, it never went any further," Searcey testified. "I do believe, if I remember right, the summonses were dismissed ... but they were dismissed on both parties."

By the time Searcey showed up at the Sheriff's Office the very next day after the bar brawl, the word was out. "It was pretty obvious when I went to work the next morning. I had an awful big lip. ... I think I acknowledged the fact that I was involved in it. Of course, that was a given. And the sheriff disciplined me by suspending me for three months without pay."

Searcey said he never contested the suspension even though it meant being docked a quarter of an entire year's salary. He also did not contest being demoted over the ordeal. Sheriff DeWitt stripped him of his rank as lieutenant. During his twelve-week-long suspension, Searcey had to turn in his weapon and badge. The suspension began in late April and ended in July of 1993.

"It was the belief of my sheriff and myself that it was probably not becoming to have had the incident happen," Searcey explained.

When he returned to duty, Searcey began at the bottom of the totem pole, as a police radio dispatcher. "But I did get my duties back as a general deputy."

Indeed, Searcey returned to patrolling county roads and he got his gun back. But he was no longer conducting criminal investigations. On November 11, 1993, Searcey wrote a letter addressed to Sheriff DeWitt and the Gage County Board of Supervisors.

"I am writing this letter to advise you that I will be resigning my commission and duties as deputy sheriff of Gage County Ne. as I am going to pursue other interests. It has been a great pleasure serving the county of Gage, and its citizens for the past six years and ten months."

Searcey put in his two-week notice. He decided to leave law enforcement to buy a liquor store in Beatrice. He maintained his three-month unpaid suspension had nothing to do with his decision to part ways with the Sheriff's Office. "I had a lot of things that I was doing. I was pursuing an interest with a new woman in my life. I started assessing what I was doing with what my job was at the time as a deputy sheriff. I had been a farmer at one time. ... So I just felt that, you know what, I think I'm going to do something different."

At any rate, once Searcey resigned in late 1993, he and his third wife began their ownership and management of the House of Bottles in Beatrice, court records reflect. Their liquor store prospered during the 1990s and Searcey made more money than he ever had as a small-town cop. "I can tell you that I was probably making back then somewhere between $50,000 and $70,000 a year out of the store," Searcey said.

***

It's remarkable how certain lives seem to intersect in small towns likes Beatrice. Tina Vath never fathomed she would take on an extraordinary role in the ultimate resolution of Helen Wilson's murder case. After all, Vath had never even heard about the slaying prior to relocating to Beatrice in the 1990s.

JOHN FERAK

Vath grew up in Scottsbluff, the same far western Nebraska community that Helen Wilson visited shortly before her tragic death. Vath graduated from Scottsbluff Senior High School in 1991 and briefly attended Western Nebraska Community College, studying business management. But by the mid-1990s, a job transfer forced her and then-husband to relocate to the far southeastern corner of the state. At the time, Vath's husband worked for a liquor and wine distributor. The young married couple left their friends and relatives behind in Nebraska's Sandhills region for a new life in Beatrice. Newcomers to town, the Vaths became acquainted with Burt Searcey and his wife, Cindy, through the House of Bottles liquor store. "We quickly became very good friends and for years would spend most weekends and even holidays together with our children," Vath pointed out.

Vath liked Beatrice. She found the community generally safe and a nice place to raise a family. During summer, local residents often sat outside and relaxed on their back porches, sipping on refreshments, mingling with neighbors, as the roar of stock car races at the Beatrice Speedway echoed in the background. During various social outings with the local liquor store owners, Vath first heard about Searcey's former career as a crime-fighting detective. He often talked about his role in solving the Wilson murder case. Vath did not know anything about the crime, other than what she gleaned during those backyard barbeques.

"I just believed that the six were guilty and ... didn't even question anything," she said.

By 1996, Vath found a job as a police dispatcher for the City of Beatrice. It wasn't long before she found it to be her calling in life. Vath took a strong interest in police work, an interest that would one-day bring her face to face professionally with Searcey – but that was still years down the road.

As for Searcey, besides owning the House of Bottles, he went on to obtain a Nebraska Realtor's license around 2000, allowing him to list and sell area properties. Unfortunately, he eventually encountered serious health issues followed by the onslaught of staggering medical bills. He declared bankruptcy around June of 2003, public records show. "I had heart attacks," Searcey said. "And I ended up having triple bypass, open heart surgery."

Searcey sold the House of Bottles for $78,000 to a woman who ran a bar in Beatrice. "That was just the business," he said. "I did not own the building."

After that, Searcey managed a deli at the Sunmart grocery store in town. He was truly a jack of all trades. He had been a grocer, a welder, a grain elevator operator, a police officer, a hog farmer, a sheriff's deputy, a liquor store owner and a Realtor. Without a doubt, his claim to fame in the community's eyes, however, was his stint as the sheriff's deputy who solved the Wilson slaying.

Unfortunately for Searcey, police incidents involving alcohol continued to dog him.

In 2005, a Gage County sheriff's deputy pulled over Searcey's vehicle and gave Searcey, then fifty-seven, a citation for disregarding a stop sign and for driving with an open container of alcohol.

"Did you have an open container?" a lawyer later asked.

"I did."

"What county attorney handled it?"

"I think it was Richard Smith."

Ultimately, the County Attorney's Office dismissed the pair of citations. Searcey recalled that the sheriff's deputy who stopped him was subsequently fired for an off-duty incident, and the prosecution had no witness available to testify against him.

***

That same year marked the twentieth anniversary since Wilson's murder rattled Beatrice. The three less culpable co-defendants, Dean, Shelden, and Gonzalez, had finished serving their prison sentences during the mid-1990s. By 2005, those three were trying to reassemble the broken pieces of their fractured lives.

The three convicted murderers, White, Winslow, and Taylor, were wasting away in different state prisons. Taylor, age forty-two, had accepted her fate. Winslow, age thirty-nine, seemed resigned to his destiny. Not so for White, age forty-two.

The Alabama native continued to deny he deserved such a fate. In his mind, he was unjustly serving hard time for a murder committed by somebody else. What little money he made at his prison job in the wood shop was squirreled away to someday prove his innocence.

White's chances of winning a post-conviction appeal were slim. The Nebraska Supreme Court already had rejected White's post-conviction appeal during the early 1990s. The state court justices found the trial testimony of his co-defendants quite convincing. Somehow, White persevered. He had to. He wanted to see his growing boy and his close-knit family back in Alabama who had stuck with him, but he felt hopeless.

White had been incarcerated for sixteen years among other caged convicts. His world revolved around no-sense prison guards who barked orders. He heard the constant sounds of slamming steel doors, prisoners screaming and uncivilized unrest. His life was dictated by the rules of the institution and standing in line for multiple daily head counts. He ate prepared meals when the prison said he could. Life beyond the massive, fortress-like concrete walls surrounding him was another world away, and it remained elusive.

While daily life inside the state pen stayed pretty much the same for White, the world outside changed dramatically. Among the historic events:

- The crumbling of the Berlin Wall and reunification of East and West Germany.

- Toppling of the Communist Soviet Union, Mikhail Gorbachev's resignation and Boris Yeltsin's election as new Russian president.

- Branch Davidian massacre in Waco, Texas.

- Election of President Bill Clinton and the first presidential impeachment since the 1868 trial of President Andrew Johnson.

- Oklahoma City federal building bombing by Persian Gulf War Army veteran Timothy McVeigh, taking 168 lives and injuring nearly 700 others.

- Narrowest presidential election in history as Al Gore captured the popular vote in 2000 but lost to George W. Bush in the Electoral College.

- Terrorist attacks on the World Trade Center and Pentagon on September 11, 2001, that killed nearly

3,000 people and wounded more than 6,000 orchestrated by Osama bin Laden, founder of al-Qaeda.

- The invasion of Iraq in 2003 by U.S. and coalition forces and the capture of Iraqi dictator Saddam Hussein who was later sent to the gallows for crimes against the Iraqi people.

By 2005, events in Nebraska took a fortuitous turn for White. He finally found a quality attorney willing to take on his appeal efforts.

Douglas J. Stratton, who graduated from Yale University in 1981, received his law degree from the University of Nebraska-Lincoln in 1984. Stratton was a native Nebraskan who chose to practice criminal law in Norfolk, a blue-collar city of 25,000 best known for its meat-packing warehouses.

Stratton's legal business was good. An attorney of his caliber and reputation wouldn't be desperate for clients, and Stratton certainly was not scrounging for money. Besides, lawyers of Stratton's credentials knew that taking on convicts serving out life sentences won't pay the bills, let alone the law office stationary and the utility bills. Even so, Stratton chose to take on convicted first-degree felony murderer White as a new client. Their post-conviction appeal would focus on modern scientific breakthroughs in DNA testing.

***

Like other states around the country, Nebraska began to recognize the emergence of DNA testing as admissible trial evidence. And around 2001, Nebraska's only black state lawmaker, Sen. Ernie Chambers of Omaha, convinced Nebraska's Legislature in Lincoln to enact a law that allowed for post-conviction DNA tests in certain older crimes. There was obvious trepidation to allowing this on the part of the state's elected criminal prosecutors, who had the most to lose under the new law. Prosecutors dreaded the prospect of being bombarded by every convict under the sun seeking this new avenue of possible exoneration. In the end, the state lawmakers set up certain criteria for convicts seeking to qualify for post-conviction DNA testing.

Although DNA petitions and exonerations had gained notoriety in Illinois and other parts of the country, they were unheard of in Nebraska, where criminal justice officials believed their system worked fine. In fact, four years after the law's passage, not a single Nebraska inmate had been exonerated due to newly discovered DNA evidence. Despite the daunting odds for success, Norfolk attorney Stratton plowed ahead in September 2005 with a rare DNA petition.

On behalf of White, Stratton notified the District Court of biological evidence that had been collected in 1985 by the Beatrice Police Department in the Wilson murder case but never tested.

"I was wrongfully convicted and sentenced of the crime for which I am currently in custody," Joseph White stated in the court papers filed by Stratton.

Vicky Johnson, a fairly new District Court judge for District 1 out of Wilber, Nebraska, was assigned the rare post-conviction petition seeking DNA testing. Now in his mid-fifties, six-term Gage County Attorney Dick Smith fiercely opposed White's push for DNA tests. Judge Johnson heard oral arguments from the lawyers on both sides during the spring of 2006 and took the matter under advisement. She would wait until August to announce her ruling.

***

An hour's drive northeast of Lincoln, White's convicted accomplice was still serving his fifty-year sentence at the Omaha Correctional Center. Tom Winslow was broke and unaware that a longtime Nebraska criminal defense lawyer who vigorously fought for the rights of the indigent was about to drop into his life.

After visiting with White's counsel, Jerry Soucie of the Nebraska Commission on Public Advocacy in Lincoln agreed to mount a DNA challenge on behalf of Winslow. The courts agreed that Winslow was poor and thus qualified for Soucie's representation, which meant any legal fees would be borne by the state. Once appointed, Soucie asked Judge Vicky Johnson to grant a DNA test for his client as well.

"I was coerced and under duress when I entered my plea in the above-referenced matter," Winslow stated in court filings. "I believe DNA testing in this case will prove my innocence."

There was a glaring difference between the two pending DNA petitions before the court. White had always maintained his innocence and took his case to a jury and lost. Winslow, on the other hand, pleaded no contest to second-degree murder. Nonetheless, Soucie argued Winslow still deserved the chance to have his case revisited. After all, Winslow was the only one of White's co-defendants who refused to testify during the trial in Fairbury. "At sentencing on January 29, 1990, the defendant and his counsel stated to the District Court that (Winslow) had no memory of the events involving the rape and murder of Mrs. Wilson," Soucie advised the judge in a 2006 legal brief. "Defendant's counsel went so far as to request that the defendant be hypnotized to assist his memory, but that motion was denied."

Modern DNA testing offered the most reliable method to show that White and Winslow were wrongly convicted, Soucie argued. He noted that the sperm belonging to Wilson's attacker had been collected during her February 1985 autopsy and could be tested.

"Now if the DNA testing in this case comes back and says that that DNA recovered from the rectum and the vagina of that woman was neither Mr. Winslow nor Mr. White, what does that say about (prosecutor Dick Smith's) case?" Soucie argued. "It says something is horribly, horribly wrong. That whoever did this crime to this woman is a free man today. That's what it says."

The Lincoln attorney told the judge Winslow and White were taking a giant gamble by pushing the court to order DNA testing that might instead prove their guilt. "If they did it, then it means that they're not going to make parole," Soucie assured the judge. "That means they're not going to get a commutation. It means they're not going to get their convictions reversed. There are consequences to our clients."

Resisting the DNA request, Gage County Attorney Smith argued that Winslow blew his chance to appeal his conviction in 1989 when he entered a guilty plea.

"He gave a statement," Smith reminded the judge. "He implicated Mr. White in this statement. He was there. He corroborated what happened from what the other witnesses had said. This is very interesting, it's interesting to talk about snitches and things like that twenty-some years later. These twelve people that were sworn to do their jobs as a jury did it in the White case. Every constitutional right that Mr. Winslow had in this case was followed. He waived all of them. He does not have a right to be asking for anything under this DNA statute. There's no judicial or legislative history that will indicate the (Nebraska) Legislature wanted to give him that right in plea cases. There is none."

***

In August of 2006, Judge Vicky Johnson released a pair of rulings rejecting the men's requests. In White's case, she stated, "The Defendant's goal is to establish by the absence of his DNA on the biological evidence that he was not present at the murder of Mrs. Wilson. There are several problems with the Defendant's theory."

She outlined that even if White's sperm had not been found inside the victim, the trial testimony put him at the scene. "Further, the jury had the opportunity to hear the defendant's testimony that he was not there and clearly chose not to believe him."

It was another stinging setback for White.

Winslow, too, was denied DNA testing by the judge.

An appeal to the Nebraska Supreme Court was the prisoners' last desperate hope. More time would pass before the seven high court jurists reviewed Johnson's rulings.

***

Interestingly enough, in 2006 the normally unbeatable Dick Smith faced a rare runoff in his Republican primary to retain job as his county attorney. Smith, seeking a seventh four-year term, had served as the county attorney since his appointment in 1980. For only the second time since taking office, Smith faced a challenger. Around Gage County, lawyer Randy Ritnour was a relatively unknown figure seeing as he was the elected prosecutor in Tecumseh in neighboring Johnson County, a sparsely populated county five times smaller than

Gage. On the other hand, Smith was a household name in Gage County and an imposing political figure.

Still, Ritnour smelled upset. He sensed the six-term incumbent was vulnerable and beatable. By 2006, Smith had worn out his welcome in the law enforcement community. He had lost a lot of respect with the rank and file police officers after more than twenty-five years in office. Smith, age fifty-four, was viewed as a bully, a belittling micromanager and a quintessential control freak. His adversaries poked fun of Smith for apparently sporting a badge with "No. 1" emblazoned on it to symbolize his power as the county's top law enforcement official. His enemies mocked him by calling him "King Richard." Indeed, the voters of Gage County were ready to dump Dick Smith in 2006.

Ritnour, age forty-six, won the GOP primary by about 400 votes. Smith was bitter about his humiliating defeat. By late summer, Smith's long-time chief deputy prosecutor, Jerry Shelton, mounted a successful write-in campaign to get his name on the November ballot. Smith, himself, mounted a petition to run for the County Board of Supervisors. It was all part of a last-ditch effort to stop Ritnour from winning the office. Shelton had worked for Smith since 1980.

"They can choose the man who had the guts to challenge Richard Smith in the primary election or they can choose the guy who publicly endorsed Richard Smith and wanted Smith to remain the county attorney," Ritnour told the *Beatrice Daily Sun*.

Ritnour crushed Shelton in the general election, capturing about sixty percent of the vote. Likewise, Smith also lost his bid to win a County Board seat.

As Ritnour eased into office in 2007, the new prosecutor was not yet up to speed on the appeal efforts of White and Winslow in the Helen Wilson murder case.

***

That year also saw a changing of the guard at the Gage County Sheriff's Office. After twenty years in office, Jerry DeWitt decided to retire in 2007, around the time he turned seventy. The new incoming sheriff was Millard "Gus" Gustafson, the long-time chief deputy sheriff. For years, Gustafson mostly had run the day to day operations of the agency. Many people around Beatrice liked Gustafson. He was easy-going, laid back and pretty friendly. A lot of people were not sorry to see DeWitt leave office. There was a general consensus that DeWitt outlasted his welcome and the Sheriff's Office needed a change in leadership.

One resident of Gage County who was pleased with the turnover at the top of the Sheriff's Office was none other than Burt Searcey.

After being away from the Sheriff's Office for thirteen years, Searcey applied for a part-time job. He wrote the following on his county job application:

"Have good management skills, have great communications skills, have very good investigative skills. I have a total of thirteen years of law enforcement experience and ten years of major case investigation experience."

He listed two references: Jerry Shelton, the long-time former chief deputy prosecutor for Dick Smith, and Paul Korslund, the former Beatrice mayor who around 1998 became the District Court judge rotating between Gage and Jefferson Counties.

Regarding his past dates of employment, Searcey wrote on his Gage County job application, "1-87 thru 2-92," court transcripts show. But Searcey was not being truthful. He clearly resigned in November 1993.

Searcey had left off his period of employment that spanned his three-month unpaid suspension handed down by Sheriff DeWitt and also his subsequent demotion from sheriff's lieutenant to patrol deputy covering most of 1993. He also left off his application that he operated the House of Bottles for many years. Searcey later testified he left off the liquor store because "that's self-employment." When asked about the discrepancy regarding his actual departure from the Sheriff's Office, Searcey would testify that, "It was a handwriting error. I can sometimes write down something and think something else."

Gage County's job application plainly stated: "In the event of employment, I understand that false or misleading information given in my application or interview may result in discharge."

In any event, Searcey was contacted for an interview soon after Gustafson took over as sheriff in January of 2007 and was interviewed by Gustafson and Chief Deputy Doug Klaus. "Maybe not together, either way, chief deputy and the sheriff had both been involved," Searcey would later recall.

The Sheriff's Office application stated the following: "Spoke to District Judge and other deputies and all seem to like him and feel he has a lot to offer. He is certified and has worked for the police department and Gage Co. sheriff's office."

The Gage County good ol' boy network overlooked Searcey's inaccurate and misleading job application.

By March 2007, Searcey was back on duty at the Gage County Sheriff's Department, working for his old friend "Gus" and Chief Deputy Klaus.

Searcey would later relate that he occasionally drank beer at their homes when everyone was off-duty.

All three men also had a connection through the notorious Wilson murder investigation. In fact, the *Beatrice Daily Sun* featured a front-page photo on March 17, 1989, showing a much younger-looking Deputy "Gus" Gustafson escorting a slim handcuffed prisoner into the stone county courthouse. The prisoner in the photo was Joseph White, who had just arrived from Cullman County, Alabama. To Gustafson's astonishment, the long ago Wilson murder case would dominate the headlines during his first term as sheriff.

CHAPTER 27
GLIMMER OF HOPE

In a blockbuster reversal, Nebraska's Supreme Court overturned the rulings of District Judge Vicky Johnson, the inexperienced judge from Saline County, against ordering new DNA testing in the Wilson murder. The court said Johnson had abused her discretion in her post-conviction rulings that shot down the appeals of Joseph White and Tom Winslow.

"We determine that a DNA test result that excluded both White and Winslow as contributors to the semen samples would be exculpatory under the DNA Testing Act's unique definition of 'Exculpatory Evidence,'" the State Supreme Court ruled on December 5, 2007.

The court ordered Johnson to determine whether the original autopsy specimens still existed. If the specimens already had been destroyed, the post-conviction appeals for the two Beatrice convicts could come to a screeching halt.

With the Nebraska Supreme Court opinion hot off the stove, Lincoln lawyer Jerry Soucie got in his car and drove to Beatrice. He met with first-year Gage County Attorney Randy Ritnour to figure out what, if any, original crime scene evidence still existed almost twenty-three years after the murder.

They were in luck. A few large cardboard boxes labeled "Helen Wilson evidence" were tucked away down in the Beatrice Police Department basement. The items contained liquid slides and blood samples taken from as many as a hundred people who were questioned or ruled out as potential suspects – before Gage County swept in and took over the case.

"Was I surprised? Yes,'" Ritnour recalled during a 2015 interview. "When we saw the basement and all the old boxes, that was pretty amazing. So the Beatrice Police Department deserves some pretty big credit."

After learning that the original biological samples existed, Judge Johnson ordered DNA tests for White and Winslow to proceed.

***

Soucie and Ritnour seemed a great match for digging into the old murder case files. As a newbie and political outsider, Ritnour had no loyalties or deep-rooted connections to anybody in Gage County who handled the original case. As for Soucie, he was probably Nebraska's premier criminal defense attorney on the complex issue of DNA evidence. The previous year, in 2006, Soucie had been directly responsible for springing two cousins wrongly accused of murder from the Cass County Jail in Plattsmouth. DNA evidence left at the crime scene proved their innocence

In 2008, Joseph White expressed optimism that the results of pending DNA testing on evidence preserved from the 1985 Helen Wilson murder would result in his exoneration.

and ultimately led to the arrests and convictions of the real killers, a pair of Wisconsin teenagers.

Coming off his stunning high-profile victory at the Cass County Courthouse in Plattsmouth, Soucie had no idea what to expect as he began dusting off the old criminal case files surrounding the February 5, 1985, murder of Helen Wilson in Beatrice.

***

Tina Vath's career at the Beatrice Police Department was on the rise from the moment she joined in 1996 as a dispatcher. By 2000, Police Chief Bruce Lang hired her as a road patrol officer. She did not disappoint. By 2002, she received two unrelated letters of commendation. One case involved a stolen property investigation and the other involved a teenager who was attempting to commit suicide. By 2004, Vath had been promoted to criminal investigator. In 2006, she garnered a commendation for solving a rash of local burglaries. Her duties ran the gamut. She often dug into crimes that had a pattern. Her caseload ranged from felony thefts and serious assaults to homicides and suicides.

In late 2007, Vath was investigating a domestic violence homicide, the shooting during a heated argument by Richard A. Griswold of his live-in girlfriend, Connie Eacret. At the same time, she was pulled in another direction when she was directed to collect DNA swabs from two convicted killers named Joseph White and Tom Winslow. Vath was vaguely familiar with their case after hearing first-hand stories from Searcey during those earlier backyard barbecues.

Vath drove to Lincoln and met with Soucie, the hard-nosed state public defender, who now was coordinating the DNA tests for inmates White and Winslow. At the state prison, they found White waiting inside the prison's medical services unit. As Soucie watched, Vath obtained a buccal swab from White's mouth. She packaged the DNA sample, sealed it with evidence tape, and marked the date, time, and her initials on the envelope.

"While I was doing this, I heard Joe White ask how long it would be before we got any results," Vath recalled.

Soucie answered the lab results would come quickly, but that he could not pinpoint a date.

"OK, because this is going to prove that I am innocent, and I will be out of here," White vowed.

After eight years as a police officer, Vath had encountered her share of conniving convicts. To her, White seemed no different.

"I specifically remember rolling my eyes and thinking to myself, 'You piece of crap, you're going to rot in here for what you did,'" Vath said.

Later that day, Vath drove to the prison in Omaha. She obtained Winslow's DNA swab and followed the same chain of custody procedures to ensure his sample was properly secured.

From there, it was only a ten- to fifteen-minute drive to the University of Nebraska Medical Center's Human DNA Identification Lab in Omaha's midtown area. At the nationally recognized medical facility, Vath handed off the DNA swabs to the laboratory scientists. A number of semen specimens were selected for the DNA comparisons from various original crime scene slides. Additionally, Wilson's aqua-blue nightgown was still preserved for comparative analysis.

At this stage, Soucie was pleased that the scientific testing was being done at the Medical Center's highly regarded DNA laboratory. The facility was independent, meaning it was not run or controlled by law enforcement. Moreover, the DNA lab was accredited by the American Society of Crime Laboratory Directors. The NU Medical Center possessed some of the finest DNA genetic technology equipment around, including the PowerPlex 16 system with the ABI Prism 310 Genetic Analyzer, the facility's bright shining star.

Lloyd Halsell, the NU Medical Center's DNA technical leader, was charged with analyzing the old forensic clues. Halsell had majored in microbiology at Southwest Texas State University and graduated in 2002. Two years later, he received his master's degree in forensic genetics from the University of North Texas Health Science Center in Fort Worth.

As it turned out, Halsell needed several months to run all the necessary DNA tests, as well as to carefully analyze and calculate the scientific results. As for Soucie, he kept busy with other criminal defense work.

"There was no reason for me to get into the investigative reports because if the DNA results showed it was Tom and or Joe, then that would have corroborated their guilt conclusively, and it didn't matter if the investigation was a fiasco," Soucie explained.

During the first half of 2008, Vath stayed busy building her murder case against defendant Richard Griswold. At trial, a jury found Griswold guilty of second-degree murder. That July, Judge Paul Korslund sentenced Griswold to life in prison for fatally shooting his girlfriend. After the sentencing, a *Beatrice Daily Sun* newspaper photo showed a white-haired Gage County sheriff's deputy in a dark uniform removing Griswold from the courtroom – and it was none other than Burt Searcey. He then worked in the jail division, handling courtroom security and prisoner transports. Searcey also had been elevated to full-time status, which meant generous fringe benefits for law enforcement, plus the opportunity to earn overtime pay.

As Searcey stayed busy in Gage County's jail division, word trickled out of the NU Medical Center that the rigorous rounds of DNA tests were finally done.

CHAPTER 28
UNEXPECTED TWIST

Gage County Attorney Randy Ritnour still remembers getting a voicemail message on his phone from defense attorney Jerry Soucie proclaiming, "that he had something."

Taking matters into his own hands, Soucie and attorney Doug Stratton disseminated the DNA testing results to the major Nebraska news media outlets including the *Lincoln Journal Star*, the state capital's lone daily newspaper after a merger of the *Lincoln Journal* and *Lincoln Star*.

Making a huge splash in the Nebraska press seemed the best tactical move on behalf of their convicted clients, Soucie said in 2015. "Our concern was that nothing was going to happen."

The lawyers assured the press that the astonishing DNA tests proved Winslow and White had never been involved in Wilson's murder. The Medical Center scientists found no DNA matches with either Winslow's or White's DNA. As a result, the defense lawyers implored Nebraska's justice system to release the pair of condemned prisoners immediately.

The press conference worked like a charm. The August 2, 2008, *Lincoln Journal Star* ran a front-page story headlined "DNA findings raise questions."

The lawyers subsequently asked a judge to dismiss the murder convictions, grant a new trial or set a resentencing hearing.

"These results are indisputable," Stratton told the media.

Meanwhile, Ritnour was not convinced of White and Winslow's innocence. "My first response was, 'Bullshit,'" Ritnour said. "I thought 'This is ridiculous.'"

The first-term Gage County prosecutor was being pressured to release two men at the same time, both convicted of the same murder.

"I thought, 'Oh boy, I better get ahold of the Nebraska Attorney General's Office.'"

Fortunately for Ritnour, he was on friendly terms with Nebraska Attorney General Jon Bruning, a fellow conservative Republican and a rising political star who had his eye on running for U.S. Senate. During Ritnour's previous tenure as the county attorney for Johnson County from 2002 to 2006, Ritnour prosecuted a state prisoner in Tecumseh who threatened to harm Bruning's family. Now it was Ritnour who needed outside legal expertise and fast. Nebraska still had an unblemished record when it came to exonerations on DNA evidence. Ritnour didn't want to make a knee-jerk reaction and allow the feisty lawyers for White and Winslow to steamroll him.

***

Until that point, Wilson's February 5, 1985, murder was not a crime on the Nebraska attorney general's radar. Jon Bruning grew up in Lincoln and was only fifteen years old when the murder horrified residents of Beatrice, some forty miles away. However, in wake of the stunning DNA test results, Bruning developed a strong interest in the case.

Bruning said he will never forget that Assistant Attorney General Corey O'Brien was instrumental in convincing him to give the decades-old small-town murder a serious new look. As Bruning pointed out, Norfolk attorney Doug Stratton did an incredible job of persuading O'Brien that White might be languishing in prison as a victim of a wrongful conviction for murder.

Bruning, who would serve the citizens of Nebraska as attorney general from 2002 through 2014, formed what would be known as the Helen Wilson Murder Case Task Force after the DNA revelations in summer 2008 to reinvestigate the Beatrice murder. It marked the one and only time during Bruning's three-term tenure that he would form a law enforcement task force to re-examine an old crime.

Bruning dispatched three of his office's most exceptional lawyers – O'Brien and fellow Assistant Generals Doug Warner and John Freudenberg to Beatrice. O'Brien became the point man for the AG's Office. He huddled with Ritnour, the Gage County prosecutor, to plot strategy. The Nebraska State Patrol also assigned a handful of its best homicide investigators to the task force. Beatrice Police Chief Bruce Lang, who had run the department since 1992, appointed two people from the Beatrice Police Department, Criminal Investigator Tina Vath and Lieutenant Mike Oliver, to leading roles as well. Gage County Sheriff's Deputy Searcey was invited to the initial meeting, but Searcey grew dismayed when he found out he would not be asked to play a leading role on the Attorney General's Task Force.

"He was clearly unhappy about it," Ritnour said. "Searcey felt he was purposively excluded."

The Gage County prosecutor preferred fresh eyes on the case to preserve the integrity of the investigation. It was imperative to have the task force represented by experienced and sharp police investigators and seasoned lawyers from the Attorney General's Office. Ritnour said he did not want the task force overrun by local officials with an obvious political agenda.

"I wanted new eyes on this. I didn't want the same old eyes on this."

That year, 2008, the task force set up a command post inside the Beatrice Police Department's large training room. In the words of Oliver, the group of about a dozen worked off the premise that Wilson's murder had just happened.

Some investigators dug through the old Beatrice police reports from February 1985. Others examined the glass vials that contained biological samples of potential suspects. Still others sifted through the three cardboard boxes of crime scene clues. The task force identified several more prime candidates for additional DNA testing.

As Ritnour dug deeper, he was amazed at how much animosity had existed between the Gage County Sheriff's Office and the Beatrice Police Department. He did not realize there was such a great divide within local law enforcement circles on the question of whether Searcey had really arrested the right people for Wilson's murder.

"I knew there were turf wars all the time, but I didn't know this particular case created a large disagreement," Ritnour said later.

Still, Ritnour, the county's top prosecutor at the time, remained pretty confident that the task force's legwork would validate the original six convictions.

"At that point, the only question on my mind was why in the world would five of them say they did it, if they didn't? So our intent was to prove these people were all involved. We thought if they say they're there, they've got to be there. Our fear was that they were going to get exonerated because of DNA that had degraded."

But the DNA evidence had not degraded. It had remained in remarkable condition.

By 2008, the Beatrice Police Department and Gage County Attorney Randy Ritnour began exploring these old cardboard boxes of evidence from the 1985 murder of Helen Wilson. Authorities needed to determine whether any undiscovered DNA evidence existed in the long-decided murder case. Photo/Beatrice Police Department

As they worked, members of the task force tried to re-interview a number of key witnesses including ex-convict James Dean. By 2008, Dean was a truck driver in his mid-forties living in Salina, Kansas. Upon being contacted, Dean was eager to provide a DNA sample to compare with the crime scene evidence.

In 1989, Dean had pleaded guilty to being an accessory in the murder. Shortly before Labor Day 2008, Dean's DNA was excluded as the source of any blood or semen found at the murder victim's apartment.

From there, the task force hunted down DNA samples for the three women convicted in the case: Taylor, Gonzalez, and Shelden.

All told, extensive DNA tests were conducted on more than forty well-preserved articles of evidence from the 1985 homicide case files. The battery of lab tests at the University of Nebraska Medical Center all reached the same conclusion: The DNA samples of convicts Joseph White, Tom Winslow, James Dean, JoAnn Taylor, Debra Shelden, and Kathy Gonzalez were not a match to any samples stored in evidence. All of the bloodstains and semen deposits collected at the crime scene and by the autopsy conclusively belonged to two people: one female and the other

Tom Winslow also petitioned the Nebraska Supreme Court for DNA testing to prove his innocence in the rape and murder of Helen Wilson.

male. The female DNA matched the murder victim, Wilson. As for the male perpetrator, his identity remained unknown. It was the most astonishing development in the history of Nebraska's criminal justice system.

"We're thinking, what's this mean, a seventh person?" Ritnour pondered. "Then, some of us are thinking, well, maybe not? Who would be so afraid of this seventh guy but not identify this mystery seventh person? Are they all protecting somebody, one unknown male?"

The conscientious prosecutor faced a quandary. He now knew the DNA tests excluded all six of the original murder defendants. He also knew that the identity of the true rapist and killer was shrouded in mystery. Meanwhile, White, Winslow, and Taylor were rotting away in state prison. Clearly, the attorney general's task force was nowhere near finished with its work. All thanks to the amazing breakthrough in modern DNA science technology, the previously open-and-shut murder case from a generation before in Beatrice was about to be turned upside down in late fall 2008.

CHAPTER 29
STARTING OVER

The top cop of Beatrice was not the least bit concerned about protecting legacies. Prior to his arrival in 1992, Chief Bruce Lang had served in the Police Department in La Vista, a growing Omaha suburb. Lang wasn't around Beatrice during the original murder investigation handled by his department let alone the investigation's contentious takeover in 1989 by the Sheriff's Department. The small-town chief just wanted to do the moral and ethical thing even if that was royally unpopular with any past and present-day movers and shakers within Gage County. Once Lang learned that

The Nebraska Attorney General's Helen Wilson Case Task Force faced the laborious task of re-testing old samples of biological evidence. Investigators hoped that one of these samples would unlock the mystery surrounding the identity of Helen Wilson's rapist and murderer. Photo/Beatrice Police Department

the new wave of DNA tests also excluded White and Winslow in Wilson's rape, he urged the Gage County prosecutor to act fast.

Lang did not want any innocent people spending another day in prison for crimes they did not commit.

"The police chief told me, 'Listen, we need to get these people out and do it soon,'" Ritnour recalled later.

White had been locked up for the murder for most of his adult life, since March 15, 1989, when he was barely twenty-six. On October 15, 2008, the Nebraska Department of Corrections opened the prison gates in Lincoln and a forty-five-year-old White walked out a free man. It had taken nineteen-and-a-half agonizing years waiting to prove his innocence. White boarded a plane bound for his hometown in Alabama.

But he was not out of the woods yet. He still faced the real possibility that the courts would order a retrial. "There was pressure on me to retry the Beatrice 6," Ritnour remembered. "As far as most people around Beatrice were concerned, these six did it. There was very much an expectation that I would retry this case."

That same week, Judge Vicky Johnson ordered a resentencing for Soucie's client, Winslow. The hearing, however, was more of a legal technicality to spring Winslow free from prison. The judge "resentenced" Winslow to a ten-year prison term, the same term given in 1990 to co-defendants Dean, Gonzalez, and Shelden. And as Winslow had already served nearly twenty years of hard time, he was granted an immediate release.

That mid-October day in Wilber, Winslow entered the Saline County Courthouse in shackles and beige prison garb. Years of prison life had taken a toll on Winslow, now forty-two and bald. In the courthouse, he read from a prepared statement. He said he hoped people listening could try to understand why he signed a plea bargain admitting to a rape and murder in which he did not participate.

"Unless someone has been accused of a crime as terrible as what happened to Mrs. Wilson and are told repeatedly by the police and the prosecutor that they have the evidence that will put them in the electric chair, you simply cannot understand the fear," Winslow said in court, as reported by the *Omaha World-Herald*. Winslow also detailed how Wayne Price, the sheriff's deputy/police psychologist, used his powers of persuasion to convince Winslow he had repressed his memories of the despicable attack.

"I spent many years in prison believing that I had actually done those terrible things," Winslow said.

Back in the 1980s, nobody would confuse Winslow with Mother Teresa. After all, he had partnered with Clifford Shelden, co-defendant Debbie Shelden's future husband, to beat a motel clerk in Lincoln during a botched 1988 robbery. But Winslow's involvement in that violent crime, though repulsive, had nothing to do with the late-night attack on the Beatrice widow.

Winslow was elated to be vindicated. His mother, Mary, always remained in his corner as he grew into a young man, and then a mature adult under the control of Nebraska's rigid prison system. Now, finally, mother and son were reunited on the outside of a prison wall.

Still, more questions lingered about the case.

"When Tom and Joe were excluded, I then became extremely curious about the investigation since, not only did we have them excluded, but with the elimination of James Dean as well, it meant the real rapist/killer was still out there," remarked Soucie, Winslow's lawyer. "It would strengthen our motion for a new trial and vacating their convictions if we could actually identify the real suspect."

Back in Beatrice, the attorney general's task force was heating up. Original crime scene photos were displayed in the war room for the keen-eyed investigators to study. The photos were eye-opening. There was absolutely no indication that Wilson had been dragged or yanked from her bedroom into the living room where she died. Aside from a toppled footstool, practically nothing else in the living room was disturbed. Those crime-scene photos painted a drastically different picture of reality when compared with the jury trial testimony offered by Shelden, Taylor and Dean against White, police investigator Tina Vath noted.

The investigators began to realize the entire criminal prosecution engineered by Gage County Attorney Dick Smith hinged on those March 1989 arrest warrants drawn up by Deputy Searcey. It became obvious Searcey had put together his investigation based on conversations he had in April of 1985 with teenager Lisa Podendorf when he was a hog farmer, not a legitimate police officer. Back in those days, Podendorf hung around with burnouts in Beatrice. But by November 1989, she became the star witness for the prosecution at the murder trial of White in nearby Jefferson County.

Now, after nearly twenty years, the task force went to talk to Podendorf, now going by her married name of Lisa Brown. She had remained in Beatrice, where she worked for the Beatrice State Developmental Center. Brown reluctantly agreed to speak with Vath and Jay Morrow of the Nebraska State Patrol.

In the words of Brown to the investigators, Taylor had alerted her around 7:30 in the morning on February 6, 1985, that there were several squad cars across the street because a woman was killed and "we killed her." According to Brown, Taylor also supposedly claimed "we smothered her" with a pillow and Taylor demanded she give her $500 so she could flee town before the police tied Taylor to the murder.

But Brown's story was preposterous. Why? No police cars were parked along Sixth Street at 7:30 a.m. because Wilson's body wasn't discovered until after 9:30 a.m. that day.

By then, she was already in class at the high school where she was a junior. She had told Searcey that she clearly knew the date that she spoke to Taylor because Wilson's grandson was pulled out of one of her classes later that same afternoon because of the family tragedy. But if she'd gone to school before the squad cars arrived, that invalidated both the time and the date of the supposed "confession."

"When we confronted her with the date and time discrepancies, she got pretty defensive and refused to take a polygraph," Vath said.

Investigators interviewed Taylor in prison. She insisted that she never, ever remembered talking with her once bitter enemy, Lisa Podendorf, outside the Beatrice public library on a frigid February morning when Taylor was in her early twenties. Taylor adamantly denied she had ever confessed to her that Taylor and White committed a murder. She agreed to take a polygraph exam with the Nebraska State Patrol. The test conducted in 2008 showed Taylor was being truthful when she denied any involvement in the murder of Wilson, Vath's report stated.

The task force realized Brown's statement was seriously flawed. "The idea that JoAnn Taylor would make a confession to Lisa Brown is pretty far-fetched," Vath wrote.

Like a poorly knit sweater, other parts of Brown's questionable trial testimony against White also began to unravel. Originally, Brown had testified that she saw Winslow driving his green Oldsmobile precisely at 10:18 p.m. as he pulled into a lot near Wilson's apartment building on the night of the murder. Brown told the jury she positively saw

Winslow, White, Taylor, and a fourth person open the doors, get out of the car and head in the direction of the murder victim's building. However, back in 1985, a bank building obstructed the view of the parking lot from where Brown said she was positioned inside her boyfriend's vehicle, the task force determined.

It wasn't long before Ritnour became convinced that Brown had concocted all of her stories implicating Taylor and White as the killers. "All of us felt it was not true," he said, speaking of the task force members.

Moreover, Brown's claim that Taylor demanded $500 from her was ridiculous and made no sense. "We found those two, Lisa Brown and JoAnn Taylor, hated each other and were actually rivals," Ritnour said.

For some reason, in 1985, in a grave and profound lapse of judgment, Searcey had taken Brown's statements as the gospel truth. The unchallenged statements became the cornerstone of his personal murder investigation as a so-called private investigator.

"Where did this thing go wrong?" remarked Beatrice Police Chief Bruce Lang in later comments about the case. "That statement by Lisa Podendorf Brown is where the thing really started to snowball. That was the beginning of the snowball. One piece of bad information sold in a convincing manner can snowball. I can see where people ran with it."

As a sheriff's deputy, Searcey emphasized the following information about Brown when he presented his arrest affidavits before Gage County Judge Steven Timm in March 1989:

"This officer believes CI #1 to be credible because of her description of the crime scene, the binding of Mrs. Wilson's body when found and the position of the step stool as described to her by Ada JoAnn Taylor. Parts of this information are still only known by law enforcement officials and not the general public," Searcey wrote.

But that wasn't exactly the case.

The public had access to the information from, for instance, a front-page article in the *Beatrice Daily Sun* on February 7, 1985, the day after police were called to the scene. The article told readers that, "Mrs. Wilson was wearing nightclothes when she was found and her hands were bound… an overturned foot stool indicated that there had been a struggle."

Searcey had also fouled up the information coming from his other unreliable confidential informant, the task force investigators easily discovered. The overeager deputy also had relied upon Charlotte Bishop's erroneous information as a critical factual basis for his conclusions:

"CI #2 would indicate that on Feb. 6, 1985, Ada JoAnn Taylor came to CI #2's apartment located in close proximity to Helen Wilson's apartment and advised CI #2 that she, Ada JoAnn Taylor, was involved in a murder. Ada JoAnn Taylor further stated to CI #2 that 'I think I killed somebody.' Ada JoAnn Taylor further stated to CI #2 'I've got to get out of here. I've got to get out of town.'"

In another act of carelessness, Searcey had not bothered to verify that February 1989 statement by Bishop before he forged ahead and built his theories on her false information. In fact, Taylor and Bishop had been evicted from their loft apartment above the Dole Floral Shop a day or two *before* Wilson's murder. That information concerning the eviction was stated in a City of Beatrice police report. Sadly, it was another critical detail that Searcey managed to overlook in his sloppiness and overzealousness to prove to everyone that he had solved the killing when, in fact, he was nowhere close to finding the real culprit.

As his work for the task force continued, Beatrice Police Lieutenant Mike Oliver made a number of disturbing discoveries as he watched some the old videotaped interviews conducted by Searcey in 1989. On one videotape, Tom Winslow asserted his innocence, strongly denying any knowledge or involvement in the widow's murder. Later, the video camera is shut off for several minutes. When the on-camera taping resumes, Winslow suddenly is able to furnish Searcey the answers that the deputy was after.

"When you look at the video interviews it becomes obvious that these defendants are getting helped by the interviewer," Ritnour explained.

***

Back in the 1980s, Gage County Attorney Smith chose to disregard the FBI's behavioral profile of the unknown attacker.

"I didn't give much weight to that FBI report," Smith would testify in 2011. "I think they were working more on the other assaults rather than Mrs. Wilson's situation. They happened to pin the report down on those results. And right off, the front page told me that, you know, this isn't scientific, and I'm not going to listen to it. I mean, I had people that wanted me to come up and have séances to see if they could talk to Mrs. Wilson and she could talk back, you know, through somebody else."

What Dick Smith had chosen to blow off, the Attorney General's Office task force treated with great importance. The original FBI profiler pointed out that Wilson's agonizing rape appeared to be connected to the series of rape attempts on other elderly women in Beatrice during the summer of 1983.

"The FBI profile said that this was one lone male," Ritnour pointed out. "You had the Beatrice Police Department saying back in 1989 that these six were not the folks. That they were the wrong people."

Furthermore, the crime scene in the living room appeared "very ritualistic," not a careless mess, he said.

"The place is not wrecked. The money is all there. Nothing had been gone through," Ritnour said. "It became obvious that we did not have the right people. You can't have six people in that little apartment room and not have other physical evidence."

There was a belief amongst the AG's task force that the killer might be right under their nose, someone whom the Beatrice Police Department pursued way back in 1985, before the hog farmer interjected himself into the murder case and set out to prove his own theory. Now that White and Winslow were released from prison, the most critical leg of the task force's journey was getting underway.

"Now, we have to find the murderer," Ritnour said.

CHAPTER 30
THE OLD SUSPECTS

Anthony C. Flowers had been one of the first potential suspects examined by the task force. A Native-American resident of Nebraska, Flowers had been in prison from July of 1981 through November 1984 for felony burglary and escape, prison records show. Flowers, who was born in 1953, also lived in Beatrice at the time of Wilson's murder.

In 1985, Beatrice Police Department detectives had backed off their suspicion of Flowers after learning he had type A blood, police reports show. However, there was a renewed interest in him by the task force after Flowers was tied to a subsequent out of state sexual assault. It also helped that Flowers' DNA had been entered in the FBI's criminal justice DNA database in the years since the Beatrice murder. However, Flowers' DNA did not match any of the samples collected in the Wilson homicide case. The task force forged ahead and eliminated Flowers as a suspect.

As its work continued, the new team of investigators gave particular interest to an old list of Beatrice police suspects with B-positive type blood. The task force noticed a young man named Randy Emery had been identified as one of the earliest original suspects.

Those police reports from 1985 showed that:

- Emery liked women who were older than he was.
- Emery acted macho in the bars.

- Emery smoked and often wore an old blue-colored chambray shirt.

- Emery underwent a sudden personality change around the time of the murder.

By the time police pursued Emery as a suspect, he had moved two hours away.

About seven weeks after Wilson's murder, two Nebraska State Patrol investigators traveled to Maryville, Missouri, to interview Emery. In Maryville, Emery worked as a janitor at a bar.

"Emery stated he was in Beatrice at the time of the homicide and was living with his mother," patrol Investigator Terry Becker stated. "Emery then changed his mind and stated he was staying with Don Rusk at 818 S. Eighth St. in Beatrice."

On the night of the homicide, Emery had maintained that he and Rusk visited a friend of theirs, Harm Ferricks, who lived on Ella Street. Emery told the patrol investigators that Ferricks drove them home between 1:00 and 2:00 a.m. Emery said he stayed up and watched television until 3:00 or 4:00 a.m. He then slept all the next day.

Back in 1985, investigator Becker came right out and asked Emery if he killed Wilson.

"Shit no, I didn't even know her," Emery responded angrily.

Emery also denied that he was into window peeping. "He stated he has never done that and he would not do that type of thing," Becker wrote in the 1985 report.

The State Patrol investigators questioned whether Emery had ever watched the women exercise at the Beatrice auditorium. "He indicated that he has never done anything like that either. Emery stated he left Beatrice due to lack of work and for no other reason."

That long ago day, Emery put up no resistance when asked to supply samples of hair, blood, fingerprints and saliva to eliminate himself as a murder suspect. A follow-up lab report at the time stated that Emery's blood type was B-positive.

***

Now that Anthony Flowers had been crossed off the suspect list, the attorney general's task force concentrated on Emery, whose biological specimen remained in the basement of the Beatrice Police Department evidence unit. Police Investigator Tina Vath brought the biological sample to the University of Nebraska Medical Center for advanced DNA tests. Emery's DNA was not a match, either, so he also was crossed off the list of suspects.

Next up, the task force revisited redheaded Clifford Shelden and a drifter named Bruce Allen Smith. Shelden maintained that he had been hospitalized for syphilis on the night of the murder.

"I believe we tested Shelden so we could positively exclude him," Vath said. That made sense. Shelden was serving prison time from 1989 through 1997 for the first-degree felony assault conviction in Lancaster County, and it was while awaiting that sentencing that Shelden implicated Winslow, White, his ex-girlfriend Taylor, and his own wife, Debbie Shelden, in the murder.

As for Bruce Smith, old Beatrice police reports showed that after his long night of excessive drinking at the bar and the trailer park, he was dropped off in a drunken stupor sometime after 3:30 a.m. about two blocks south of where Wilson was murdered. Vath found that the State Patrol's Becker and

Beatrice Police Lieutenant Bill Fitzgerald had traveled to Oklahoma City in March 1985 to interview Smith. But while they were there, Joyce Gilchrist, the Oklahoma City Police Department lab technician, told them that Smith had type B blood but was a secretor -- and they were in search of a non-secretor.

The rest was history. Becker and Fitzgerald left Oklahoma without interviewing Smith in connection with Wilson's rape-murder and also without questioning him in connection with the string of still-unsolved rape attempts upon three different elderly Beatrice residents during that terrorizing summer of 1983. Once the two Nebraska police officers returned to Beatrice, Smith was crossed off the list of prime suspects.

"Blood samples, pubic hairs, scalp hairs, and saliva was kept at the Oklahoma City Police Department and was picked up by myself Lt. Fitzgerald at 10:09 a.m. on March 8, 1985, transported to the Beatrice Police Department and placed in our refrigerator until it was tagged on Saturday morning March 9, 1985," Fitzgerald wrote in a report about the trip.

The task force learned that, over the next few years, Beatrice police hit a brick wall in their dogged quest to identify the perpetrator until January 1989, when Searcey convinced his boss at the Sheriff's Department that he had figured out the murder mystery.

***

As the task force continued to investigate the Helen Wilson case, in September 2008 Tom Winslow's lawyer offered to help identity the elusive perpetrator. Jerry Soucie utilized his investigative resources within the Nebraska Commission on Public Advocacy in trying to track down a list of former juvenile offenders who were involved in sex crimes during the 1980s, thinking one of them might be the real culprit.

"I had brushed over Bruce Smith because I saw the serology exclusion, but I missed that it was done by Joyce Gilchrist," Soucie said, identifying that name as a red flag.

During the 1980s, Dr. Reena Roy of the Nebraska State Patrol crime lab handled practically all of the serology testing in the Wilson murder case, but the blood sample from Bruce Smith had never been sent to her after it was apparently analyzed in Oklahoma City by Gilchrist. Over the years, Smith's hairs, saliva and blood samples remained preserved in the cool basement of the Beatrice police station.

Ritnour, the Gage County prosecutor guiding the task force probe during the fall of 2008, pointed out that the March 1985 investigative excursion out to Oklahoma was telling.

"When you look at the original case," Ritnour pointed out, "this case went cold once the investigators went to Oklahoma."

On October 21, 2008, Beatrice Police Lieutenant Mike Oliver drove the specimens collected from Clifford Shelden and Bruce Smith all those years before to the NU Medical Center in Omaha for advanced scientific tests. A week later, the DNA comparisons were done. One definitely did not match the DNA of Wilson's attacker.

The other, however, was a definite match.

***

One of the most significant documents that the task force uncovered was the jury trial stipulation presented by prosecutor Dick Smith at Joseph White's trial. The task force deemed the document misleading and false, yet back in 1989 it slipped past the defense attorneys and got introduced as evidence before the judge and jury.

The stipulation stated that Dr. Reena Roy of the Nebraska State Patrol's crime lab "would testify that there was human blood found on the gown of the victim similar to that of Kathy Gonzalez. Stains in the carpet revealed semen from a person who were similar to the blood type of Tom Winslow ... Sperm from the vaginal swab could not be positively identified being that of Joseph White."

Unbeknown to them, the twelve honest citizens on the jury from Fairbury were misled on the blood and semen deposits by the power hungry Gage County prosecutor. "The full serological profile of Kathy Gonzalez actually excluded her as a source on the Gc subgroup, even though her blood profile was similar in the ABO group and other subgroups," Soucie stated later.

Additionally, the "stipulation" informing White's jury that the rapist's semen at the crime scene was "similar to co-defendant Tom Winslow" could not be true. This "was absolutely false," Soucie pointed out. "Mr. Winslow was a blood group type A and could be excluded as the source of the semen."

Indeed, the task force's work was done. It was now time to make an astounding announcement to the public through the watchful eyes of the Nebraska media.

CHAPTER 31
REVELATION TIME

The State Capitol in Lincoln was buzzing on November 7, 2008, after Nebraska Attorney General Jon Bruning alerted the news media that a major announcement was coming that day.

Bruning was one of the Cornhusker state's most recognized state politicians, and he was an old pro at holding press conferences and talking in front of a room of television cameras. But this media event was unlike any other. In fact, Bruning invited a number of public officials to join him as he addressed the press from the podium. They included Gage County Attorney Randy Ritnour, Beatrice Police Chief Bruce Lang, Beatrice Police Lieutenant Mike Oliver, Beatrice police Investigator Tina Vath, Nebraska State Patrol Investigators Jay Morrow and Kevin Knorr, and current Gage County Sheriff Millard "Gus" Gustafson.

What happened next was something that Ritnour would never forget.

As the attorney general's special guests stood and waited for the press conference to begin, Ritnour noticed that State Senator Ernie Chambers had walked into the hallway and joined them. Chambers had a reputation as Nebraska's most polarizing political figure. He was in his early seventies at the time and the only black lawmaker serving in the Nebraska Legislature. Chambers had nobly served his constituents from a predominately black and impoverished district of north Omaha since 1970. Many of the state's white conservative lawmakers viewed Chambers as obstructionist. He was notorious for holding up bills he did not believe were logical. On numerous occasions, Chambers and Bruning had epic political battles over issues on which they did not see eye to eye. Although many people across conservative and predominantly white Nebraska disliked the often misunderstood black senator, Chambers had a following. His supporters considered Chambers "The Defender of the Downtrodden."

On this momentous day, Bruning, the face of Nebraska's Republican Party, a staunch conservative and rising political star, wanted Ernie Chambers, an independent, standing alongside him. Bruning wanted to recognize the lasting accomplishment of Chambers, who spearheaded the passage of the 2001 state law that allowed for advanced DNA testing in certain post-conviction appeals.

"Today is a day of mixed emotions," Bruning said into the sea of media microphones on the wooden lectern. "On one hand, I am enormously proud of the team of prosecutors and investigators from a number of law enforcement agencies who gathered with the single-minded intention of finding the truth. I am proud of that, in my opinion, because of their efforts we now at long last know the truth. On the other hand, I am disappointed that twenty years ago, in their zeal to make a community feel safe again, to solve an unthinkable crime, the former county attorney and some members of law enforcement bullied six innocent people into admitting crimes they didn't commit."

The newspapers snapped dozens of photographs as Bruning delivered an uncomfortable but heartfelt message from inside Nebraska's Capitol.

FAILURE of JUSTICE

"Because of the well-intentioned but misguided actions of a handful of people, the noble goals of our judicial system were twisted and perverted and turned upside down. If there is a lesson to be learned, it is that every one of us entrusted with enforcing the laws must never forget our sacred oath to protect the Constitution of this great country. As the English jurist William Blackstone said, 'Better that ten guilty persons escape than that one innocent suffer.'"

In November 2008, Republican Nebraska Attorney General Jon Bruning convened an extraordinary press conference. Bruning revealed that the three men and three women who were sent to prison in January 1990 for the February 6, 1985, murder of Helen Wilson were all actually innocent.Photo/Jon Bruning

Bruning explained that his office personally became involved in the Beatrice murder case three months earlier, at the request of Ritnour, the first-term Gage County prosecutor.

"While there is no doubt today that six people innocent of this crime have indeed suffered, we are doing now what we must and that is to give the public the unvarnished truth. It is they who will judge those who made these mistakes."

Bruning said he accepted the responsibility to obtain justice and seek the truth. "Justice for both Helen Wilson and for the six people wrongly convicted in this case. Today we believe that we have found the truth and are taking the steps to see that justice is done."

The attorney general remarked that the Beatrice Police Department "did a good job" of collecting physical evidence that "ultimately led us to the real killer."

"In 1985, Burt Searcey, a former Beatrice law enforcement officer and friend of the victim's family, began a private investigation into the unsolved murder," Bruning said, explaining the origin of the errant theories of the crime. "Searcey's investigation focused on a loosely connected group of six people. Searcey took his theory to Sheriff Jerry DeWitt and County Attorney Dick Smith. County Attorney Smith and Beatrice law enforcement conducted numerous interrogations of the suspects, including methods that have now been discredited and discarded."

Bruning noted that during the spring and summer of 1989, four defendants under the threat of first-degree murder charges, Ada JoAnn Taylor, James Dean, Debra Shelden and Kathy Gonzalez, all confessed to participating in Helen Wilson's murder.

"Each of these four pled guilty to lesser charges," the attorney general said. "Based on the testimony of Taylor, Dean, Shelden and Gonzalez, Joseph White was convicted of first-degree murder in November 1989. White was sentenced to life in prison."

The sixth individual, Tom Winslow, pleaded no contest to aiding and abetting second-degree murder after White lost his jury trial.

"Fast forward to August of this year," Bruning said. "Preliminary results of DNA tests on the evidence collected by the Beatrice Police Department show that the blood and semen at the crime scene did not match any of the original six defendants. The blood and semen belonged to an unknown male. After additional tests were run in September 2008, it was clear that none of the DNA evidence at the scene matched Mr. White or Mr. Winslow. Mr. White's conviction was vacated and Mr. Winslow was resentenced to time served."

With that, the moment had arrived for the most stunning public announcement at any point in almost twenty-four years regarding the Wilson murder.

"Today, we are here to announce that Helen Wilson's killer is Bruce Allen Smith," Bruning informed the press. "In addition, none of the six convicted of this crime had any connection with Bruce Allen Smith and with this murder."

The attorney general's statement triggered all kinds of reactions. Back in 1989, Beatrice public defender Paul Korslund had represented Debbie Shelden when she became the first defendant to sign a plea bargain presented by Dick Smith.

"It never entered my mind that her story, although believed by her to be the truth, was actually not the truth," Korslund said in a 2016 interview. Of all six of the co-defendants, Shelden spent the least amount of time in prison. Korslund noted that she had been paroled after serving about four and a half years of a ten-year prison term.

"The other defense lawyers were quite experienced and questioned Debbie thoroughly in a deposition, and she was of course questioned on the stand before a jury in the White case by experienced lawyers," Korslund noted. "Judge William Rist, who took her guilty plea, was very experienced and extremely thorough."

Korslund, who went on to become the Beatrice mayor during the 1990s before his appointment as the district court judge for Beatrice and Fairbury, said he never fathomed that the DNA evidence would tie the crime back to someone else such as Bruce Smith.

"That news stunned me," he said.

**

After the historic press conference in the Capitol, the *Lincoln Journal Star* rightfully credited Omaha State Senator Chambers for playing a leading role in the events that led to the recognition of the six wrongful convictions. After all, Chambers' political persistence had sparked the creation of the new state law that let convicts pursue DNA testing under certain circumstances.

"In this case, justice was wounded, she had a lacerated face, the blindfold had tipped akimbo. Well now, justice is probably dancing," Chambers said, in a *Lincoln Journal Star* report.

Chambers told the newspaper that he could never remember a time during his storied career in Nebraska politics when he was more exuberant.

From Ritnour's perspective, Bruning never winced about uncovering the real truth in the Helen Wilson murder case, even though the truth would be incredibly unpopular in Gage County.

"The Attorney General's Office and Jon Bruning said, 'Let's just rip the Band-Aid off," Ritnour said. "And Senator Ernie Chambers, he deserves a lot of credit as well. Without that legislation, Joseph White, JoAnn Taylor and Tom Winslow would still be in prison, and all six would still be under that cloud of that murder. They were the usual suspects … for one thing."

Because of the extraordinary turn of events, JoAnn Taylor, who remained incarcerated in Omaha, would go before the Nebraska Board of Parole within a few days.

"My office will testify in support of granting Ada Taylor parole," Bruning vowed at the announcement. "This afternoon, Gage County Attorney Randy Ritnour has dismissed the charges against Joseph White."

Lastly, the Nebraska Pardons Board would convene in the coming weeks to consider full pardons for all of those wrongly convicted for Wilson's murder.

The stunning news coming out of Lincoln caught several people off-guard. For a number of years, public defender Lyle J. Koenig had continued to visit JoAnn Taylor while she was housed at the Nebraska Correctional Center for Women in York. In retrospect, Koenig said he put forth his best effort as Taylor's lawyer, given her unusual circumstances.

"While she may make a different tact now, Jo did not exactly proclaim her innocence back then," Koenig said. "Indeed, given her psychological profile, I am not sure Jo actually knew whether she was present or not when Helen Wilson was killed. However, that is not much help. Juries are not particularly persuaded by the suggestion that someone was crazy when a particular event occurred."

Also, Koenig pointed out it was "well-documented Jo wanted to accept a plea."

"Believe me when I say that if you hold someone's life in your hands, as you do when they are facing the electric chair, you are not inclined to persuade them to run the risk of dying, when you have the ability to avoid that result, even if you suspect that they are innocent. This would be hubris to the ultimate degree, and frankly, it is my opinion that Jo's blood would to some extent be on my hands."

During the historic press conference, Bruning unveiled a large blown-up mugshot of Bruce Allen Smith. The bushy-haired, scrawny young man with a mustache wore an unbuttoned short-sleeved shirt exposing a large tattoo etched across his chest. At the time of Wilson's brutal slaying, Smith was only twenty-two.

"When this case was brought to me three months ago, we could not have predicted that we would find no DNA evidence tying any of the defendants to the victim or the crime scene," Bruning explained to the assembled media representatives. "And we could not have predicted that the good investigative work and preservation by local law enforcement twenty-five years ago would help us find the sole perpetrator, Bruce Smith, who brutally raped and murdered Helen Wilson."

However, despite the damning evidence, Bruce Smith would not be prosecuted for beating, raping, sodomizing and suffocating the defenseless widow during the early morning hours of February 6, 1985.

CHAPTER 32
WICKED LIFE

After slipping out of Beatrice on a Greyhound bus in early February 1985, Bruce Smith got away with the hideous crime that cost Helen Wilson her life – and subsequently sent six other people to prison.

Smith left his crime behind and lived out his troubled, wicked life in Oklahoma.

Smith was born on August 22, 1962, to Clifford Smith and Clara Beth Womack. He grew up in Beatrice, where he lived with his mother. By fifteen, he ended up at a juvenile detention facility in Kearney, Nebraska. After that, he lived around Oklahoma City, mostly with his mother and other times finding shelter wherever he could.

Smith's first known adult crimes happened in 1980, when he was eighteen. That October, Oklahoma City police arrested him for concealing stolen property. He received a deferred two-year sentence and was ordered to pay restitution. Two months later, Smith was arrested for auto burglary. Police reports also showed Smith had three outstanding bench warrants for traffic offenses. In the car burglary, Smith stole a .22 caliber automatic pistol, a box of .22-caliber ammunition, an orange hunting jacket, a hydraulic jacket, a bowie knife, a CB radio, and a socket set. While in jail, Smith agreed to show a detective where the gun, jacket, and CB radio were hidden by some railroad tracks. The district attorney in Oklahoma ultimately declined to prosecute Smith for the burglary.

The Oklahoma State Bureau of Investigation noted that Smith had been charged with committing a rape on December 14, 1981, but little appears to be known about the crime. A criminal history for Smith does not reflect how or why the case in this serious crime was resolved. The file for that incident was supposedly destroyed years ago by flooding. At any rate, Smith couldn't have been incarcerated for that sexual assault very long. By March of 1982, he and his future wife, Patricia Alexander, were arrested in Oklahoma City for possessing dangerous drugs, carrying a concealed weapon and public drunkenness, police reports show.

The following year, in 1983, the couple married and Smith's wife had triplets, but only one daughter survived the birth. That year Bruce Smith was arrested for at least the fifth time in Oklahoma City, records reflect, in a case involving public intoxication and two outstanding traffic warrants. By August of 1984, Smith and another man were arrested for riding in a black Mustang that had been reported stolen out of rural Merrill County in far western Nebraska.

When he wasn't breaking the law, Smith was busy getting lots of tattoos. He preferred scary ones: spider webs, skulls and crosses. Most notably, he had a large tattoo of an eagle etched across his chest. Police reports from the 1980s indicate Smith may have served as a confidential informant for the Oklahoma City Police Department during that time frame, but it is not clear to what extent.

In February of 1985, Smith took a bus to his Nebraska hometown. On Monday, February 4, he dropped in at the Beatrice home of his half-brother, Gary Orth, who lived on Herbert Street. Smith stayed the night, police reports indicate.

On Tuesday, February 5, Smith wandered over to visit Michael Hyatt, his old childhood chum. That evening, Smith and Hyatt met up at the rowdy R&S Bar downtown. By midnight, Smith was inebriated. Nearing 3:00 a.m., Smith's raging sexual impulses were in overdrive. After passing out, he awoke at the after party at a trailer outside town and tried to force himself on a young woman.

"Bruce Smith became angry and threatened to rape (her) and made statements that he always gets what he wants," police reports from the time state. "Bruce Smith also made a statement that he was 'going to get a piece of ass, no matter what it took.'"

Smith was angry and threatening revenge against everyone at the trailer. A half-hour later, Hyatt dropped off Smith in Beatrice. In all probability, Smith invaded Wilson's apartment shortly after his friend sped away, breaking the door jamb and ripping her from sleep into horror and pain.

By 6:00 a.m., Smith showed up at the convenience store on Sixth Street where he was caught trying to steal two bags of Doritos by a store clerk who suspected he saw blood on the man. By 6:30 a.m. Smith began banging on the door at his half-brother's house. Frightened by the pounding, Gary Orth's wife, Cindy, refused to answer. Smith left and wandered around more. He returned after 8:00 a.m. Once inside, Smith complained that he had injured his nose in a fight with Hyatt. Almost immediately, Smith dozed off to sleep.

That same morning, one of the women that Smith tried to rape at the trailer in Blue Springs discovered that her wallet was missing. Beatrice police later found the woman's wallet in an alley near the 600 block of Court Street, not far from where Smith had been dropped off. The only thing missing was $60, which Smith probably stole.

During the next couple of days, Smith met up with old girlfriends and frequented the bars. He never, ever, said a word to anyone about the deadly rape he committed inside the old Lincoln Telephone & Telegraph Building.

On one of those nights that he was still lurking around his hometown, after a night of heavy drinking, Smith joined a few friends at the Marshall's Truck Stop restaurant at around 2:00 a.m. One of the young women at Smith's table noticed that he had several scratches on his hands, police reports state. Two nights after the widow's rape, Smith met up with some young women he knew at The Little Bar in Beatrice. When one of the women returned from her boyfriend's place to her residence at 5:00 a.m., she was shocked to find Smith fast asleep on her couch, reports show. He apparently had slipped into her place through an unlocked door.

Smith scrounged up his belongings. He boarded a bus and left Nebraska. It was just few weeks later, however, that he came within a whisker of being arrested in Oklahoma City for Helen Wilson's murder – which would have happened if not for the apparent botched blood test performed for visiting Nebraska law officers by the yet-to-be nationally disgraced Oklahoma City police crime lab specialist, Joyce Gilchrist.

"I had looked at Smith, and I had excluded him on the serology," Soucie recalled later. "When someone said they got a hit on Smith with the DNA, that's when Joyce Gilchrist's name jumped out. I said, 'Joyce Gilchrist, Joyce Gilchrist, why does that name ring a bell?'"

Back in 1985, nobody in Nebraska realized Gilchrist's limited role in the chemistry analysis for one out-of-state prime suspect would have such disastrous consequences for the Wilson murder probe. Her erroneous conclusions unavoidably sent the Beatrice murder investigation down a bunch of rabbit holes for the next few years.

Gilchrist's name now is immortalized in America's forensic science community for scandal and misconduct.

But in 1985, she had become the Oklahoma City Police Department's "Employee of the Year," the very year she handled the biological sample of Bruce Allen Smith and relayed inaccurate test results to the pair of anxious Nebraska police investigators prepared to arrest Smith, their prime suspect, for rape and murder.

Gilchrist, an African-American woman, was known around Oklahoma City police circles as "Black Magic" thanks to her ability to shore up the prosecution's cases on the witness stand, several media outlets have widely reported. But her errors caught up with Gilchrist in 2001, when an FBI investigation exposed years of shoddy performance and the Oklahoma City police fired her.

That year, *CBS News* correspondent David Kohn brought Gilchrist's case to the national spotlight in a news piece entitled, "Under the Microscope." Evidence routinely disappeared in major violent crimes, including capital murder cases, *CBS News* reported, and a crime lab freezer once broke, contaminating evidence in numerous crimes. While Gilchrist worked in the crime lab, blood analysis files from 1980, 1981 and 1990 went missing. The Oklahoma City police lab also had a reputation for destroying specimens in rape cases after only two years, *CBS News* reported. Other lab chemists reported Gilchrist would refer in her notes to a number of crime victims or defendants as "fags" or "faggots" to jog her memory about their cases.

Despite being fired, Gilchrist denied any wrongdoing and later filed a lawsuit against Oklahoma City alleging wrongful termination.

"My administrators are the ones who make the decisions about the operation of the laboratory," Gilchrist told *CBS News*. "I don't make that decision. I just carry out those orders. That's why I can't comment right now."

***

It's debatable whether Gilchrist was even qualified to be hired straight out of college to work in Oklahoma City's crime lab, given that her college grades were so poor. According to court transcripts, Gilchrist had earned a D in general chemistry at the University of Oklahoma. After transferring to the University of Central Oklahoma, she got Cs and Ds in chemistry, general physics and quantitative analysis. She was put on academic probation and academic suspension, lawsuit depositions note. However, in May of 1980, she received a bachelor's degree in forensic science and had a job lined up in the Oklahoma City crime lab where she had interned in college.

Gilchrist remained a fixture at the crime lab for the next twenty-one years, attaining the rank of forensic chemist supervisor in 1990. But her police forensics career was mostly a sham. Her errors and outright falsehoods put several people into Oklahoma's prison system for violent crimes they did not commit.

David Johns Bryson was one of many men whose lives were ruined by Gilchrist, the Innocent Project has reported. In 1982, a woman was blindfolded near an Oklahoma City law firm parking lot, forced into her car and violently raped. Gilchrist later testified at Bryson's trial that hairs found on the victim were consistent with his. More damning, Gilchrist testified that Bryson's blood type matched the rapist. Bryson received an eighty-five-year prison term. He appealed, but in 1988, Gilchrist wrongly claimed that additional forensic tests were impossible because biological evidence from the case had been lost. An appeals court ordered a new search and sure enough, the semen samples were found, the Center for Wrongful Convictions reported. In 1999, a new battery of forensic tests determined Bryson was not the rapist. He was exonerated, but not before spending sixteen long years in prison for a vicious rape he did not commit.

The case of Jeffrey Pierce also exposed Gilchrist to the national forensic science community as an incompetent fraud. Pierce had been convicted in 1986 of raping and robbing an Oklahoma City woman at an apartment building where he worked on a landscaping crew. Pierce's conviction was largely based on erroneous testimony from Gilchrist. He remained imprisoned for the next fifteen years until 2001, when the FBI determined that Gilchrist's hair analysis was mistaken. DNA testing cleared Pierce and implicated a different man, the Innocence Project noted. Because of Gilchrist, Pierce lost more than fifteen years of freedom.

After Gilchrist found herself under siege, plagued by a litany of federal lawsuits, her civil attorney once told journalists that aside from Oklahoma City bomber Timothy McVeigh, only the name of Joyce Gilchrist elicited more disgust and outrage around their metropolitan city. The fallout from her atrocious work at the Oklahoma City Police Department lab seeped into Nebraska, but it didn't come to light until seven years after her firing. Still, her role in the mishandling of the Wilson murder investigation can't be ignored or underplayed.

"That blood was mishandled, and they gave us the wrong information," retired Beatrice Police Chief Donald Luckeroth told the *Lincoln Journal Star*. "Had they given us the right information on the blood at the time, we'd probably have had the case closed in a couple weeks."

Make no mistake: Gilchrist was not responsible for putting Joseph White and his five cohorts in prison. But she prevented Wilson's actual rapist and murderer, Bruce Smith, from being linked to the crime long before those convictions after he emerged as the Beatrice department's prime suspect.

Although Bruce Allen Smith emerged early as the prime suspect in Helen Wilson's slaying, he was eliminated as a suspect in March of 1985 because of botched laboratory test results from Joyce Gilchrist of the Oklahoma City Police Department. Gilchrist's costly mistake paved the way for the eventual wrongful convictions of the Beatrice 6 four years later. Photo/Jon Bruning

The lawyer who won Winslow's exoneration said there are a couple of scenarios to explain how the blood foul-up occurred.

One, Gilchrist simply messed up the basic serology test on Bruce Smith's status as a non-secretor. The other distinct possibility, he said, is that she never conducted the serology test to begin with, thereby faking the lab results and giving the Nebraska authorities the wrong information. Soucie said his own research into the case file raises a strong possibility that the Oklahoma City Police Department considered Smith a valuable confidential police informant around that time frame and didn't want to lose him to Nebraska.

Regardless of her intentions or ambivalence, Gilchrist fouled up the results of a basic serology test. By the time her colossal errors were detected in late 2008, it was too late to matter.

Bruce Allen Smith had already been dead for more than sixteen years.

***

In Oklahoma, as Bruce Smith lived with the dark, terrible secret of Helen Wilson's murder, he continued on with his carefree life of crime.

Roughly three weeks after being cleared by Gilchrist's shoddy lab work for the Nebraska rape-murder, Smith was arrested in Oklahoma City for auto theft and marijuana possession. For those crimes, Smith got a suspended two-year prison sentence, instead receiving court probation.

Two years later, in March of 1987, under the cloak of darkness, Smith scaled a wrought iron fence intent on crimes that he never had a chance to commit. Armed security guards on night patrol nabbed the prowler. Smith began screaming at the top of his lungs, calling the guards, "motherfuckers" and vowing they would be fired, police reports show. Officers discovered Smith had a .77-caliber Marksman

BB pistol inside a shoulder holster tucked underneath his coat. He also had eight BB pistol darts and a small dagger in his pockets bearing the inscription, "Mexico." Besides trespassing, Smith was arrested for disorderly conduct and public drunkenness.

"I would beat you motherfuckers' asses if ya'll weren't in those monkey suits," Smith sneered at police. When Smith doubled up his fists back at the jail, the police threw him against the floor.

It wasn't long before Smith was out of jail and back on the street committing more crimes.

Four months later in 1987, Smith was involved in another prowler incident. A man who lived alone told police he heard one loud knock on his front door around 3:00 a.m. When he got out of bed, a shadowy figure was trying to pry off the screen off his front window at the Old London Town Apartments. Several minutes later, Smith slipped inside the man's apartment through a ceiling duct. Smith kneed the man in the stomach and shoved him into the door, blaming the victim for not answering his door when Smith knocked.

The police learned that Smith used to live in the apartment complex. The victim told police he knew Smith was a problem and probably had come by to cause trouble. "Upon asking suspect Smith how he got in the ceiling he stated he went into his old apartment and climbed up into the attic and kicked down the ceiling into (the victim's) apartment. He stated he was merely checking on the welfare of (the tenant.)"

Smith's lucky run was over. This time, he got convicted of two first-degree burglary counts. In August 1987, Smith drew a four-year prison term. He went to state prison until December 15, 1989.

In 1990, after Smith's release from prison, a woman claiming to be his girlfriend notified police that Smith had busted the windshield on her 1979 Chevette with his fists after she gave him a ride home, reports show. It marked one of the few police calls where Smith was not taken into custody.

That December, Smith was arrested for drunken driving. Just two months later, while driving on a suspended license, Smith was busted for another drunken driving offense after his white van was seen weaving all over the road. At the jail Smith was offered to take a sobriety breath test. "I know my constitutional rights. I don't want to take it," he responded.

That October, Smith was back in jail, this time for four outstanding arrest warrants. Officers also slapped Smith with a total of eight citations including another driving under suspension offense. In January of 1992, Smith was jailed for more outstanding arrest warrants. He stayed in jail about five weeks. Then, on February 20, 1992, Smith was freed. A notation in a jail booking log revealed that his life of crime would soon be over. Smith had AIDS, the log said.

Smith stuck around Oklahoma City and survived for several months. Once Smith reached his thirtieth birthday, his health rapidly deteriorated. On September 25, 1992, Smith was given a ride to a hospital in Oklahoma City. Five days later, at 4:49 a.m., he gasped his last breath of air. His death certificate confirms Smith died of AIDS.

Around October 5, 1992, a hole was dug and Smith's casket was lowered into the ground at Rose Hill Burial Park in Oklahoma City. Decorative flowers were etched into the headstone. The epitaph referred to Smith as a "Loving Son."

Toward the tail end of 2008, Beatrice police investigator Tina Vath went to Oklahoma City to gather up police reports and glean more about Smith's troubled lifestyle and background.

She visited Rose Hill Burial Park and took a handful of photos of Smith's tombstone. Prior to first learning of Smith's death in 2008, Vath had wanted to be the first police officer to confront Smith. She wanted to watch his reaction when she broke the news that he was going to be prosecuted for killing Helen Wilson after more than twenty years thanks to irrefutable DNA evidence.

"I remember feeling so disappointed at knowing we would never have the opportunity to confront him and try to get answers for the family," Vath said. "I'm sure he did go to his grave knowing he got away with the murder."

It was a crime Smith got away with in life, but not in Smith may have escaped a death sentence for murdering Helen Wilson, but he could not escape death.

"It was some comfort to know that he only lived seven years after the murder and died alone, essentially," Vath said. "If he did know that the wrong people were convicted for something he did, I don't believe he ever told anyone about it."

Vath, a skilled police investigator, said she was convinced Smith knew that Wilson died during his crime, even if rape alone was his motivation. "By the placement of the hand towel over her face, which was already covered with the scarf wrapped around her face, that would make me think that he knew she was deceased."

Just how many other crimes Bruce Smith got away with is anybody's guess. Smith had been arrested around Oklahoma City at least thirteen separate times. Consequently, authorities in Nebraska never determined whether Smith was the elusive serial rapist prowling Beatrice's neighborhoods and terrorizing older women back in 1983. It does not appear Smith had been jailed in Oklahoma at the time of those crimes in his hometown, which would have been shortly before he turned twenty-one.

"Bruce Smith's family talked to us about how Bruce would disappear for periods of time and then show back up wherever his mother was living at the time," Vath said. "So it's interesting to see that his mother and him are buried next to each other and share a double headstone."

In November of 2008, Vath and Beatrice Police Lieutenant Mike Oliver interviewed Smith's former wife, various relatives, plus his closest friends. Paul Orth, Smith's half-brother, said that Smith was always in trouble and Orth had little contact with him. "Paul stated that he knew that Bruce that stolen from him," interviews state.

Paulette Orth, Smith's half-sister, remembered that the family lived Beatrice when she and her siblings were young.

"Paulette stated that she knew that Bruce Smith had AIDS after getting released from prison in 1989. Paulette stated that Bruce never told her that is what he had, but she knew by the types of medication that he was taking."

Dale Stephens, one of Smith's friends in Oklahoma, remembered that Smith mentioned Beatrice from time to time. He thought Smith might have traveled back to Beatrice to visit a girlfriend. "Stephens stated that it did not surprise him that Bruce Smith had killed and raped a woman," his interview stated. Smith's relationship with his wife, Patricia Alexander, was short-lived. "Patricia stated that she was married to Bruce Smith in 1985, however, they were not together for very long."

The police interviews in Oklahoma City painted a disturbingly accurate picture of the deviant young man who terrorized the Beatrice widow.

"It seemed like his entire life he was either running the streets, in trouble, and then finding his way back to his mom when he thought he was in trouble or had nowhere else to stay," Vath said. It "seems to have stayed that way even to his death."

Thanks to legwork of the attorney general's task force, Nebraskans now knew the truth about the Wilson murder, and history was being rewritten. The next order of business was to correct the terrible injustice that played out in the community of 12,000 for far too long, ruining so many lives over a twenty-year period.

Bruce Allen Smith only lived seven more years after getting away with the rape and murder of Helen Wilson in Smith's hometown of Beatrice, Nebraska. Smith died of AIDS in 1992 shortly after turning 30. He was buried at a cemetery in Oklahoma City. Photo/Tina Vath

CHAPTER 33
BEYOND ALL DOUBT

On January 26, 2009, the three-member Nebraska Board of Pardons -- comprised of Attorney General Jon Bruning, Governor Dave Heineman, and Secretary of State John Gale -- met to wash away an enormous stain on the state's criminal justice system that none had been involved with. In the blink of an eye, Nebraska was about to go from zero DNA exonerations to six.

In this case, the Nebraska Attorney General's Office was not the least bit ashamed.

The pardons board applications told of six loosely connected people whose fractured lives were derailed by one Gage County sheriff's deputy and those who blindly trusted in him. Not one of the wrongly condemned six, however, could regain their lost years.

Dean was incarcerated from April 15, 1989, until he finished his prison sentence for aiding and abetting a second-degree murder on August 12, 1994.

After serving his time for a crime of which he was innocent, Dean resettled in Salina, Kansas, and found his calling in life as a truck driver. He worked a couple years for Payless Trucking. He drove for a year with H D Trucking, also in Salina, before it, too, went out of business. By 2009, when he was exonerated, Dean had driven a truck for the past eighteen months with Great Plains Trucking in Salina.

After his prison release, Dean had run afoul of the law only once, around 2001, in Wichita. For receiving stolen property Dean was given court probation. He had been divorced twice and he had two daughters at the time of his exoneration.

On his pardon application, Dean wrote, "I was innocent of the charges for which I was convicted. The DNA established beyond any reasonable doubt that Bruce Smith committed the rape and murder of Helen Wilson and that he acted alone."

**

Tom Winslow was twenty-three when he was put in jail on March 17, 1989, in connection with the Wilson murder. Winslow was finally freed on October 17, 2008, in the midst of serving a fifty-year prison term. Winslow was in his early forties at the time of his pardons board hearing. On his pardon questionnaire Winslow admitted that he pleaded "no contest" but chose to answer "No" at that time on whether he was admitting guilt.

"Based on the false statements and confession of Ada JoAnn Taylor, Clifford Shelden, Debra Shelden and James Dean, I made an admission that I had been present at the rape/murder in exchange for a five-year sentence and to avoid the death penalty. Ada Taylor, Debra Shelden and James Dean then testified false in Joseph White's trial that myself and Mr. White had raped Helen Wilson while Taylor smothered her. DNA testing in 2008 established that we were all innocent and that Bruce Smith was solely responsible," Winslow stated.

Winslow had lived at the Lincoln Correctional Center, a medium/maximum-security prison facility, from 1990 to 2001. From 2001 to 2003, Winslow went to the new maximum-security prison in Tecumseh, Nebraska. From

2003 until his release in October 2008, he served time at the Omaha Correctional Center.

Winslow wanted the pardons board to realize that he was not an angel while growing up around Beatrice. He dropped out of high school, and things spiraled downhill. "I abused alcohol from 1984 to 1989," he wrote. He also was convicted of an unrelated serious offense, first degree assault, in Lincoln's Lancaster County. "I received a sentence of six to twelve years in 1989."

But upon regaining his freedom just a few months before the pardons board hearing, Winslow said he was making up for lost time and wanted to be a decent man. He quickly found a job at Omaha's Humboldt Specialty Manufacturing plant, performing quality control tests. It didn't pay much, but it was a step in the right direction.

***

On November 10, 2008, JoAnn Taylor, forty-five, was the last of the Beatrice 6 officially freed from prison. Like White, she had been taken into custody around March 15, 1989. Prison life tamed Taylor. She earned her GED. And after her release from prison, she stayed around Omaha and enrolled in a bachelor's degree program at nearby Bellevue University.

"I abused alcohol and drugs when I was younger before I was arrested on this offense," she told the pardons board. "I may have been convicted of some minor offenses such as disturbing the peace before this offense. I'm not sure."

Like Dean and Winslow, she too had admitted "guilt" and "pleaded guilty" in Wilson's murder. Taylor spent seventeen years at the Nebraska Correctional Center for Women along

Recharge Road in York. She then spent her last twenty-one months of imprisonment in Omaha.

***

Of the six finally exonerated, Kathy (Knehans) Gonzalez had the hardest time dealing with the sudden statewide attention surrounding the long ago Beatrice crime. The former Hebron (Neb.) High School graduate had been arrested and pulled from the life she was building in Denver in May 1989, and sentenced to ten years in a Nebraska prison on January 26, 1990. At age thirty-four, she was released from prison on October 19, 1994, prison records show. In sum, she had been robbed of about five and a half years of her life thanks Gage County's broken criminal justice system.

Gonzalez served her entire sentence at the Nebraska women's prison in York.

Afterward, she stayed in York to rebuild her shattered life in relative anonymity. In the days before the Internet and cellphones, practically nobody in York had even heard about Helen Wilson's murder. Beatrice and York were ninety miles apart.

In York, Gonzalez stayed single and led an ordinary existence. She resided in the same apartment for the next fourteen years. She worked at a Gas 'N Shop, Arby's restaurant, Valentino's Pizza and, finally, the Grand Central Grocery. But by 2009, on the verge of her pardons board hearing, Gonzalez was in her late forties and suddenly unemployed.

For Gonzalez, the reopening of the Wilson murder case caused lots of unwanted headaches and worry. Many in York who never knew anything about it began connecting Gonzalez to the ghastly crime that began dominating the Nebraska news cycle, and they glossed over Attorney General Jon Bruning's declaration that the original six were innocent. It was not a surprise. Many Nebraskans just could not wrap their heads around the idea that five people would plead guilty – implicating a sixth person -- and allow themselves to be branded as convicted murderers and shipped off to prison knowing they were truly innocent all along.

On her pardon application, Gonzalez checked the box, "No," on whether she ever admitted to the crime.

***

Debbie Shelden's pardon application was the strangest of them all. The easily manipulated woman clung to the false belief that she was an accomplice in her great-aunt's death. Her bizarre pardons board application stated, "An elderly woman, Helen Wilson, was raped and murdered on Feb. 6, 1985. I was present and observed Joseph White and Thomas Winslow on top of Helen Wilson. I testified truthfully at the trial of Joseph White. I have been told that DNA evidence from the crime scene matches that of Bruce Smith. I do not know Bruce Smith. To my knowledge, Mr. Smith was not present at the time I was in the apartment."

Obviously, the fifty-year-old Shelden was a troubled soul. She had been treated as a young adult for an assortment of mental health problems. Her first child was taken away by the courts and given up for adoption. Shelden's pardon application indicated she had never been convicted of a crime except for the Wilson murder.

She had been taken into custody on April 13, 1989, and let out of prison on September 6, 1994. By 1998, she reunited with her husband after Clifford Shelden finished out his prison term for the October 1988 assault at a Lincoln motel. According to her pardon application, Debbie Shelden was unemployed, her husband was unemployed and she recalled having previously worked in nearby Waverly, Nebraska, at MBA Poultry, but she did not know the year or dates of employment. She and her husband had a daughter who was age twenty-one at the time of the pardons board hearing.

As for Joseph White, technically, he did not need to fill out a pardon application because his first-degree felony murder conviction was overturned by the courts in October 2008. Nonetheless, for all intents and purposes, the wrongful conviction exonerations of the pardons board included White as an integral part of the group now known as the Beatrice 6.

***

Assistant Nebraska Attorney General Corey O'Brien's detailed seven-page summary given to the pardons board explained how not a single shred of physical or DNA evidence connected any of the Beatrice 6 to the attack inside Wilson's four-room apartment on February 6, 1985.

O'Brien outlined Bruce Allen Smith's actions on February 5, his night of excessive drinking, his attempted rape at the Blue Springs trailer park and his appearance at the downtown convenience store with bloodstains around six the next morning.

"Finally, based on its review of the crime scene, the task force concluded that rape and not robbery was the sole motive for Mrs. Wilson's murder and that Bruce Smith acted alone in fulfilling that motive," O'Brien told the pardons board. "In reaching this conclusion, the task force deemed it significant that the apartment was left in such immaculate condition and so much easily accessible money was left behind."

As for the DNA evidence, "Results indicated that the probability of someone other than Smith being the lone contributor of the semen, blood and hairs collected from

Mrs. Wilson and her apartment was nine hundred fifty one quintillion to one (that is 951 followed by 18 zeros)," O'Brien advised.

"The DNA evidence not only clearly demonstrates Smith's involvement but also tells an unfathomable tale: That if any of the original six defendants were present inside that small apartment, none of them left behind even the tiniest shred of DNA. DNA testing was conducted on approximately forty separate hairs, bloodstains and semen samples that were collected from Mrs. Wilson's apartment. Results showed only Mrs. Wilson's and Mr. Smith's DNA was present."

If the evidence that former Gage County Attorney Dick Smith presented at White's jury trial was even remotely accurate, traces of blood DNA belonging to Debbie Shelden and Kathy Gonzalez would have been found by the advanced DNA tests. "Furthermore, there would have been traces of White's and or Winslow's DNA in the semen and pubic hairs found on or around Mrs. Wilson's body," O'Brien said. "Instead, these results show that White, Winslow, Dean, Shelden, Taylor and Gonzalez are absolutely excluded as contributors of any blood, semen and public hairs found inside Mrs. Wilson's apartment."

What's more, there was another reason why the Gage County investigation driven by Burt Searcey was an outright fiasco.

"Additionally, in all their years of collective experience and training, no member of the task force had ever heard of a rapist who committed his crimes in the presence of so many witnesses, especially when so many of those witnesses were women," O'Brien pointed out. "Undoubtedly, all of these things were equally significant to the FBI when they prepared an offender profile in 1985."

Retired FBI Special Agent Pete Klismet's 1985 profile of the killer had stood the test of time, now twenty-four years later. He had predicted all along that Wilson's elusive rapist was a lone white male, in his early to mid-twenties.

"A profile we now know matches Bruce Smith and the horrendous rape and murder of Helen Wilson in every conceivable way," O'Brien said. "Satisfied beyond all doubt that Bruce Smith acted alone in perpetrating the horrendous rape and murder of Helen Wilson, the task force unanimously supports the pardon applications pending before this body and asks you to consider granting each of these requests."

***

For the first time in decades, the Beatrice 6 found themselves treated with the utmost respect and dignity as they visited the state's Capitol in late January of 2009. The *Lincoln Journal Star* reported that Taylor showed up at the pardon hearing with her new husband, Fred Duncan. Dean traveled from Kansas, accompanied by his fiancee. Gonzalez made the hour-long drive from York, joined by her sister. The former objects of shame and punishment received a certificate with a gold seal proclaiming their convictions had been officially wiped off the books by the State of Nebraska.

"I believe the evidence is overwhelming and conclusive that we should grant a pardon today," declared Governor Dave Heineman, as reported by the *Lincoln Journal Star*.

It was a beautiful yet awkward day for the state of Nebraska. Until the Wilson murder case came along, Nebraska had no exposure to exonerations through DNA testing. The state's two most powerful conservative Republican stalwarts, Governor Dave Heineman and Attorney General Jon Bruning, had leading roles as crusaders for the six wrongfully convicted from Beatrice.

Gage County District Judge Paul Korslund remembers how he got a phone call around the time of the momentous pardon board hearing. On the phone was Debbie Shelden, the client he defended twenty years earlier and who remained falsely convinced of her role in the crime.

"She was upset because one of the attorneys for the others said she was a liar because she was standing by her testimony at the White trial," Korslund said.

In turn, Korslund did not hesitate to offer the clearly confused woman his wisdom. "I told her that she was not guilty, that she should get legal counsel and pursue any remedy she could obtain."

***

Back in November 1989, inside the Fairbury courthouse, the most profound event of Joseph White's trial happened when prosecutor Dick Smith handed the murder defendant the portrait of Wilson. White studied the photo and blurted out, *"That's just some old lady."*

White's remark sounded rude to the courtroom, but it was right on the mark. Joseph White really did not know Helen Wilson at all.

Now twenty years later, the time had come for a new quote to summarize the Helen Wilson murder case. It would come from the mouth of Assistant Attorney General Corey O'Brien, the dedicated Nebraska public servant who stood on the side of decency, righteousness and integrity. O'Brien had devoted several months working hand in hand with the task force to uncover the truth, all in the vigorous pursuit of justice.

As he addressed the Board of Pardons, O'Brien stressed that each and every member of the Beatrice 6 was truly innocent.

"Not beyond a reasonable doubt, but beyond all doubt," O'Brien declared.

Applause rang out within the State Capitol as the governor, the attorney general and the secretary of state voted unanimously to erase the murder convictions of the Beatrice 6 from their records.

It was now time to throw a party to celebrate the six exonerations.

In January 2009, the Nebraska Board of Pardons gave pardons to all six men and women who had been wrongfully convicted of the 1985 homicide of Helen Wilson. Nebraska's action marked the largest-ever mass DNA exoneration in the United States. Photo/Jon Bruning

CHAPTER 34
JUBILATION

Downtown Lincoln's Cornhusker Marriott Hotel is one of the crown jewels of Nebraska hospitality. The luxury hotel features marble floors and a grand piano in the lobby. Nearby is a bookcase replete with hardcover books about famous Nebraskans. The Cornhusker is the premiere destination for dignitaries and VIPs who visit Lincoln, the state's second-largest city, with a fast-growing population of 260,000.

Inside an exquisite ballroom, JoAnn Taylor and the others gathered for cake and punch. The frosting on their decorated cake proclaimed," Justice for the Beatrice Six," the *Lincoln Journal Star* reported.

In light of the six exonerations, the Nebraska Innocence Project developed an immediate interest in the case. The organization wanted to help the Beatrice 6 reassemble their damaged lives. The Nebraska Innocence Project hosted the gala at The Cornhusker, which was attended by four of the six. The nonprofit entity gives free legal assistance to people who have been wrongly convicted of crimes in Nebraska but who don't qualify for court-appointed lawyers, according to the organization's website.

White was unable to fly back from Alabama for the occasion, and Gonzalez left Lincoln after getting her formal pardon. She remained uncomfortable with being in the media spotlight. It was another reminder that she pleaded no contest and went to prison for a crime – a heinous murder – that she had no part in committing.

At the gala, the four smiled and posed for photographs. They enjoyed the attention. Most had come from broken homes, difficult upbringings or endured a myriad of psychiatric problems. Some of their past demons were illicit drugs and alcohol. For much of their lives, they were frowned upon. They were vulnerable, easy targets for opportunistic public officials from Gage County looking to be exalted as hometown heroes for getting a horrendous unsolved murder case off the books and off the community's mind.

Nebraska's only black state senator, Ernie Chambers, had an instrumental role in the exonerations of the Beatrice 6. Years earlier, Chambers convinced the Nebraska Legislature to pass a law allowing prisoners convicted in older crimes to pursue DNA testing. In 2009, Chambers attended a party for the Beatrice 6 after they were pardoned by the State of Nebraska. Photo courtesy of Lincoln Journal Star

High society types would never think of inviting the likes of JoAnn Taylor and Tom Winslow over for dinner. For much of their lives, the individuals who came to be known as the Beatrice 6 were accustomed to being dealt the table scraps off other people's dinner plates. But on that one memorable day in late January 2009, they were treated with respect. The decorative cake symbolized a time in their lives of redemption.

Nebraska's legendary lawmaker from Omaha, State Senator Ernie Chambers, made it a point to head over to The Cornhusker to attend the exoneration party for the Beatrice 6. His legislation had paved the way for two of the wrongly convicted -- White and Winslow -- to pursue the DNA testing that reclaimed their innocence.

On this milestone occasion, the mood inside the hotel was celebratory. Collectively, the Beatrice 6 had sacrificed more than seventy years of their lives behind bars in Nebraska – while Bruce Allen Smith never served a single day for the despicable rape and suffocation of an older woman in the sanctity of her home. Twenty years after their erroneous convictions, the Beatrice 6 had grown up. They matured. They moved past their wild and crazy nomadic lifestyles that symbolized their destructive lives during from the 1980s.

Before the party at The Cornhusker wound down, James Dean, age forty-four, spoke with a *Lincoln Journal Star* reporter.

"Good ending to a bad nightmare," Dean told the journalist. "A lot of people lost their lives. A lot of people lost everything they had over this. Can't put a price on it, though."

Dean heaped praise upon his old co-defendants Winslow and White. From behind their respective prison walls in Omaha and in Lincoln, the men won an uphill legal battle to get

DNA testing of the evidence, even when the lower district court denied their petitions.

"Some of us gave up, some of us didn't," Dean told the newspaper. "The ones that didn't are the heroes here."

For White, especially, his was an excruciatingly hard-fought and lonely battle to achieve victory. All he ever wanted to do was reclaim his stolen life. He had spent nearly half of it sharing quarters with other lifers in Nebraska's prison system. He was among other cons claiming they got shafted and railroaded by an unfair justice system, perhaps blaming their race, a bad judge, a tough as nails prosecutor, a jaded cop, an angry ex-girlfriend, or a manipulative spouse. Somehow White, one among them who truly had been innocent, persevered and triumphed.

Tina Vath remembered how she once came across an old police report that coincided with White's March 1989 arrest in Cullman, Alabama.

"He was asked to give a blood sample. White agreed and made the statement, 'My blood will set me free.' I find it interesting that it did but, unfortunately, nineteen years later."

CHAPTER 35
POTHOLES AHEAD

Eventually that evening in early 2009 at The Cornhusker Marriott Hotel, the lights were turned off and hotel staff swarmed into the ballroom to toss away the empty plates and plastic cups. Once the exoneration party ended, the individuals known as the Beatrice 6 were free to most likely resume their lonely lives of despair.

The State of Nebraska had no policies in place, no laws on the books, to award restitution to the wrongfully convicted, to offset their years of heartache and unjust incarceration, regardless of who deserved blame. This, ironically, came from the same state that proudly posted a large green and white welcome sign high above the raised concrete bridge crossing the Missouri River into Omaha that proclaimed, "NEBRASKA ... the good life." To the members of the Beatrice 6, Nebraska symbolized anything but the good life. The state symbolized agony, pain and lots of bureaucratic red tape. Gage County's twisted justice system stole a total of seventy-plus years from their lives. Nebraska was prepared to give the six nothing for their troubles. It was like the scabs were being ripped off their wounds once again.

After the pardons, Nebraska scrambled to adopt legislation so that anyone wrongfully convicted of a crime had an opportunity to collect restitution from their state government for their pain and troubles.

Talk of shelling out state tax money to the Beatrice 6 was more than the family of murder victim Helen Wilson could stomach. The exonerations of the Beatrice 6 put the family through an emotional wringer and disrupted their healing process. For nearly twenty years the Wilsons -- who sat through White's jury trial – had been convinced that all six were guilty. Then out of nowhere a new team of unfamiliar prosecutors and police investigators were telling them Bruce Smith – someone the family had never even heard of – was the real rapist who terrorized and killed their loved one.

On January 30, 2009, the *Beatrice Daily Sun* published a seven-paragraph letter to the editor from Jan Houseman. The letter was headlined. "Daughter of Helen Wilson opposed to compensation for Beatrice 6." It would go down as one of the most well remembered letters to the editor in the hometown newspaper in quite a long time.

"While there may be merit to such a bill for those who are truly innocent and who have been wrongfully charged and convicted, it has no place for those who have already admitted their criminal involvement, which the investigation and trial has confirmed ... We are not convinced the Beatrice 6 were not involved ... To allow compensation in their case would serve a great injustice to our family as well as to the taxpayers of this State," Jan Houseman wrote.

At the time, Beatrice Police Lieutenant Mike Oliver lived for years behind the home of Helen Wilson's daughter and son-in–law, Jan and Wayne Houseman.

"Wayne would talk to Mike in the backyard and say that they did not believe the six were innocent, and they believed that they were all involved," Tina Vath said. "Wayne eventually just stopped talking to Mike at all."

The Wilsons would put forth a strong political lobbying effort inside the State Capitol. The family did not want Nebraska lawmakers cutting the Beatrice 6 a blank check as a tradeoff for all of their years of incarceration.

Joseph White testified in February 2009 that he lost more than nineteen years of his life because of his wrongful conviction for the murder of Helen Wilson. Sitting behind White inside the Nebraska State Capitol were Helen Wilson's daughter and son-in-law, Janet and Wayne Houseman. The Housemans continued to cling to their belief that the Beatrice 6 were guilty. Photo courtesy of Lincoln Journal Star

On February 19, 2009, nearly a month after the Beatrice 6 were granted pardons, State Senator Kent Rogert of Nebraska's 16th Legislative District proposed Legislative Bill 260, otherwise known as the Nebraska Claims for Wrongful Conviction and Imprisonment Act.

Rogert, who represented Tekamah, a small town an hour north of Omaha, proposed a flat $50,000 per year stipend for an unlawful incarceration, plus a higher payment if that innocent person spent time on Death Row. Rogert was following the recommendations previously put forth by President George W. Bush and Congress. The adoption of compensation for the wrongly convicted was left up to each state to decide.

"It is my sincere hope that Nebraska join the twenty-five other states that have statutes that compensate the wrongly convicted," Rogert urged fellow lawmakers in Lincoln. "Reintegration into society upon release is difficult, regardless, but even more difficult when we have robbed that person of their life, their happiness and their trust in a system that may have crippled their chance at a fair shot in life out of no fault of their own."

At the hearing that day in the Capitol, a tall Southerner in jeans and a black T-shirt stepped forward to speak after traveling more than 900 miles to Lincoln. He had been incarcerated by Nebraska from March 15, 1985, until October 15, 2008, for Bruce Allen Smith's rape and murder of Helen Wilson.

"My name is Joseph White. I'm not a politician. I may have fought twenty years to prove the truth that I was put in prison for a crime I did not commit. I worked every day to earn the money to hire lawyers. I've spent over $50,000 in attorney's fees, and I still owe $40,000 in attorney's fees just to prove my innocence. I've got a doctor's bill from two hours in the emergency room. Because I don't have a job, I don't have insurance. I got a $3,000 bill just because I had a slight chest congestion."

At the legislative hearing, White took a moment to display a portrait of his son, Brandon Poteete, for all of the senators to see.

"I lost twenty years of my son's life. When I was arrested, they took the father away from his baby. When I reunited with my son four months ago, it was just before his twenty-first birthday, which was just three days ago."

These days, White said, he leaned on his parents, Carroll and Lois White, to reassemble his broken life back in Alabama. When White went to prison, they were about fifty years old.

"They're retirees. They don't have the money to support me now. I've got no home, except for what they give me. I have no retirement. I can't get back what I've lost. I can't go back and teach my boy how to ride a bicycle or how to drive a car. All I'm asking for (is) the dignity to be able to support myself. I can't find a job because I've got a conviction on my record. I have no retirement. I have no equity in my home. I don't have one. All I have is a place to stay with my parents.

"I have no recourse in the state of Nebraska because the tort, the Nebraska Tort Act bans legal action of this sort. It has to go federal. I have nothing except my pride to fight. I never gave up on the truth, and I cleared my name. I've got bills to pay, no way to pay it.

"I don't know if this bill will help or not," White said in closing.

***

The hearing on Legislative Bill 260 marked the first time in twenty years that White had crossed paths with JoAnn Taylor. The two had first met by chance during the early 1980s, a period of Taylor's wild life marked by constant drug use and alcohol abuse. Out in Hollywood, Taylor snorted cocaine and dropped acid, working as a stripper and a model. There, White was also trying to make it as a nude male model in the pornography industry.

About six years later, in November 1989, White sat at a defense table, on trial for the murder of a complete stranger. He listened as Taylor furnished false testimony against him, claiming that she had seen White beat and brutally rape Wilson while she held a pillow over the woman's face – when the crime scene evidence contradicted such a scenario.

The rest was history. Taylor, White and Tom Winslow all lost the next eighteen years of freedom to the Nebraska Department of Corrections. Now two decades later, White and Taylor were together again, fighting to right a terrible wrong done to them and four one-time acquaintances during their long ago days of carefree living.

Taylor followed White at the hearing in testifying to the lasting impact of a wrongful conviction.

"My name is Ada JoAnn Taylor. I am part of the Beatrice 6. And no matter how much we get pardoned or cleared, that's how people are always going to remember us and assume who we are. The profound losses we've had, we've all lost family members that we couldn't go to funerals for. I had a brother that died fighting this government's war and was told that the military was not secure enough to support me, transport me to his funeral. He was my baby brother!"

Taylor said her family was broken up because of her imprisonment.

"I've got one of my three children back in my life because she found me. I have a son out there that's twenty-one years old that nobody knows where he is because of this whole situation. I can't find him. I can't get him back. I can't bring back his childhood. I can't get insurance. I have doctors that I need to go to because I have a chiropractic problem due to being in the prison, due to injuries there."

There were other money problems, she said.

"I can't obtain credit because I've never had credit and I'm forty-five years old. People look at me and say, 'Well, why haven't you had credit?' It's hard to explain twenty years of your life when it was taken from you for a wrongful conviction. But this pardon and everything that has gone on, it's made my life a little easier. But people still look at me and say, 'Oh, you're part of the Beatrice 6. You're unemployable. You're not good enough.' But I'm just as good as anyone else that's out there."

At many times in her life, Taylor was no angel. She abused drugs. She battled a host of severe psychiatric problems.

"We've made our mistakes. We've been wrongly judged for that. I can't get housing because I don't have credit to even go get a loan for a house or an apartment or anything of that nature. I can't get a car for the same reasons."

In closing, Taylor implored the state senators to pass LB 260. It would be a great step forward to help the Beatrice 6 rebuild their lives, she said.

"I pray that this bill goes through and we get some compensation. Houses and cars can be replaced, but childhood and lives can't. Thank you."

Back in 1984, Taylor convinced White to abruptly leave California to help her find her young daughter, who had been put into foster care in Gage County.

Now, a quarter-century later, Taylor, White and Taylor's daughter were all together.

And that little girl, Rachel Leigh Morgan, now twenty-six, had driven to Lincoln from her home in Kansas to testify on behalf of legislation that could give her mother a chance to salvage her wretched life.

"Good afternoon. My name is Rachel Morgan. I am the daughter of Ada JoAnn Taylor. We lost many, many years and many, many memories. That's obvious. But my concern is for my mother at this time. She doesn't have a way to become a normal human citizen like everybody else has the opportunity to. Everybody looks at her and says, 'Oh, I've seen your face in the paper. You're one of them people.' And after taking her to my hometown last evening, she saw that there are people that are there to support her, but there's more against her than there is for her."

***

As could be expected, there was a contingent of angry looking people who showed up in the State Capitol to make their feelings about the bill known.

Steve Olsen, a lawyer from Scottsbluff, addressed members of the Legislature's Judiciary Committee, announcing that he represented the Beatrice murder victim's family. Several of Helen Wilson's relatives traveled to Lincoln from across Nebraska to attend the hearing. The Wilsons fiercely opposed the compensation bill aimed at helping the Beatrice 6.

"For twenty years, this family has not had a voice," Olsen said. "They've not chosen to have a voice or have their voice heard, and now they do. And the reason they do is because they believe they've been harmed as well ... Many of the Beatrice 6 told stories that they were involved, that they participated in what happened to Helen Wilson, that they were there. They provided graphic details about what went on that evening. That continued throughout the trial in even more graphic description of how Helen Wilson spent her last moments and then died."

Now, he said, twenty years since the murder trial of White, the Wilsons were being told they must understand that all of six were innocent.

"But yet their testimony at trial, their untruths at trial all served as untruths against the system, the court and this family. And we don't believe that the bill properly addresses the harm and damage and the injury that this family has suffered."

Federal civil rights lawsuits, not claims on the State of Nebraska, were the proper way for the Beatrice 6 to pursue relief for their perceived injustices, the Wilsons' lawyer said. "And in that lawsuit, the trier of fact is the sole judge of credibility and can determine in a way the claims of the Beatrice 6 for the fact that they have been wrongfully imprisoned and also weigh in the other side of the case, and that is what they did. The lies they told. The positions they took during the trial to determine whether in fact compensation is proper and to what extent."

Next up, the murder victim's grandson, Shane Wilson, addressed the senators. His family just could not accept Nebraska Attorney General Jon Bruning's stunning press conference declaration three months before that the real culprit was a man named Bruce Allen Smith, who had died of AIDS many years back in Oklahoma City.

"The problem that we have is trying to get rid of the idea that the Beatrice 6 had something to do with this because of the testimony that was given," Shane Wilson told lawmakers.

The pardons board hearings had not convinced him that the Beatrice 6 were innocent.

"I don't have to probably tell you what a pardon does, but a pardon says that you are forgiven from this day forward. It does not, however, say that you didn't do what you were convicted for," he said. "The reality is the Beatrice 6, I would love to know whether they were there or not … it is possible that those six were there because nobody has proven to us that they weren't there. Nothing in the court system has proven that they weren't there. All it proved is that they didn't rape my grandma. That's all it proved, because DNA proves that. But it does not prove that they weren't there watching, that they weren't a part of it, they didn't do anything to stop it, they didn't do the things that I guess I'd like to think would do and anybody in this room would do, would try to stop such a horrific act … This bill will compensate them for that before they have to prove their innocence."

The testimony of Wilson's family stirred a hornet's nest within the legislative chambers. A widow in her seventies from Gage County took her turn to address the Judiciary Committee.

"My name is Mary Winslow, and I am the mother of one of the victims in the case of the Beatrice murder of Helen Wilson. My son spent a lot of years in jail, sentenced to fifty years for a crime he did not commit, nor was involved with. The investigation techniques used in this case were very questionable, if not illegal, at the very least, immoral. The FBI profile of the case was pushed aside and brainwashing techniques used to convince people to commit perjury and plea agreements to save their lives. The same brainwashing was used on the public and the members of the Helen Wilson family. The hate and bitterness they have harbored for nineteen years is now hard to let go. This is very sad."

Mary Winslow begged the senators to pass the bill on behalf of the wrongfully convicted. For them, the clock of life could never be rewound.

"My son pleaded no contest to the crime. He received a very harsh sentence. It could have been much shorter had he been willing to commit perjury. He wasn't. I am very proud of him for what he stood for then and what he stands for now. My son, Thomas Winslow, and the other five, Joseph White, Ada JoAnn Taylor, Kathy Gonzalez, James Dean, and Debbie Shelden, did not deserve what happened to them, and the Wilson family did not deserve what happened to them nineteen years ago at the hands of the investigators, the law enforcement, and the Gage County Attorney's Office.

"I sincerely hope and pray that no one will ever have to endure what these individuals and their families have suffered ever again for such a horrific miscarriage of justice. Thank you for allowing me a few moments of your time."

Tom Winslow could not be at the Capitol because missing work might cost him his job. Instead, his sister Tina Kaminski traveled to Lincoln to read a statement that he prepared.

"During my time in prison, I went through many difficult things. I could sit here and explain them to you, many horrific things that I saw in prison," Winslow wrote. "That's not why I'm here. What I'm here to do today is to share with you why I think this bill is important. Due to my wrongful conviction, twenty years of my life was taken. I can't get those twenty years back. All I can do is try to rebuild my life."

Since his release, Winslow had found work in Omaha in the quality control division at a manufacturing company.

"I have got a job. It's not a great job. It's a job without health insurance. It's a job that barely makes the rent in my apartment. But I do it and I make it, but I know it's not a job I can spend the rest of my life at."

Winslow said he dropped out of Beatrice high school in the early 1980s when he was in eleventh grade. He now wanted to resume his education and desired mental health counseling. "I want to be able to deal with some of the pain and issues, the lies, and the loss of people who took twenty years of my life. ... I need insurance to do that or I need money to do that. I want to be able to help my mother who was there to support me for twenty years unconditionally."

Above all, Winslow desired happiness within his newfound life. "I lost time with my father. I wasn't able to be there when my dad died. ... I'm not asking you guys for a handout. I'm asking you to give me a hand up and to continue to help me build my life because I've already started the process. All I need is the help to continue."

After the hearing ended, the political arm-twisting in the Capitol got underway. It became clear that the state lawmakers ultimately gave more weight to what the Wilsons had to say than the emotionally reeling testimony of the wrongly convicted Beatrice 6 and their supporters.

CHAPTER 36
RITNOUR'S WRATH

As time went on, many state senators grew reluctant about cutting a blank check for the Beatrice 6. For them, it was cut and dried: Five of the six pleaded guilty and several of them gave false testimony at White's trial. On the other hand, the phenomenon of false confessions was less convincing.

State lawmakers apparently gave little weight to testimony about that phenomenon by Dr. Richard Wiener, director of the psychology/law program at the University of Nebraska-Lincoln. Across the nation, he told lawmakers, people who are innocent confess to a violent crime about five percent of the time. But in cases of DNA-backed exonerations, about 25 percent involve a false confession. He noted that the Beatrice 6 case involved not one but four separate false confessions from Dean, Taylor, Winslow, and Debbie Shelden.

"In compliant false confessions, suspects acquiesce in order to escape from a stressful situation, avoid punishment, or gain a promised or implied reward," Wiener stated. "The interrogators implied to the Beatrice 6 that they would likely suffer the death penalty unless they confessed to their crimes and testified against each other."

He argued that the Gage County authorities – not the Beatrice 6 – warranted the blame for the travesty of justice that arose in the Wilson murder case.

"The interrogators included showing the suspects pictures of the crime scene and challenging their memories of the events, relying on the services of a police psychologist to help the defendants recover memories that they were too traumatized to recall," Wiener stated. "The criminal justice and psychology literature is replete with reports illustrating that innocent people can and do come to believe in their own guilt and even create memories for their alleged crimes. Some people resist the later suggestion that they created these memories, even when later evidence such as DNA tests or later confessions exonerates them."

At the time of her pardon, Debbie Shelden was one of those who still doubted her own innocence.

With the strong political influence of Wilson's family at the hearing on the measure, it was probably no surprise that many state lawmakers backed away from the original wrongful compensation legislation. The bill that became law was far short of the $50,000 annual package previously endorsed by Congress and President George W. Bush. The Nebraska Claims for Wrongful Conviction and Imprisonment Act signed into law by Governor Dave Heineman that spring of 2009 set a $500,000 cap as a maximum payment for anyone exonerated for a wrongful conviction. Furthermore, the new law attached several caveats to make it tough for anyone to get restitution in such a case.

The Nebraska Innocence Project was greatly disappointed with the outcome. The organization had lobbied in support of the initial bill asking for the $50,000 per year of incarceration as a fair restitution payment for members of the Beatrice 6. "The statute that passed effectively re-victimizes the exonerated by requiring them to reprove their innocence by 'Clear and Convincing' evidence," the advocacy organization posted on its website.

The group said it found some aspects of the new law insulting. "This statute requires exonerees not only to reprove their innocence they must do so in the very district court and community where they were wrongly convicted and sentenced. In the case of the Beatrice 6, they would have to return to a community where some residents, including the victim's kin, still insist upon their guilt despite overwhelming evidence of innocence. The district court judge in that community would run the risk of not being retained if he or she awarded compensation against public sentiment. In sum, unless the Attorney General quickly settles their claims, recovery of damages under the new Act could be long, hard and costly."

The Nebraska Innocence Project's words were prophetic. A long, bumpy road remained ahead for the Beatrice 6 in their efforts to seek redemption.

Even though they each had a piece of paper from the state pardons board declaring their innocence, the court of public opinion – back in Beatrice – remained against them. Investigator Tina Vath recalled later that the Wilson family members initially accepted the task force findings, only to change their minds shortly afterward.

"I remember calling all the family into the Police Department to tell them about our findings before it was released to the media," she said. "I specifically remember, of course, some shock, but most importantly Jan Houseman (the victim's daughter) saying that they owed six people an apology because they were innocent. I actually received a thank you card from the family a short time later. I'm not sure at what point they decided that the six were not innocent and still had something to do with the case at all."

Gage County Attorney Randy Ritnour had a similar experience. He remembered huddling with about a dozen members of the family to break the news to them that White and Winslow were being released from prison.

"It was an interesting discussion," Ritnour recalled. "I'm feeling bad for them, and I could genuinely tell that they actually felt some remorse that the wrong people had been convicted. There was absolutely no doubt that there was real sadness, remorse and confusion on the part of the dozen or so family members. But then within about a week or so, the Nebraska Attorney General (Jon Bruning) and his minions were the Devil himself."

In 2009, the main public officials responsible for the Beatrice 6 debacle – prosecutor Dick Smith, Sheriff Jerry DeWitt, police psychologist Wayne Price and Deputy Burt Searcey – all very much remained a vital cog of the Beatrice community. The six murder convictions that they had worked so hard to achieve had unraveled. Their work had been thoroughly discredited by the Nebraska Attorney General's Office and across the statewide news media. Their legacies were tarnished, and Searcey became a laughingstock and the poster child for the ineptitude of small-town police.

When asked for comment about Searcey's performance, Ritnour remarked, "His methods of investigation and quality of investigation speak for itself."

As for the former prosecutor, Beatrice attorney Dick Smith (who was no relation to the real killer, Bruce Smith) gained sudden infamy. His name was now attached to one of the worst miscarriages of justice in modern American history. The case of the Beatrice 6 marked the country's largest known mass DNA exoneration in a single murder case.

So who was the fall guy for the Beatrice 6 spectacle?

If you guessed Searcey, you were wrong. His boss and longtime friend, Sheriff Millard "Gus" Gustafson stood behind him and even promoted him to corporal in the jail division. In fact, Searcey helped oversee the application process when the jail had job openings, according to the Sheriff's Office website.

Instead, the town's vitriol was directed toward County Attorney Ritnour, who wasn't even in office at the time of the Wilson murder case. He said a "whole choir" of locally connected people insisted that the DNA testing did not mean a thing. These constituents were royally displeased that Ritnour had publicly supported the exonerations of the Beatrice 6.

"I knew I was dead for the next election by backing the story. I'm kind of an outsider, and I'm a prime target. Nobody was happy."

Back in 1985, Searcey had endeared himself to the Wilsons. The rural Gage County hog farmer gained their trust and confidence as he engineered his own investigation, one that later sent a half-dozen local misfits to prison for killing their precious loved one. The only thing the Wilsons knew was that the murder case stalled in the hands of the Beatrice Police Department. They didn't know the back story about the botched blood test done by Joyce Gilchrist at the Oklahoma City police lab that had screwed up the investigation.

"This family, they worshipped the ground of Burt Searcey," Ritnour said. "For them, he was the person who caught the people who killed their mother and their grandmother."

Despite keeping the Wilsons' respect after the Beatrice 6 were freed, Searcey was like a deer caught in the headlights as his role in the case came to light. Then in his early sixties,

Searcey was recipient of widespread unflattering front-page newspaper articles across Nebraska.

It was only a matter of time before now Sheriff's Corporal Burt Searcey and Gage County were sucked into an ugly and unflattering civil rights depravation lawsuit accusing Searcey and a host of others of conducting a reckless murder investigation that led to six wrongful convictions and more than seventy years of unjust imprisonment.

The lawyers representing the Beatrice 6 in the lawsuit were no slouches. Consider some of their resumes: Herbert J. Friedman of Lincoln graduated from the University of Nebraska College of Law in 1960, civil rights litigation was one of his primary areas of expertise, and his bar admissions included the U.S. Supreme Court; trial lawyer Maren Lynn Chaloupka of Scottsbluff had tried around sixty personal injury, civil rights and criminal cases dating back to 1997, her law firm bio notes, and in 1999 she attended world-famous lawyer Gerry Spence's monthlong trial school in Wyoming; Robert F. Bartle of the Bartle & Geier Law Firm in Lincoln, who graduated from the NU Law College in 1976, specialized in civil litigation and civil rights lawsuits; and Jeffry D. Patterson was a 1995 NU Law School graduate whose areas of practice included professional negligence.

In July of 2009, Gage County was smacked with the federal lawsuit and Corporal Searcey was named one of the lawsuit's co-defendants. Searcey, the fallen hero, had put the county seat at the center of the legal firestorm for the state's largest-ever miscarriage of justice in its entire history.

Days later, Searcey requested permission to purge some unfavorable documents from his personnel file at the Sheriff's Office.

CHAPTER 37
BACK IN SOCIETY

Days after being served with official legal papers notifying him that he was the subject of a federal civil rights lawsuit on behalf of the Beatrice 6, Searcey chose to write the following memo to Doug Klaus, the deputy chief sheriff of Gage County.

Chief Klaus:

I am requesting that all reports and documents contained in my personal file pertaining to the disciplinary action reference April 21, 1993, be purged from my file.

Cpl. (Corporal)

Burdette Searcey

Gage County Sheriff

Klaus went ahead and dated Corporal Searcey's memo "July 29, 2009." During the pretrial discovery process, the memo was later turned over to the trial lawyers suing Searcey individually, "Doc" Price individually, retired Sheriff DeWitt individually, and Gage County as the public entity with the deepest pockets. By now, Maren Chaloupka, the tenacious trial lawyer from Scottsbluff, represented Debbie Shelden, the low-functioning woman who came to be brainwashed into thinking she had been involved in her great-aunt's murder.

Eventually, Chaloupka came to face to face with Searcey during a pretrial deposition. She asked him why he had not previously sought to purge any of his disciplinary record, say, between the time of his re-hire in March of 2007 until July 2009, prior to the filing of the civil rights lawsuits against Gage County and himself.

Gage County Sheriff's Deputy Burt Searcey's abysmal performance in the Helen Wilson murder case caused six innocent people to lose between five and nineteen years of their lives to wrongful imprisonment. In July 2009, Searcey sought permission to purge documents about an unflattering incident from his personnel file. His request was granted. Photo courtesy of Lincoln Journal Star

"I have no answer for that. It's just something that never crossed my mind," Searcey told her.

"So why did it cross your mind on July 29, 2009, after you'd been served with a summons and complaint in this litigation?"

"I don't know."

"Are you saying that one had nothing to do with the other, that being served with this summons and complaint in this lawsuit had nothing whatsoever to do with your decision to ask your chief deputy to purge documents from your file?"

"No. I think it was because I probably wanted to see my file. And when I seen my file, I made that decision."

Searcey testified that he approached Klaus because he was following chain of command procedure.

"Why did you think that you had the right to ask that anything in your file be destroyed when there was a lawsuit pending against you?"

"I never entwined the two ... I just knew I had a right. Doesn't have nothing to do with the lawsuit."

She reminded Searcey that he had been "busted down in rank." He lost a quarter of an entire year's salary.

"There was no criminal, nothing charged. And so I wanted it out of there. And I had a new sheriff," Searcey responded.

"And this document had sat in your file without any concern on your part from March 21st of 2007 until July 29th of 2009?"

"It was always on my mind. It was something that I wasn't very proud of."

"And not until after you got sued did you ask to have it torn up?"

"That's not correct. Had nothing to with that."

Searcey claimed that he was not sure what his sheriff's administration did after he wrote Klaus the memo.

"Did he say, 'We've got a lawsuit pending against our agency. This is not a good time to be shredding documents'?" Chaloupka asked.

"That wasn't said. No, ma'am. That wasn't said."

"You ever hear the phrase, it's not the crime, it's the cover-up?"

"I've heard of that."

Astonishingly, Klaus had accommodated Searcey's request. Any internal affairs reports surrounding the three-month-long unpaid suspension and demotion were removed from Searcey's personnel file, lawyers for the Beatrice 6 later learned.

It's probably no wonder that Searcey wanted the off-duty bar brawl removed from his Sheriff's Office personnel file. Witness statements taken by the Beatrice Police Department in the spring of 1993 reveal the following information surrounding the violent incident:

Back in 1993, the bar at the local country club was known as the Gateway, and Searcey's future wife, Cindy Saathoff, was a waitress there. One evening, Sheriff's Lieutenant Searcey was off-duty and drinking at the bar with Saathoff and another friend. Words were exchanged between Searcey and the bartender, who was identified in police reports as Chris Garcia. Searcey later told Beatrice cops that Garcia pushed him off his bar stool, and when Searcey got up, Garcia decked him. Searcey indicated he got off the floor and left the bar. A short time later, Garcia was found in the entryway, lying on the ground, with blood coming out of his face. By the time Beatrice officers responded to the melee, Searcey's girlfriend begged another waitress not to say anything for fear that Searcey would lose his job, reports indicate. However, her conversation got put over the Gateway's loudspeaker and the Beatrice police officers were able to hear her plea.

At first, everyone denied witnessing the incident. Once Beatrice police re-interviewed everyone, a different scenario emerged: Searcey and the bartender were pushing each other and they punched each other. Another waitress heard the commotion and saw Searcey's friend on top of Garcia as Searcey's girlfriend tried to pull Searcey away. Searcey denied that he ever went to the entryway or that he saw the bartender being assaulted. He also denied punching Garcia, but other witnesses told Beatrice police that they saw pushing and punches thrown by both Searcey and Garcia. Both men received a citation for fighting by mutual consent, and Searcey's friend was cited for assault.

Less than four months after serving his unpaid suspension, Searcey resigned from the Sheriff's Department – only to return more than thirteen years later when Gustafson became sheriff.

***

After becoming Nebraska's first prisoner exonerated by DNA evidence, White was in his comfort zone back in Cullman County, Alabama. The community of Holly Pond had grown to around 800 people since White graduated from high school in 1981. In his mid-forties, White had traded in his beige state prison garb for Western wear. He preferred black cowboy hats, blue jeans, leather boots, and black T-shirts. While some of the Beatrice 6 didn't like the media attention, White remained welcoming and gracious toward journalists. Through the press, White was able to let others know that he was bound and determined to make something of the life he had lost.

On October 19, 2009, *The Cullman Times* newspaper published a comprehensive story headlined, "Back on his feet." Reporter Patrick McCreless had interviewed White at the Holly Pond Café.

"Today, just a little over four minutes from now, was when I walked out of the penitentiary a year ago," White told the newspaper. "Things like that just stick with you for some reason."

During the interview, White laughed a lot and conveyed a sense of optimism. He decided not to sink his head and wallow in despair. White had joy in his life. He reconnected with a woman named Paige Latham, a former high school classmate, and a romance blossomed. For the first time ever, White was able to celebrate his only son's birthday – a special milestone, turning twenty-one. Father and son, Brandon Poteete, savored the special moment, trying to make up for so many lost years. "I took him to a bar for the first time he took his first drink of alcohol," White told *The Cullman Times*. "I do see a lot of me in him. And he looks just like me when I was arrested."

White told the newspaper he had taken up smoking cigarettes – a habit he kicked seven years earlier while stuck in prison. "People tell me you shouldn't do that, but ... I was told for twenty years what I could and couldn't do."

After one year of freedom, White still had a ways to go. His release from prison came at a terrible time – in October 2008 the United States had plunged into a severe economic recession. Companies were eliminating workers left and right. On occasion, White picked odd jobs doing roofing for old friends, but the work wasn't stable and the construction industry was taking a beating.

White also couldn't completely turn his back on Nebraska. Besides the federal civil rights lawsuit against Gage County, White filed a tort claim seeking $500,000 in restitution under Nebraska's new wrongful incarceration law. But a month after LB 260 officially became law, White had not received any payments for the misery that Gage County officials put him through. White knew he was in for another long and frustrating journey. He had been there before. It took him almost twenty years to prove his innocence. He had no idea when he would ever be compensated for the travesty of justice done to him.

"I have learned that when dealing with the state and government, it's a shot in the dark," White told *The Cullman Times*.

***

When White went to prison in 1990, people didn't own laptops. When he was set free, practically everyone had a desktop computer, Internet access and cellphones.

Barely a year out of prison, White set up a Facebook account. He introduced himself to everyone on social media on New Year's Eve, December 31, 2009:

> "New to Facebook, just learning how it works. If I lose you in chat, that's cause I didn't know how to get back to chat."

His goofy personality shined for everyone to see. His Facebook status updates were downright hilarious.

> "I corrupt the innocent," White declared January 20, 2010.

"Has found a new calling in life ... wait for it ... Professional Procrastinator! Now if I could only get paid for it, I'd be a billionaire!!" (January 26)

"My body is a divine temple. My brain on the other hand, is home to twisted, perverted, nasty thoughts of impurities." (February 26)

"Is having coffee with his invisible friends and making sure none of them steal his cups." (March 14)

"Is going to go running through the street naked while throwing Skittles at everyone screaming, "TASTE THE FREAKING RAINBOW!" (March 18)

"If you see an onion ring - answer it! I did and it made me cry." (March 21)

Some of White's Facebook wall posts came straight from the heart.

"To me my mother is the most splendid woman I ever knew. If I have amounted to anything, it would be due to her. I LOVE YOU MOM!" (April 25)

His mother, Lois Powell White, was touched and posted a reply on his Facebook wall:

"You are so sweet, always have been, knowing how to make Mama feel good. I still have the poems you wrote for me."

His social media posts revealed that White had fallen in love – with a genuine, caring person. He posted several photos on his Facebook wall, beaming about his engagement to Paige Latham.

"AIN'T SHE GORGEOUS?"

White often smiled in his Facebook photos. Life was good. He bought a Kawasaki 500 motorcycle. He and his fiancee clowned around at the beach. He spent time tending to a large garden. And he kept his friends laughing with his clever Facebook posts.

But everyone so often, White unleashed a blunt post on social media that drew upon his bottled-up pain and inner heartache. He reflected on his three years of service in the U.S. Army, including a tour in Korea. And he couldn't escape his nightmare in Nebraska.

"I hope none of you ever have to face the choices I made for this country. I sacrificed part of my soul and part of my sanity to secure the rights and freedoms enjoyed in this country. Yet for nearly twenty years those same rights were denied me for a crime I didn't commit. To have people preach the word at me all the time just reminds me what I've lost and can never regain. I can't go back and change those choice (sic) and wouldn't even if I could. Thank you and love to all." (July 15)

Then in September, White had a major life event to announce on Facebook. He landed a new full-time job.

"Third day on new job, work easy, just hot and still learning ropes but going great so far." (September 26)

White splurged. He bought a new car for the first time in his life – a dark gray 2010 Dodge Challenger RT.

White felt blessed. He was happily engaged. He owned a slick new sports car. He now belonged to Local 12136 in District 9. He was a proud member of the United Steelworkers union.

His new job meant something. He was part of a special tight-knit brotherhood.

Above all, more than anything, the man in the black cowboy hat who sported a bushy horseshoe-shaped mustache was thankful to be free.

> "Yesterday was the second anniversary of the day I walked out of prison, free after 19 years, 7 months, 23 days and 18 hours for a crime I didn't commit." (October 16, 2010)

Around Halloween, White was at it again. He painted his nose black. He grew out a grizzly beard. His smile bore fake fangs. He dressed as a wolf and posted a selfie on Facebook. Since his early twenties, White relished his nickname of Lone Wolf. The wolf symbolized White and remained one of his favorite creatures.

Two years removed from prison, White had found his inner self, reunited with old friends, his loving, caring family and his faithful fiancée, Paige Latham, a thin blonde who wore glasses. They were in love. Everyone looked forward to their fast-approaching wedding date of May 7, 2011. White and Latham made plans to return to Holly Pond and build their dream house. For the time being, Latham held down a steady job at the Ridgeview Health Services in Jasper, Alabama, about fifty miles from Holly Pond. Ridgeview provided short and long-term skilled nursing services.

White's job in Tarrant, an hour's drive from Holly Pond, brought stability and fulfillment. He was a hard worker who strived to excel. In many ways, life was clicking on all cylinders for White at age forty-eight. And as 2011 hit, White took a brief break from Facebook. The new full-time job at an old coal factory along Highway 79 kept him preoccupied.

CHAPTER 38
TROUBLE AT TARRANT

A local landmark with a towering smokestack, the Alabama By-Products Co. plant was a fixture around Tarrant, population 6,000, since the early 1900s. In more modern times, people commonly called the plant ABC Coke. The coal delivered by rail to Alabama By-Products was dumped into the scorching ovens to create a refined byproduct known as foundry coke.

The Alabama By-Products Co., also known as ABC Coke, was a fixture in the coal-mining region of North Birmingham, Alabama, since the early 1900s. Around September 2010, Joseph White was hired to operate the heavy machinery inside the industrial coal plant located along Highway 79 in Tarrant. Photo Courtesy of U.S. Library of Congress

"With its trademark flame of fire shooting from a high tower overlooking Tarrant, ABC processes coal into coke, which is then used by customers as a burning agent to melt scrap steel and limestone into iron and steel," reported the *Birmingham Business Journal*.

General Motors was the plant's largest customer, the Birmingham newspaper noted. According to the Drummond Company, the parent owners of Alabama By-Products, its foundry coke also served the construction, smelter, rockwool insulation and sugar industries. Alabama By-Products Co. was a round-the-clock factory. The plant employed about 400 workers, several media outlets reported. Tarrant sat on the northern edge of Birmingham, population about 215,000.

The industrial plant was an enormous local economic engine for Jefferson County, Alabama. However, environmentalists were constantly at odds with the company concerning air pollution issues. Within the factory, ABC used transports -- known as Larry cars - to drop large piles of black coal down the vertical chutes and into the coke ovens with orange flames topping 2,000 degrees Fahrenheit.

Obviously, this was not a suit-and-tie job. But this kind of grimy, greasy factory work was right up Joseph White's alley. He liked to sweat. He did not mind getting his hands dirty with soot and coal dust. The work was stable, and White got along great with his co-workers.

During the last week of March 2011, White had a lot on his mind – but much to look forward to. The Nebraska Legislature was days away from giving White a large lump-sum payment as restitution for his wrongful imprisonment. At the moment, White had only received $25,000 of the full $500,000 payment that Nebraska had agreed to compensate him for his nineteen lost years of freedom. For White, the big six-figure check could not come at a better time. He and Paige Latham were only six weeks away from their much anticipated wedding date. That money could help build their dream home back in their native Holly Pond.

Only days shy of receiving the rest of his restitution payment from Nebraska, White volunteered to work a double shift on March 26. It was a noble gesture on White's behalf. A fellow ABC worker had recently injured himself, so White stepped forward to pick up the slack. As most of Alabama slept comfortably, White worked fervently through the middle of the night. He manned his control center. His eyes scanned the mechanized Larry cars delivering the coal that fueled the fiery coke ovens.

Suddenly, White identified a problem. A coal chute on one of the Larry cars was blocked. White knew if the coal was not loaded properly into ABC's ovens, foundry coke could not be made, pure and simple. So, White left his perch at the operator's control station to dislodge the blocked coal with his hands. The time was now around 3:30 a.m.

Several hours later, his mother, Lois Powell White, took to her Facebook wall to make an announcement to friends.

> "All Friends It is my regret to inform you this way. We lost our oldest son in an industrial accident last night. We will share details when we know more." (March 27, 2011)

Joseph Edgar White, the first prisoner ever released from the Nebraska Department of Corrections by the testing of old DNA evidence, had died instantly during an unforeseen work accident, just a matter of days shy from receiving a $475,000 check from the State of Nebraska to redress his wrongful conviction. He was forty-eight.

Family and friends of White, in Alabama and back in Nebraska, just could not believe the tragic news. Everyone was devastated.

CHAPTER 39
LIGHT BEHIND DARKNESS

Death leaves a heart ache no one can heal
Love leaves a memory no one can steal

—Lois Powell White, April 1, 2011, Facebook

On Wednesday, March 30, 2011, heartbroken mourners flowed through the Holly Pond Funeral Home chapel to pay their final respects to an honest, forgiving and all-around good guy who was robbed of twenty years of his life, all because of a vicious rape and murder committed by someone else in Beatrice, Nebraska.

The newspaper obituary was simple: White died on Sunday, March 27, 2011, in Jefferson County, Alabama. He was born in Cullman, Alabama. He worked at Alabama By-Products and served in the U.S. Army. His survivors included his father and mother, Carroll and Lois Powell White, plus one brother and three sisters: Jason White, Evelyn Cox, Nancy Aspinwall, and Margaret White. His other survivors were fiancee Paige Latham and his grown son, Brandon Poteete.

Brandon was jarred by the shocking news of his father's untimely death. "He's very upset," White's mother, Lois, told the *Lincoln Journal Star*. "Yesterday, he said, 'I just got a daddy, and now I don't have a daddy again.'"

White's burial took place at the Union Grove Church Cemetery, a beautiful cemetery out in the country, a tranquil place for loved ones to take pause, to grieve and remember the dearly departed. He was buried near the tombstone of his younger brother, Jeffery. While Joseph White had been marking his fifth full year of wrongful imprisonment, Jeffery died in 1994, just days short of his thirtieth birthday.

During his limited time of freedom, Joseph White made it count. He harbored no ill will. He forgave. He made people smile. He made a positive difference in the world. In fact, shortly after his release from prison, White made amends with his fellow co-defendants in the Beatrice 6, notably JoAnn Taylor and James Dean, whose damning testimony was crucial in convicting White of first-degree felony murder in late 1989.

"Hearing that testimony and everything was irritating. I knew it was a lie," White told *The Cullman Times*, during a 2008 interview. "Those people, as I've known all along, were threatened with the death penalty. They were told that if they testified, they'd work out a deal with them."

While unjustly imprisoned, White studied Christianity, Buddhism and other religions. He went on his own spiritual quest, which led him to shamanism and Wicca. He believed the divine could be found in nature, the Lincoln newspaper reported.

Ernie Chambers, the legendary Nebraska state senator responsible for Nebraska's DNA exoneration law, said some might say it was Shakespearean that White fought for nineteen years to prove his innocence, only to die shortly after winning his freedom.

"They would say he served a very noble and high-minded purpose," Chambers said. "But I don't see it that way at all."

Chambers said the individuals responsible for the Beatrice 6 wrongful convictions were all cruel-hearted people, who took advantage of people who were suffering from mental disorders and other problems. Chambers said the interrogators more or less frightened the Beatrice 6 into implicating themselves and others "as part of perpetuating a great big lie" upon Nebraska's criminal justice system.

"It's shameful for what they did," Chambers said. "They are unrepentant, they're engaged in self-deception, they have no remorse for what they have done, or if they do, they want to keep it very hidden."

Of the Gage County law officers, Chambers said, "these people doing this stuff are so cruel. They are cruel like little children who pull wings off of butterflies and stick pins in beetles' eyes."

The longtime Nebraska lawmaker took enormous pride in the fact that one of his laws set the wheels in motion for releasing three innocent people still housed in state prison for a crime they did not commit. In sum, Chambers' legislation achieved six exonerations total, all for the same murder case.

"Joseph White and these other people are all innocent. All of the heartache, all of the years of wasted lives, all because of a corrupt system," Chambers said. "I'm glad it helped these people but it's regrettable that our system would even allow for something like this to happen. I try to address things that will help people. But a law is no better than those who administer it."

The Beatrice 6 case was a great awakening for the people and politicians across Nebraska. Before, most people lived in denial of such deeds, presuming their cops, prosecutors and judges were all righteous and always got it right. Chambers said there is no doubt that there are other Joseph Whites still mistakenly locked away somewhere in Nebraska and elsewhere, serving hard time for somebody else's violent crime.

"I know these things happen," said Chambers, who has a law degree from Creighton University in Omaha. "It really bothers me that people are suffering. America is a horrid place in many ways."

***

White's untimely death prompted the federal Occupational Safety and Health Administration to show up at the Alabama By-Products facility in Tarrant. All told, federal safety regulators smacked the industrial facility with around two dozen serious violations and $115,000 in proposed fines. Those fines were later reduced to $82,000, OSHA records show. The vast majority of safety lapses were unrelated to White's fatality, OHSA records indicate, but the violations were uncovered as government inspectors trolled the coal factory because of White's work-related death. OSHA cited the company with one serious safety violation tied to White's death: ABC failed to develop and utilize lockout/tag out procedures for its coal transport vehicle "which would have prevented it from moving while the worker was un-jamming the coal chute," OSHA regulators stated.

White's workplace fatality was covered by the Industrial Safety & Hygiene News, a prominent business-trade publication: "Coke ovens are filled from above by means of transport vehicles, which drop coal down through chutes into the ovens. In this case, a coal chute became jammed and the operator left his controls to attempt to un-jam it. Through miscommunication, another employee took the controls and moved the transport vehicle, which hit the worker, crushing him between a guardrail and the jammed coal bin chute."

In 2011, OSHA issued a public statement regarding White's death.

"This fatality could have been prevented had the employer ensured that proper procedures were developed and implemented," stated Roberto Sanchez, the OSHA area director for Birmingham, Alabama. "It is the employer's responsibility to assess workplace hazards and ensure corrective measures are taken to protect employees."

***

White's shocking death left a giant hole in so many hearts. Since White had so much fun in life on Facebook, it was fitting that his loved ones set up a Joseph White Memorial Page to keep his memory alive on social media. The Facebook memorial page proved especially therapeutic for his reeling fiancee, Paige Latham, his grieving mother, Lois Powell White, and his devastated sister Nancy Aspinwall. They visited the page regularly to keep Joseph in their hearts.

> "So everybody asks how I'm doing, well to be perfectly honest, I'm mad. You joined the army straight out of high school and were gone. You got out of the army and you went on your adventure and you were gone. You finally came home and then the state of Nebraska stole 20 years and you were gone. Finally you came home again and now you are gone again and this time you are never coming back. I wasn't ready to lose you again, definitely not forever. We just got you back. So I am mad about the years we lost and the years we will never have. I Love You!
> – Nancy Aspinwall, April 10, 2011

"Hey Joe, your folks came out to visit me this morning. It was a good visit … It hurt to see your car drive away as they rode away in it, it always made a special purr sound when you drove it, for some reason, I didn't hear the purr … Gosh I miss you Joe, don't think I will ever be the same. – Paige Latham, April 19, 2011

On April 27, 2011 – exactly a month after White's death – his hometown made national headlines due to another tragedy. Anchor Diane Sawyer of *ABC News* showed the world glimpses of a killer tornado that decimated Cullman. Downtown was destroyed. Churches were leveled. Two people had died.

"Cullman is a unique community. Cullman is tough and resilient. It will shock people how fast this community will come back," the Rev. Bob Kurtz, pastor of the toppled St. John's Evangelical Protestant Church, assured the *ABC News* camera crew filming the devastation.

Cullman would rise from its ruins. And even from the grave, Joseph White helped the community heal and pick up the broken pieces, as his fiancée posted on Facebook:

"The nursing home is taking up donations for tornado victims. They need clothes, canned goods, etc. I am going to donate some of Joe's clothes for them. Was wondering how I could ever part with them, but I know what Joe would say. There may be someone tall and skinny enough to wear them. I'm keeping some, but a lot of good clothes will go help victims, I hope it pleases you Joe, I love you!!! – Paige Latham, May 4, 2011.

White's fiancee had given up many of his cherished clothes to help ravaged tornado victims just days before their wedding had been scheduled. Now, she had to wrestle with the direction of her life after White's work-place tragedy shattered their dreams.

> "Well, Joe, I've decided to keep my job at Ridgeview and stay here in Jasper. It was our dream to move to Holly Pond and build a house there, but that was our dream together. I've already lost you and I just don't think I can bear losing my job and all the friends I've made there also ... Me and the kids are going to rent an apartment in town and they are going to the city school. We miss you a lot Joe! – Paige Latham, June 8, 2011

***

Nearly six months after White's death at the ABC coal factory, a large truck delivered a new marble tombstone to the countryside Union Grove Church Cemetery. The tombstone was unlike any other. One side showed a howling wolf with its head tilted up toward a bright full moon, along with the following epitaph: *"When tomorrow starts without me, try to understand, an angel came and called my name, then took me by the hand."*

On the other side, *Joseph E. White* was etched in cursive along with the dates December 8, 1962, and March 27, 2011. The middle of the slab displayed a large black-and-white photo of White, his hair slicked back and a slight grin emerging over his thick mustache. The stone contained one large black vase for mourners to place their flowers to pay their respects.

Joseph Edgar White had sacrificed his self-worth while locked away in Nebraska for a hideous murder he did not commit. But he never gave up his fight to prove his innocence.

"My bullheadedness has cleared us all," White proudly told *The Cullman Times* in 2008. "They found the guy who did it. I've been completely cleared. I can't wait to get my life back on track again."

In the end, White did prove his innocence. He will forever be known as Nebraska's first prisoner exonerated because of Senator Chambers' law allowing new testing of DNA evidence.

In 2009, the *Lincoln Journal Star* had interviewed White for an award-winning eight-day special series called "Presumed Guilty." White told reporter Joe Duggan that the "Beatrice 6" label conjured up by the lawyers and the media to refer to the co-defendants was his greatest pet peeve about the case.

"It was the Beatrice 5. The 'Beatrice 1' never said he did it," White said, referring to himself.

Not surprisingly, Joseph White died without receiving a personal apology from Searcey or any of the other Gage County criminal justice officials who caused White to be wrongly convicted.

"They have to answer for their own actions, if not here, then in the next life," White told the *Lincoln Journal Star*.

***

Back on February 19, 2009, Amber Weinacht, an articulate young woman with short brown hair, stood at the podium inside the Nebraska Capitol. She was aspiring paralegal student who had learned about the Beatrice 6 case as part of an academic term paper assignment. She was moved to give testimony in support of LB 260, the legislation proposing compensation for those wrongly convicted or crimes they did not commit. Nearly four years later, Weinacht found comfort sharing her thoughts on Facebook's Joseph White Memorial Page:

> "I wish you were here so I could tell you how you have truly changed the course of my life. I have applied to Grace University for Pastoral Ministry and this was the writing sample I just submitted for acceptance." (November 26, 2013)

She titled her paper, "An Angel Wearing a Man's Shoes." She posted the four-page document on Facebook for everyone to read. Here are some excerpts of her heartfelt writing:

> "There are many people whom I admire in this world, but one stands out from the rest. His name is Joseph White and he was one of six people wrongfully convicted and incarcerated in the rape and murder of an elderly woman in Beatrice, Nebraska in the late 1980s. What I learned from Joseph, and what this case taught me, forever changed the course of my life. I grew up wanting to be a prosecution attorney, but because of Joseph, I now want to minister to those in prison, and help families with restorative justice through the forgiveness of Christ."

Weinacht's research pointed out that White had been the 225th person to be exonerated across the country thanks to post-conviction DNA testing, but Nebraska's first. Still, she noted, the Beatrice 6 became the single largest mass exoneration in modern United States history, all thanks to advances in DNA testing.

> "No one ever offered an apology to White for taking away a good portion of his life. With sadness in his

voice and tears in his eyes, after he was released from prison, he talked about the heartbreak of missing nineteen out of twenty years of his son's life … He remembered relatives and family friends that he lost that passed way while he was incarcerated. Amazingly, White blamed no one in particular for the nineteen years he spent behind bars."

Weinacht called White a "true Southern gentleman." She said she learned two valuable lessons from the only member of the Beatrice 6 to defy the odds and continuously proclaim his innocence: Foremost, that the truth will always set you free. Secondly, you must always get back up, no matter how hard life tries to knock you down.

"My goal now, because of Joseph, is to help all God's lost children through Pastoral Ministry, whether it is others like him, or other secondary victims of homicide. There is light behind the darkness. It just has to be found," Weinacht wrote.

White made the most of his limited time of freedom. He reconnected with his only son. He fell in love with a former classmate. He found a job that gave him pride and respect. Then he died – just weeks before his marriage and a matter of days before the large six-figure check from Nebraska arrived in his bank account. Circumstances beyond his control first robbed White of his freedom and irreparably damaged his reputation then cost him his life far too early.

"He may have been a petty criminal at one time, but certainly he was not guilty of this murder," said Ritnour, the prosecutor whose efforts led to exoneration of the Beatrice 6. "Joe White goes to jail for twenty years, gets released, is told he's getting $500,000 from the State of Nebraska, only to die before he gets it. How unfortunate can you be? You breathe your freedom only to get killed yourself. Can you imagine a more tragic life?"

With White deceased, the remaining members of the Beatrice 6 carried on without him as their slow-moving federal lawsuit slogged through the U.S. District Court system in Lincoln, Nebraska. About the only people being paid were the high-priced Nebraska law firms hired to put up a fierce and prolonged legal battle in the hopes of blocking the Beatrice 6 from achieving a sizeable financial settlement against Gage County's government and thus its taxpayers.

CHAPTER 40
LASTING TRIBUTE

The federal lawsuits brought uncomfortable notoriety to some in Gage County, and among them was Dick Smith, the former towering prosecutor. Smith grew defiant. He refused to concede the Beatrice 6 had been innocent. Initially, the plaintiffs had tried suing Smith, but he was later dropped as a defendant. Criminal prosecutors are typically afforded what's known in the legal system as absolute immunity. Nonetheless, Smith was still deposed by the lawyers during the pretrial evidence-gathering process.

Richard T. Smith served as the Gage County Attorney from 1980 until 2007. He holds the dubious distinction of having prosecuted the only murder case that resulted in six DNA exonerations. Six innocent people lost between five and nineteen years of their lives. Photo courtesy of Beatrice Daily Sun

"I feel confident in the jury verdict," Smith testified in a sworn deposition. "I believe nothing's been shown to me that would say that they did not do what was testified to at trial."

In preparation for trial in the federal civil rights suit, the Beatrice lawyer was asked to respond to the finding that Bruce Allen Smith was the lone rapist and true killer of Helen Wilson.

"He could have been there. I mean, there's no doubt about it," Dick Smith testified.

More than anything, Dick Smith did not want Nebraska's legal profession to view him as incompetent or lazy. So now that the truth had been exposed, he dreamed up an outrageous alternative theory to justify his original prosecution. He remained of the mindset that all of the Beatrice 6, including White, were still responsible for the brutal attack and murder of Helen Wilson, suggesting it had occurred between 10:30 p.m. and midnight, rather than sometime after 3:00 a.m., when Smith had been left in the area by Hyatt, the former classmate.

"And I think they ran out of the place with the door open," Smith testified. "I think JoAnn finally told that to Searcey that she had left some money there. They never found the money that was in the dresser in the bedroom ... And the DNA, it's his stuff (referring to Bruce Smith), and he was in there afterwards."

The discredited Beatrice 6 prosecutor suggested Bruce Smith then wandered into the old three-story apartment building around 3:30 a.m. "So that's probably a building he might want to go to if he was cold on the street ... because he had a family member or somebody that lived around there and might have known Mrs. Wilson lived there, and I think he found the door open after the rest of them ran out. I think they raped her, too."

The former prosecutor's theory of two completely separate violent rapes upon the body of the elderly widow within a four-hour span in her apartment was preposterous, but a good percentage of gullible locals easily bought into that tale.

A former member of the Wilson murder case task force, Tina Vath, said she and Beatrice Police Lieutenant Mike Oliver, who have since married, still encounter plenty of skeptics around Beatrice.

"Community members seem surprised when either of us express that we one hundred percent believe the six are totally innocent," Vath said. "In my opinion, I think a lot of the community still thinks they were somehow involved. The popular theory is that Bruce Smith showed up after the murder and just raped Helen Wilson after she was deceased."

Pete Klismet, the retired FBI profiler who now lives in Colorado, said it's absolutely ludicrous to even suggest the idea that Bruce Smith arrived and committed another rape on the body of Helen Wilson some four hours after the Beatrice 6 raped and killed her.

"Judging from the way the second investigation went, it doesn't surprise me in the slightest," Klismet said during a 2015 interview. "Again, I come to the notion of 'common sense.' It was a small apartment. Having six or seven people in it doing everything they were supposed to have done would have been like a herd of buffalo stampeding through the living room. This was one of the considerations I made in my profile when I said it was only one person who committed this crime."

The retired FBI agent said he once had considered a scenario in which two sexual predators had raped Wilson, but he believed that deviant act would not have included onlookers.

"Would two or more young guys have committed a violent sexual assault on an older woman, while the others watched?" Klismet asked. "I doubt it. It's a macho thing and not even something you'd tell any of your friends if you'd done it, let alone having your friends watching. Bruce Smith was an 'anger retaliatory' rapist. His anger stemmed from an incident which happened at a bar earlier in the night. Any woman could have been his victim. He was releasing anger for one person to another, Helen Wilson."

***

In January of 2016, Searcey declined to be interviewed for this book, citing the ongoing federal lawsuit against him that had yet to be decided by a jury.

Koenig, who was JoAnn Taylor's former public defender and is a dead ringer for KFC's Colonel Sanders, has an interesting perspective on the former hog farmer's role.

"Burt Searcey is a friend. He was not particularly a friend when this happened twenty some odd years ago. I believe he and the Gage County Sheriff's Office pursued this case very aggressively and to this day, Burt Searcey, despite all of the evidence to the contrary, actually believes that Jo and the other five had something to do with Helen Wilson's death. That belief is literally unshakeable in him."

Koenig suggests that Searcey's refusal to accept reality is probably "convenient on his part."

"I would imagine it would be hard for someone to reconcile themselves to the notion that they had put six innocent people in jail for fifty some odd years in the aggregate, without some feeling of remorse. Of course, the other side of that coin is to believe that you did nothing wrong and that the parties are actually guilty of the original charges. I suppose that is the way one psychologically deals with that problem."

***

Over the years, the pricey law firms being bankrolled by Gage County tried a number of legal tactics in the hopes of having the Beatrice 6 civil rights lawsuits dismissed. The lawyers argued that their law enforcement clients should be entitled to qualified immunity in the federal judicial system. In layman's terms, this means the investigators would be considered to have acted more or less in good faith at the time they charged the Beatrice 6 in the murder.

The pivotal decision in the case came from U.S. Senior District Judge Warren K. Urbom of Lincoln, who released an eighty-eight page ruling on August 8, 2011. Urbom qualified his comments, noting he was only judging the evidence in the White case and not evaluating the merits of the cases.

Here were some of the highlights reached in the federal judge's conclusions:

Searcey submitted misleading arrest affidavits involving White and Taylor in March of 1989. Of particular note, Searcey's arrest affidavits submitted to the Gage County judge stated that Taylor implicated herself to Lisa (Podendorf) Brown "within twenty hours of the Wilson homicide discovery" even though Brown actually gave multiple statements suggesting Taylor confessed at 7:30 or 8:00 a.m. on February 6, 1985 – which was impossible because Wilson's body wasn't found until 9:30 a.m. By that time, Brown would have been in class at the high school.

"It is reasonable to conclude that Searcey's affidavit was left deliberately vague in order to lend plausibility to Podendorf's statement," Judge Urbom concluded.

There was no evidence Searcey had ever produced a single written report at the time his sheriff let him take over the Beatrice Police Department's unsolved murder case in January of 1989. "It appears that (Sheriff) DeWitt asked Searcey to write a report about his investigation in 1987 or sometime during the first half of 1988, but there is no evidence that Searcey drafted a report prior to February 28, 1989."

The federal judge cited numerous instances in which Searcey's conduct appeared improper. "Perhaps most seriously, there is evidence that Searcey fed information to White's alleged accomplices, coached and led interviews, and pressured these interviewees using threats, deception, and manufactured evidence to act as if they had independent knowledge of Searcey's version of events," Judge Urbom wrote. "Many of these interviewees may be fairly characterized as psychologically vulnerable, if not disturbed. Using these tactics, Searcey was able to generate compelling cases against White and others that culminated in White's erroneous conviction."

Just as troubling was Searcey's role in regards to accounting for the actual rapist's known blood type. "The record supports a reasonable inference that Searcey manufactured evidence so far that he could account for the type B blood found in Wilson's apartment without collapsing his case against White," Urbom wrote.

The sharp-minded eighty-six-year-old Lincoln judge, who already had more than forty years on the bench, made the following observation in regards to Searcey's mistake-riddled investigation: "As each new suspect's blood was tested, and the test results excluded them as possible sources of the blood found in Wilson's apartment, Searcey obtained modified statements implicating new suspects."

After all, the true perpetrator's blood type did not match White, Winslow or Taylor when they were all thrown in jail in March 1989. By April 14, Debbie Shelden was jailed only to find out she had type AB blood. James Dean was arrested on April 15, and a report noted he had type O blood. Then more than a month would pass. Finally, Searcey met separately with prisoners Dean and Shelden. He obtained an old Beatrice Police Department mugshot of Kathy Gonzalez, the young woman who lived directly above the murder victim. Searcey showed that mugshot to Shelden and Dean. Each went along and agreed to change their earlier interview statements. Both identified Gonzalez as being present and suffering a bloody nose during a skirmish inside the victim's bedroom. Days later, Searcey flew to Denver to arrest Gonzalez.

"And after Gonzalez was found to have blood type B, Searcey did not target any other suspects in the case," Judge Urbom observed. "In short, the record is replete with evidence showing that Searcey manipulated witnesses' statements in order to build a false case against White and a number of his alleged accomplices."

On the other end of the spectrum, Searcey ignored leads and evidence if they were helpful toward White or called into question interview statements from others. For example, Tom Winslow's wife, Beth Johnson, gave her husband and JoAnn Taylor an alibi during the night of the homicide, but Searcey discarded her story, noting it "did not lead to any helpful information."

"The question is not close," Judge Urbom determined. "It is reasonable to infer, based on the evidence in the record, that Searcey knowingly fabricated evidence to convict White wrongfully. Searcey's conduct shocks the conscience and he is not entitled to qualified community."

Besides Searcey, the depravation of civil rights suit would proceed against police psychologist Wayne Price, retired Sheriff Jerry DeWitt and their employer, Gage County. However, before the federal lawsuit went to trial, DeWitt died of illness at age seventy-five. The lawyers for the Beatrice 6 thereafter sued the deceased sheriff's estate.

Finally, on the verge of the federal trial, Searcey underwent another deposition with the Beatrice 6 lawyers in November 2013. He denied being stressed out about the lawsuit or wavering in his belief in his own theory. "I'm saying that I think the DNA only points to one person. I don't think it answers questions about the other people that I think are involved," Searcey testified.

Debbie Shelden's lawyer, Maren Chaloupka, asked Searcey whether the attorney general's task force had exonerated all of the Beatrice 6.

"No."

"You don't think that's what the task force found?"

"No."

As the deposition questions persisted, Searcey's ineptness was revealed. He acknowledged he had sent serology samples -- blood, saliva and clumps of hair -- from his suspects White, Winslow, Taylor, and Gonzalez to the Nebraska State Patrol's chemistry lab back in 1989. Lab reports had proved that the semen-depositing rapist had type B blood group and what's known as a GC 1 genetic marker. This came to light after analyzing the bloodstains in Helen Wilson's bedroom.

"And none of those factors fit Joe White, Tom Winslow, JoAnn Taylor, Kathy Gonzalez, Deb Shelden, or James Dean, is that correct?" Jeffry Patterson, the Lincoln lawyer representing the estate of White's family, asked Searcey.

"According to these reports, yes," Searcey testified.

"Do you have any reports that say different?"

"No."

"This is scientific evidence?"

"It's lab evidence, yes."

"Was there something wrong with this evidence in your view?"

"No."

"Did you ignore this evidence?"

"No."

"Didn't it indicate that you did not have the person arrested who was the source of the semen?"

"Yes."

"So there was still somebody else there. There was somebody out there?"

"Yes."

"Right?"

"Yes."

Patterson asked when the Wilson murder investigation was considered closed at the Gage County Sheriff's Office.

"I think once we completed the court actions, the trial, everything as the prosecutor did. When there was dispositions is how I would answer that."

"Okay, after the prosecution were you still looking for the guy who was the source of the semen in Helen Wilson's rectum?"

"No."

"You didn't convict that person?"

"No."

"You didn't convict the person who was the source of the blood?"

"No."

Before wrapping up, attorney Chaloupka asked whether Searcey expected to prevail against her and the other trial lawyers representing the Beatrice 6.

"Well, you know, I believe in what I'd done. I guess if that's a yes, that's a yes. ... I haven't thought about losing."

"Have you ever had a conversation with your sheriff, just you and him, about what happens if you lose?" Chaloupka followed up.

"We've probably talked about things. But I don't know if we specifically talked about what happens if I lose, if we lose, quote."

***

Two months later, January 2014, marked the start of the federal civil rights trial at the Robert V. Denney Federal Building and U.S. Courthouse in Lincoln. Five years had elapsed since Nebraska pardoned the Beatrice 6 for Gage County's colossal errors. Now, the five surviving members of the wrongfully convicted individuals, plus White's widowed mother, were trying to hold the powers of Gage County government financially liable for a miscarriage of justice.

James Dean's attorney, Herb Friedman, remarked that Searcey "was absolutely obsessed with this" case, taking up his questionable investigation into Wilson's unsolved murder when Searcey was not even employed as a police officer, back in 1985.

"The only good thing I can tell you about this case is that no one was electrocuted," Friedman told the courtroom.

***

Upon completing his in-depth behavioral profile of Wilson's unknown assailant, FBI Special Agent Pete Klismet had asked the Beatrice Police Department to let him know if a suspect was ever arrested. That call never came. And in the days before the Internet, Klismet never knew what became of the murder case in Nebraska. He presumed it had gone down as a cold case, as many murders sadly do. He had no idea that the local police rival Sheriff's Office down the street had hijacked the murder investigation four years later and then netted an astounding six convictions – six wrongful convictions, nonetheless.

"I never would have found out the case had been solved until I got a call from a reporter at the *Omaha World-Herald,*" Klismet said. "When she asked me if I knew what the outcome was, you could have knocked me over with a toothpick. It was probably the biggest surprise I ever received in a thirty-year law enforcement career."

Klismet said that the Lisa Brown statement implicating Taylor and White "was spurious at best and it should have been vetted through the original investigators."

"What she told the deputy simply could not have happened. ... It appears they accepted the information on its face without question and ran with it."

Also, why didn't anybody at the Gage County Sheriff's Office verify Brown's other highly dubious claim that she had seen the Beatrice 6 piling out of Winslow's Oldsmobile near Wilson's apartment building on the night of the murder?

"Once they did none of that, they reached the point of no return," Klismet added.

Soucie, the public defender who obtained Winslow's exoneration, said the mystery of Lisa Brown's statements may never be known. He said it's entirely plausible that Brown was running around telling other people Taylor and White were the murderers without realizing that her statements would be taken seriously, let alone reach the ears of a local hog farmer setting out to solve the murder.

"How much of this was just Burt Searcey fanning the flames?" Soucie asked. "That's the part I don't get. Why does Lisa Brown go to Burt Searcey when Searcey is not in the Police Department (in 1985)? Why isn't she going to the real cops for three to four years? That's what's incredible. There is just something that is not right on the whole deal."

In January of 2016, Brown did not respond to a letter sent to her residence in Beatrice seeking an interview for this book.

The retired FBI agent who came up with the near-perfect original suspect profile said the mistake-riddled Wilson case traced back to inadequate police officer training and lack of sophistication. The small-town Gage County Sheriff's Office only has about a dozen sworn deputies working under the sheriff.

"Let's face it," Klismet said, "the smaller police and sheriff's departments in the USA don't pay that much, so they don't get the pick of the litter in candidates or people they may choose from an academy class. The ones at the top go to the higher paying jobs. Small departments get the bottom of the barrel generally."

As for Searcey, "he was probably a 'cop wannabe' and wasn't trained to do what he did," Klismet said. "He learned what he 'knew' from TV and movies in all probability. The Nebraska State Patrol should have been called in at some juncture. At least they had trained people who could have made more accurate determinations and decisions on how to proceed."

Klismet said it's unfathomable that six innocent people lost a combined seventy-plus years of their lives at the hands of Gage County's misguided justice system. There was no way on earth six people would have been present at the widow's rape and murder, he confidently declared.

Klismet said the portrayal of the ripped five-dollar bill as White's "calling card" during the jury trial also was preposterous.

"Even the 'calling card' conjures up some mysterious story they may have seen in a murder movie. Problem with that is, if a killer is going to leave a calling card, that's usually a sign there are other murders to come. And that didn't happen. It was simply a bunch of naive people being led down the primrose path," he said.

"The Helen Wilson case was simply an 'Imperfect Storm' of unimaginable consequences, which effectively ruined the lives of six people and which will let a thirty-year-old solved case fade into obscurity with absolutely no justice served in the slightest."

***

Beatrice, to this day, remains haunted by the truth, and many movers and shakers wish that lawyer Randy Ritnour had never come to town and been elected county attorney. His one and only four-year term as the Gage County prosecutor reshaped the community's standing in the national criminal justice world. The Beatrice 6 case is now well-known throughout the country among academic scholars, psychologists and lawyers who study false confessions and wrongful convictions. There are extensive write-ups on the Beatrice 6 case at the Innocence Project and at the National Registry of Exonerations.

"I am not well-liked in a lot of places in Gage County by people who hold the opinion that we're wrong and stupid," Ritnour said during a 2015 interview. "I'm sure Burt Searcey still believes that I'm wrong and that a real travesty has occurred here. But I'm absolutely sure we did the right thing."

Ritnour, a longtime Republican conservative, said his direct involvement in unraveling the Beatrice 6 case had a profound impact on his own belief system.

"I was always a firm believer in the death penalty, but I am no longer. And I'm a very conservative guy," he said. "Clearly, there are mistakes with administering capital punishment. Life in prison is fine.

"As far as the Beatrice 6, we now know that they're obviously not guilty, and they could have all suffered the death penalty. For me, I don't believe in the plea bargain system. Clearly, there were five plea bargains, and they were all trying to avoid a death penalty. Plea bargains encouraged them to plead guilty to something they didn't do."

In the aftermath of the findings of the attorney general's task force, Tina Vath had a mural created on a wall of the Beatrice Police Department's large training room. Vath recalls how she went out on a whim and paid for the lettering herself and worked with her future husband, Lieutenant Mike Oliver, to put up the vinyl lettering on the wall.

The lettering on the wall now reads, *"What do you think ... What do you know ... What can you prove ... in memory of Helen Wilson."*

"I had heard the quote said many years before the Beatrice 6 case, and for some reason it had always stuck in my head," Vath said. "I was always taught throughout my career that a confession alone is never enough, so after this case I thought it would be nice to have something like a quote on the wall in the investigations office in the hopes that if I worked every case or investigation, whether it be a murder, a robbery or a simple theft, that something like the Beatrice 6 case would never happen again."

She said that if every Beatrice police officer followed those three simple guidelines, "that maybe tunnel vision could be avoided."

Vath said the only person around Beatrice who had a negative reaction to the wall mural was Dick Smith, the prosecutor of the Beatrice 6.

"He made some type of comment that it should not be allowed to be in the office because it's city property and he felt offended by it, and as a member of the public he didn't feel it was appropriate," Vath said.

When the Beatrice Police Department underwent remodeling roughly a year ago, workers were instructed to paint around the vinyl mural. The city later hosted a community open house to show off the new and improved downtown police station on North Fifth Street.

"Many members of the public commented on the saying and loved that it was there and the idea of it," Vath said. "So my guess is it will be staying for a very long time."

Tina Vath said this mural in the Beatrice Police Department's training room has been well-received in the community. One of the only people to offer sharp criticism was Dick Smith, the Gage County Attorney who successfully prosecuted six innocent people for Helen Wilson's murder in 1989.Photos/Tina Vath

EPILOGUE

At the time of this book's publication, the Beatrice 6's federal civil rights lawsuit still has not been decided by a jury. A tentative federal trial – scheduled to be a month long -- had been set for June 6, 2016, in Lincoln, Nebraska.

The first civil rights trial, lasting three weeks, ended in a hung jury in January 2014 and included a stunning ruling by federal Judge Richard Kopf. During the middle of the trial, Judge Kopf dismissed all claims against Gage County. The jury was left to deliberate whether remaining co-defendants Burt Searcey, Wayne Price and the estate of the late sheriff, Jerry DeWitt, should be held financially liable for reckless misconduct. The jury deadlocked after roughly three days of deliberations. The hung jury was a huge letdown for the Beatrice 6 and their lawyers seeking at least $14 million in damages.

The jury forewoman, Jan Anderson of St. Paul, Nebraska, told the *Lincoln Journal Star* that she cried after hearing the judge announced a mistrial. The newspaper reported that the jury had to consider as many as thirty-six different verdicts, with six possible scenarios for each of the Beatrice 6.

In sum, the mistrial began the whole jury trial process over. The Beatrice 6 lawyers immediately appealed Judge Kopf's unexpected midtrial decision. Finally, on August 31, 2015, a three-judge panel of the U.S. Court of Appeals 8th Circuit overturned Kopf's decision. The fourteen-page ruling was a stinging rebuke of Kopf, who has a reputation in Nebraska's judicial circles as an aloof and activist judge who likes to draw attention to himself.

The appeals court ruling reinstated Gage County as the principal defendant in the Beatrice 6's civil lawsuit.

"Whether these policy decisions resulted in a violation of constitutional rights is a question for the jury in the second trial," the appellate judges concluded.

It remains to be seen what will happen when the case is retried. No matter what, the Beatrice 6 case has been a pot of gold for a number of Lincoln-based law firms and at least one California-based expert witness consultant who have been hired to defend the actions of Gage County over the wrongful conviction fiasco. Since July 2009, the Gage County Board of Supervisors has spent an astonishing $1 million in taxpayer funds to retain outside legal counsel. The primary recipients of Gage County's excessive spending on legal fees have been: attorney Jennifer Tomka of the Boucher Law Firm; Patrick O'Brien of Butler Galter O'Brien & Boehm Law Firm; Melanie Whittamore-Mantzios of Wolfe Snowden Hurd Luers & Ahl; and defense expert witness Ron Martinelli of Martinelli & Associates, a justice and forensic consulting firm in Temecula, California.

Officials who work in the Gage County Courthouse continue to support Searcey, and that's primarily why the small, rural county continues to spend gobs of money on costly legal fees at their taxpayers' expense, month after month. The current group of elected officials, notably current Gage County Attorney Roger Harris, hopes to prevent the Beatrice 6 from prevailing in their civil rights lawsuit against Gage County

***

Though Nebraska Attorney General Jon Bruning championed the Beatrice 6's innocence, he opposed awarding compensation to the members of that who gave false testimony at White's 1989 murder trial. Bruning did not oppose the $500,000 maximum settlement for White, $350,000 for Kathy Gonzalez and $180,000 to Tom Winslow under the state's wrongful imprisonment act. The three pardoned ex-prisoners being shut out of compensation from Nebraska were James Dean, JoAnn Taylor and Debbie Shelden.

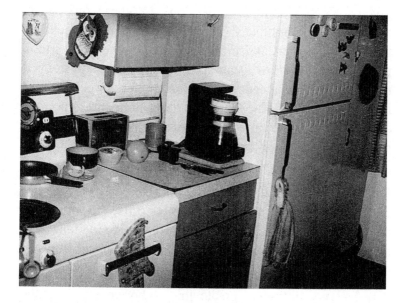

To bolster his flawed murder case against the Beatrice 6, Gage County prosecutor Richard T. Smith suggested at Joseph White's trial that the six co-defendants sat around and brewed coffee inside Helen Wilson's apartment after raping and killing her. In 2008, Smith's theory was completely discredited. Photo/Beatrice Police Department

A few years later, lawyers for Dean and Taylor argued their cases at a bench trial before Gage County District

Court Judge Daniel E. Bryan Jr., a former prosecutor in Geneva, Nebraska, with a reputation of being a hard-lined conservative jurist. The Attorney General's Office stood in opposition. Its lawyers argued that Dean and Taylor forfeited their right to a reparation payment because they, in effect, had committed perjury at White's 1989 trial.

But Judge Bryan saw things differently. During the September 2012 trial, the jury heard testimony from Dr. Richard Leo, a nationally recognized academic scholar and expert witness on false confession cases. Leo concluded that Dean had given a "persuaded false confession." In other words, Dean had come to be brainwashed into believing he was actually involved in Helen Wilson's homicide. Judge Bryan took particular note of how Dean finally broke down and stopped maintaining his innocence after spending three weeks locked in the county jail. "No one, including his court-appointed attorney, Richard Schmeling, believed what he was saying," the judge wrote in his ruling.

Judge Bryan found by clear and convincing evidence that Dean did not commit perjury, did not fabricate evidence nor did Dean otherwise make a statement to cause the conviction of anybody else. The veteran Nebraska judge made a clear distinction that Dean never sought out police investigators to confess to the crime.

"He had no motive to create this elaborate story ... the blame or cause for Dean's belief of guilt rests primarily on law enforcement's mistakes, whether intentional or unintentional."

"Dean had his freedom taken from him for five years, five months. He has had and will have the effects of this event permanently with him for the rest of his life. He suffered the embarrassment, humiliation and degradation of being charged with the most heinous of crimes and he was held in a 9-by-5 cell. He did vigorously claim his innocence, only to be told by everyone he entrusted that he was involved," Bryan concluded.

Knowing that the Nebraska Legislature enacted a $500,000 cap to redress the wrongful convictions of exonorees, a $300,000 payment to Dean in damages was appropriate, the judge ruled.

In Taylor's case, the judge noted that she had suffered from delusions and schizophrenia before being arrested and assured by police that they could prove she was involved in Wilson's death.

"As the cliché goes, 'The path to hell is paved with good intentions.' The path to Mr. Dean's and Ms. Taylor's hell was led by a narrowly focused, almost obsessed, rush to judgment to solve a murder which, while well intended in its goal, nonetheless resulted in grave errors in practice, procedure and conclusions," Judge Bryan wrote. "Taylor had her freedom taken from her for nineteen years, seven months and twenty-six days. To try to attempt to place any value on one's liberty to be free is a Herculean task. To even attempt to rationalize a method of valuation would be foolish at best. But this court has been given this task. ... It finds by a preponderance of evidence that Taylor shall recover damages found to proximately result from the wrongful conviction in the amount of $500,000."

Rejecting an appeal by the defendants in the suit, the Nebraska Supreme Court agreed that Dean and Taylor did not knowingly commit perjury. The court upheld restitution awards for them totaling $800,000.

Finally, on December 17, 2014, Scottsbluff attorney Maren Chaloupka negotiated a $300,000 payment for Debbie

Shelden, the *Omaha World-Herald* reported. At that time, Shelden lived in Lincoln, but was homeless, her lawyer said. A trust fund was set up so that others would not take advantage of her.

"I think about Debbie Shelden often," Paul Korslund, her former public defender, said in January 2016. "I have the utmost regard and sympathy for her. She relied on what she believed to be the truth and stood ready to accept the consequences. As a result, no one in the case had any ill feeling towards her, including the family of Helen Wilson. Debbie is a truly good and innocent person. I hope she has a happy life and that she derives much joy and satisfaction from her family and is able to enjoy a good home."

All told, the Beatrice 6 received a combined $2.13 million from the State of Nebraska thanks to the wrongful imprisonment fund restitution fund.

But for Kathy Gonzalez, the $350,000 payment she received for spending more than five years warehoused in prison was not worth the tradeoff. No amount of compensation could make up for the ruined life and emotional trauma caused by the ordeal to Gonzalez, who had been uprooted from Denver, where she had a stable job working at an upscale restaurant.

"They just found a bunch of suckers," Gonzalez once told the *Lincoln Journal Star*. "They weren't getting anywhere so they found a bunch of disposable people -- and that was us." Whether the Beatrice 6 will receive a sizeable punitive settlement for their still ongoing federal civil rights case remains to be seen.

To this day, Wilson's family still clings to their mistaken belief that the Beatrice 6 – along with Bruce Smith – were all in some way involved. Some relatives are so desperate that they base their belief upon the fact that a pot of cold coffee was discovered inside Wilson's kitchen. During White's trial, Katie Wilson, Helen's daughter-in-law, had claimed that there was no coffee in the pot when Katie and her husband left the apartment around 9:45 p.m. – about six hours before Bruce Smith broke into the apartment and terrorized the widow while the rest of Beatrice was sound asleep.

"Could the family be mistaken about the circumstances surrounding the coffee?" asked Tina Vath, the task force investigator. "I didn't put a whole lot of thought into the coffeepot during our investigation because I didn't feel it was relevant at all, and I knew they made a big deal of it back then. I don't think it can be shown or proved at all who made or when that pot of coffee was made. I think it's possible (Bruce) Smith could have made it. Helen could have decided to make some after her family left."

***

It's important to remind readers that the Wilson family never, ever deserved the cruel series of events that left them in a state of confusion. Helen Wilson was a wonderful woman, a loving family member and a well-respected member of her community. She was involved in several clubs and civic groups at the time of her horrific tragedy. Her family went four long years without justice, then they thought it came -- only to discover two decades later that someone named Bruce Allen Smith was the true perpetrator, and that he's long since died. All they were left with was a catastrophic miscarriage of justice, one of the worst in the country's history.

It's surely no wonder the Wilsons have never been the same. It's easy to see how this good, well-intentioned family has been put through the criminal justice system ringer.

"Her children were very happy adults and their personalities now have been changed," said Edie Wilson, the daughter-in-law of Helen Wilson who lives in Scottsbluff. "You don't go through what they have and be the same people."

Edie Wilson is spot on when she says that the family feels like it has never gained justice for Helen's awful rape and murder back in 1985.

"She set a good example for us to lead our lives," the victim's daughter-in-law said. "She would be so proud of her family and how we have all held our heads up high and went through the trials and all the other disappointments from her death with dignity with pride of our mother, sister, grandmother, great grandmother ... we don't feel we have truly had closing."

***

Here's an update on key people associated with the Helen Wilson murder:

In March 2010, **Tina Vath**, the Beatrice police investigator who served on the attorney general's task force, joined the Nebraska Attorney General's Office as an investigator in the criminal and consumer protection units.

Randy Ritnour was defeated in his bid for re-election as county attorney by the voters of Gage County in 2010. Ritnour returned to private law practice in Lincoln, where he mostly concentrates on criminal defense. "As far as the Beatrice 6 case, I feel very good about the outcome. I tell myself I did a good thing, so I'm proud of that," he said.

Dick Smith, the former longtime county prosecutor largely responsible for the travesty of justice in the Wilson murder case, remains in private practice in Beatrice, operating the Smith Law Office on Court Street. Smith is now in his mid-sixties. In January of 2016, Smith did not respond to a letter sent to his law firm seeking an interview for this book

Wayne Price, the police psychologist suspected of manipulating a number of the co-defendants into believing they were guilty, retired in 2006 as director of the Blue Valley Mental Health Center in Beatrice. Price has remained active in the field of psychology, working in both Lincoln and Beatrice. Now in his seventies, "Doc" still works part-time at the Gage County Sheriff's Department, mostly handling courthouse security. Besides Searcey, Price remains the only living member of the Sheriff's Department still being sued in his individual capacity as part of the Beatrice 6 federal lawsuit. In 2011, U.S. District Court Senior Judge Warren Urbom ruled that Price, among other things, convinced James Dean that he "had repressed his memories of the crime and that he could benefit from therapy sessions with Price even though Price was a deputy sheriff ... Dr. Price also complained that city detective Sam Stevens was not trying to obtain a confession from White, who was actually innocent, of the murder. In short, there is evidence that Price knowingly participated in a conspiracy to ... manufacture of false evidence against White," the judge wrote. Price, who continues to live in Beatrice, did not respond to a letter asking for his comments regarding the Beatrice 6 case.

As a teenager, **Lisa (Podendorf) Brown** was the primary confidential informant for Searcey. She was responsible for concocting the story that JoAnn Taylor had confessed the murder to her. Now in her late forties, Brown continues to reside in Beatrice. Brown did not respond to a letter asking for her comments for this book.

Charlotte Bishop was Searcey's second unreliable informant used to secure the faulty arrest of White and Taylor. It was ultimately proven that Bishop gave a false statement claiming Taylor had confessed the murder to her. Bishop was also known as Charlotte Mendenhall, Charlotte

Crumb, Charlotte Watkins and, when she died in 2009 at age fifty-three in Milford, Nebraska, she was known as Charlotte Troupe. Her obituary noted that she attended Beatrice Public Schools through eighth grade and suffered from varying disabilities. "For those who knew Charlotte, she was a very loving person yet showed a tough personality in spite in her failing health and fight with diabetes," her obituary stated.

Paul "Jake" Jacobson, operator of the Jacobson Polygraph Services firm in Lincoln, had been a highly respected Lincoln Police Department homicide detective for many years before getting involved in the Wilson murder case in 1989. After retiring from the force, he opened his successful polygraph company in the 1980s in Lincoln. He died in 1994 at the age of sixty-eight. However, it wasn't until 2008 when the attorney general's task force looked into the Wilson murder case that it became evident Jacobson had done incredibly shoddy polygraph work on the case. Jacobson's pretrial polygraph examinations flunked co-defendants Joseph White, James Dean, and Kathy Gonzalez. It's now clear they were telling the truth when they denied involvement in the homicide. Jacobson also determined that co-defendant Debbie Shelden passed her polygraph test with flying colors when she implicated herself and the others in the crime when the opposite was true. Besides Burt Searcey and Wayne Price, Paul Jacobson's role in furthering the false murder cases against the Beatrice 6 cannot be forgotten. It's clearly a dark mark on Jacobson's otherwise stellar professional career in Nebraska law enforcement circles.

Joyce Gilchrist, the Oklahoma City crime lab technician who botched the serology blood test involving Bruce Allen Smith, thus leading Nebraska investigators to wrongly exclude the actual killer from their list of suspects, was fired in 2001. Gilchrist then found employment as an administrative assistant at a dental clinic, court records show. *The Oklahoman* reported that Gilchrist later moved to Houston and worked at a candle-making company. In June of 2015, she died at age sixty-seven.

Pete Klismet, the Cedar Rapids, Iowa-based FBI profiler who came up with the near-flawless profile of Helen Wilson's unknown killer, worked for the FBI from 1979 through 1999 with assignments in Los Angeles, Cedar Rapids, Omaha, and Grand Junction, Colorado. These days, Klismet lives in Colorado Springs, Colorado, and runs Criminal Profiling Associates, a consulting firm. He has authored a number of books, *FBI Diary: Profiles of Evil, FBI Animal House: What Really Happened Inside the FBI Academy and FBI Diary: Homegrown Terror.*

The most important legacy for **William B. Rist,** the judge in Beatrice who presided over Joseph White's trial and handled the proceedings for the Beatrice 6,was his decision to spare White's life and not send him to the electric chair. In January 2016, just a month shy of turning ninety-three, Rist died at a hospital in Lincoln. Rist's obituary in the *Beatrice Daily Sun* noted that Rist practiced law in Beatrice from 1948 through 1971, and served as county attorney from 1949 until 1958. Rist served as the 1st Judicial District judge from 1971 until his retirement in 1998.

Ralph "Sam" Stevens, the Beatrice Police Department detective who was told to stay out of the Beatrice 6 murder investigation by early spring of 1989, retired from the department during the late 1990s. Now in his early eighties, Stevens continues to call Beatrice home.

Donald C. Sass, who was appointed as Kathy Gonzalez's lawyer, provided a lackluster effort that resulted in Gonzalez pleading no contest and serving more than five years in prison for a crime she did not commit. Sass, who was a public defender in Fairbury, died in 2009 at age seventy-five.

John Stevens Berry, founder of the Berry Law Firm, represented Tom Winslow as one of the Beatrice 6. Back in 1989, however, Berry was already defending Winslow in connection with the brutal tire-iron clubbing at the Harvester Hotel in Lincoln. Berry is regarded as one of Nebraska's most prominent criminal defense attorneys. In 2014, Berry co-authored the book, *The Twelfth Victim: The Innocence of Caril Fugate in the Starkweather Murder Rampage*. Berry continues to remain an active member of the Nebraska bar. His law firm website notes that Berry has appeared in court in 24 states and in two foreign countries. An incredibly experienced trial lawyer, Berry continues to travel, speaking at legal seminars across the country.

Toney Redman, lead public defender for Joseph White, retired from law in 2015 after 42 years as a criminal defense attorney in Lincoln in an unforgettable manner. According to the *Lincoln Journal Star*, Redman, age sixty-nine, yanked off his tie and tightly tied it around the courthouse flagpole. "Redman. 3/4/15 42 years. Adios," he wrote on the tie. Redman now runs Toney Redman Metal Sculpture artistic services out of his rural acreage. "It beats the hell out of being a lawyer," he told the newspaper.

Douglas J. Stratton, the criminal defense lawyer who took up White's post-conviction appeal that led to Nebraska's first DNA exoneration, remains a partner at his private law firm in Norfolk. According to his firm bio, Stratton received the George H. Turner Award in 2009 from the Nebraska Bar Association related to proving the innocence of the Beatrice 6.

Jerry Soucie, the Nebraska state public defender responsible for obtaining the exoneration of Tom Winslow through testing of DNA evidence, became the point man working with Gage County Attorney Randy Ritnour to re-examine the false confessions and wrongful convictions of the rest of the Beatrice 6. Soucie has recently moved to Georgia, but he still frequently travels back to Nebraska where he has operated the Soucie Law Office in Lincoln, specializing in criminal defense and civil rights litigation.

Alan Stoler, the lawyer who served as the defense co-counsel at White's jury trial in Fairbury, had a profound contribution to the case when he convinced Judge William Rist not to impose the death penalty against White. Stoler remains a criminal defense lawyer in downtown Omaha. Stoler obtained his bar admission from Nebraska in 1978 and a bar admission from the U.S. Supreme Court in 1992. Stoler also practices in the federal court system.

Donald Luckeroth, the former longtime Beatrice chief of police, died in July 2013 at age eighty-one. Like Sam Stevens, Luckeroth always harbored grave doubts about the legitimacy of Burt Searcey's investigation into the Wilson murder. Luckeroth lived long enough to see all six of the wrongly convicted individuals released from prison and Searcey's professional reputation sullied by the shocking turn of events that unfolded in 2008.

Richard Schmeling was the public defender who represented James Dean, who pleaded guilty and spent more than five years in prison though he was innocent of any role in Wilson's death. In 1999, the Nebraska Supreme Court upheld the disbarment of Schmeling's law license in two unrelated cases pertaining to his civil practice. "The charges in the instant case are not isolated events," the court wrote. "Schmeling has been afforded past opportunities to monitor his compliance with the Code of Professional Responsibility, including three private reprimands and a one-year suspension from the practice of law … we determine that Schmeling must be, and hereby is, disbarred effective immediately." In 2011, Schmeling wrote a column published in the *Lincoln Journal Star* headlined, "Consider Rail as a Safe Alternative to Keystone XL [pipeline]." The column identified Schmeling as a retired lawyer and an expert on transportation issues.

Ada JoAnn Taylor has been the most active member of the Beatrice 6 in terms lending her name to advocacy groups for the wrongly convicted. Taylor has remained active with the Nebraska Innocence Project, and she participated in several video interviews that were posted on the Cornell University School of Law website in November 2012 in conjunction with a national study on false confessions. In one video, Taylor talked about the difficulty of life after exoneration:

"I have a lot of people who tell me I should put it behind me. Well, I'm sorry, I lost twenty years of my life. How do you put that behind you? They say that when you are locked up, you mentally stop growing. Well, at forty-nine, I should be able to do a whole lot more than I did, but I'm still stuck at that youngster age."

Even four years after being exonerated, Taylor said in that 2012 interview she still had difficulty finding her place in society. About the only positive aspect of prison was getting an education. "I love computers and I never thought I would. I got fourteen years of data entry experience. I've got my associate's degree and I'm halfway through my bachelor's now. The weird thing is, I'm a psychology major," Taylor said, erupting in laughter.

Tom Winslow made a rare public appearance in 2015 to open up about the Beatrice 6 case. Winslow traveled to the Innocence Network Conference in Orlando, Florida. A year earlier, in 2014, Winslow testified during the Beatrice 6's federal trial. He told the courtroom that he had been repeatedly sexually assaulted by other inmates during more than half of his time in state prison, the *Omaha World-Herald* reported. "I was sexually assaulted after three days. If I hadn't been labeled as being involved in the sexual assault of Helen Wilson, I probably wouldn't have got picked on as much," Winslow testified.

Winslow, who recently turned fifty, now resides in Tulsa, Oklahoma, with relatives, where he works as a nursing assistant. **Lyle J. Koenig**, the public defender for Taylor, remains a criminal defense attorney in Beatrice. Koenig said it's worth pointing out that when he represented Taylor on first-degree murder charges, he was in the dark about the FBI's criminal profile of the unknown offender and unaware that the Beatrice Police Department had pursued Bruce Allen Smith to Oklahoma City in 1985. "We were never advised of the fact that there was a suspect that had been developed," Koenig said. "Had that information been disclosed, I would have been on a plane to Oklahoma City in a heartbeat. Obviously, had defense counsel been informed of these two facts, it would have been formed a potential defense about which none of us knew."

Paul Korslund, the public defender for Debbie Shelden, went on to have a highly successful tenure as a southeastern Nebraska judge, handling both civil and criminal cases. In January 2016, Korslund, age sixty-six, announced he would retire from the bench on April 1. Korslund served as the District Court judge for both Gage and Jefferson Counties in Beatrice and Fairbury, after Rist retired in 1998. On the

JOHN FERAK

bench, Korslund crusaded to greatly improve public and electronic media access to the courts, and in 2008 he won the Nebraska Supreme Court's Outstanding Judge Award.

Jon Bruning, the Nebraska attorney general responsible for overturning the convictions of the Beatrice 6 and endorsing their pardons, said he is incredibly proud of his office's work on the Wilson murder case. He considers it one of his proudest accomplishments during his three-term tenure in one of Nebraska's most powerful state political offices. Bruning also singled out the performance of Assistant Attorney General Corey O'Brien in the case. A staunch Republican conservative, Bruning ran for U.S. Senate in 2012, but lost in a primary upset to Valentine rancher Deb Fischer, who went on to be elected to the Senate. In 2014, Bruning ran for Nebraska governor. Although he was endorsed by the departing two-term governor, Dave Heineman, Bruning narrowly lost in the GOP primary to the eventual next governor, Pete Ricketts, whose family founded TD Ameritrade and now owns the Chicago Cubs. After twelve years as the attorney general, Bruning left political office in 2015. He opened the Bruning Law Group in Lincoln.

Ernie Chambers, the longtime Omaha state lawmaker, is now seventy-eight and showing no signs of slowing down. Chambers was responsible for Nebraska's DNA law that allowed condemned prisoners like White to retest newly discovered DNA evidence. Chambers joined the Nebraska Legislature in 1970 and served for many decades as its only black lawmaker. After being forced to leave political office after a term-limit law was enacted, Chambers successfully reclaimed his old north Omaha seat in a tough battle in 2012. Once again, Chambers remains one of the most powerful figures in the State Capitol. In 2015, in an historic vote, Chambers led the Legislature's crusade to abolish the state's death penalty, securing enough votes to override Governor Pete Ricketts' veto.

The historic vote created furor across the largely agrarian state, outraging the Legislature's predominantly conservative constituency. A quickly mobilized citizen petition drive netted enough signatures to put the measure on the November 2016 election ballot. Voters will be asked whether they want to repeal or maintain the law that eliminated the death penalty. Despite the uproar by pro-death penalty advocates, Nebraska has not carried out an execution since 1997. Given that many rural Nebraskans are not the most sophisticated of folks, I expect the death penalty ballot measure will probably pass by a wide margin. It's also likely that thousands of Nebraska voters who head to the polls will be completely oblivious to the negative lasting impact that Nebraska's capital punishment law had in the investigation of Helen Wilson's rape-murder.

It's also unlikely that Nebraska death penalty proponents will remember the foolish words uttered in the courtroom by the Gage County prosecutor during the sentencing arguments for Joseph White. Dick Smith argued in 1990 that "everyone's heart would like, at least on this side, a death sentence."

"His participation was major," Smith said of White that day. "He was the one that planned it. He was the one that got them together. He was the one that went there. He was the one that committed the sexual assault first ... and he was the one that basically was the ring leader. I would say that's what the evidence showed."

Today, the nation now knows the six-term former prosecutor was on the wrong side of justice and history. Dick Smith had supported the imposition of Nebraska's electric chair against Joseph Edgar White – a truly innocent and wrongly convicted man. And thanks to Smith, Nebraska holds a dubious distinction in the wrongful conviction arena, a record that may stay on the books for decades, a record that no criminal prosecutor in Nebraska or any other state will probably want to take away from Beatrice's Dick Smith.

"This was the worst miscarriage of justice in the history of the state of Nebraska and probably the entire country," remarked Herb Friedman, the lawyer for James Dean. "This was pretty bad."

Use this link to sign up for advance notice
of new books from John Ferak.
http://wildbluepress.com/AdvanceNotice

Word-of-mouth is critical to an author's long-term success.
If you appreciated this book please leave a review on the
Amazon sales page:
http://wbp.bz/foja

Other Exciting WildBlue Press
Books By John Ferak

DIXIE'S LAST STAND: *Was It Murder Or Self-Defense?*

BODY OF PROOF: *Tainted Evidence In The Murder Of Jessica O'Grady*

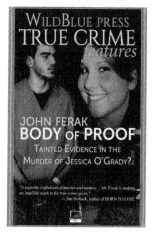

http://wbp.bz/dixie

http://wbp.bz/bop

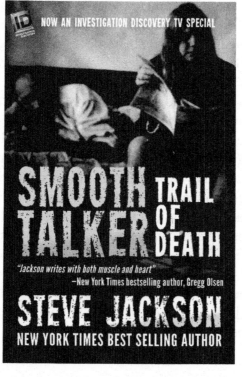

SMOOTH TALKER: Trail of Death
by STEVE JACKSON

In July 1974, Anita Andrews, the owner and bartender at Fagiani's Bar in Napa, California was found one morning in her bar raped, beaten, strangled and murdered. She'd befriended a stranger that night, but no one knew if he did it, and he'd disappeared. A month later, young Michele Wallace, was driving down a road in the mountains near Crested Butte, Colorado, when she gave two stranded motorists, Chuck Matthews and a man named Roy, a ride. Dropping Matthews off at a bar, she agreed to take "Roy" to his truck. She was never seen alive again. The trail for her killer grew cold. Fourteen years later, Charlotte Sauerwin, engaged to be married soon, met a smooth-talking man at a Laundromat in Livingston, Parish, Louisiana. The next evening, her body was found in the woods; she'd been raped and her throat slashed. But like the other two women above, her killer had simply disappeared. In fact, not until the early 1990s, when a Gunnison County sheriff's investigator Kathy Young started looking into the still-unsolved Wallace Case, would a single name eventually be linked to the murder of all three women. That name was Roy Melanson, a serial rapist considered to be a prime suspect in the rape and murder of several other women as well. Smooth Talker is the story of Melanson, his depredations and the intrepid police work that went into bringing him to justice.

Read More About SMOOTH TALKER At:

http://wbp.bz/smoothtalker

www.WildBluePress.com

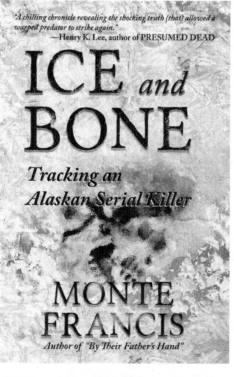

ICE AND BONE: Tracking an Alaskan Serial Killer
by MONTE FRANCIS

In the Fall of 2000, in Anchorage, Alaska, a series of murders captured headlines, stoking fears a serial killer was on the loose. Six women, mostly Alaska Natives, were found slain, all under similar circumstances. An anonymous tip led investigators to a thuggish, young drug dealer, who would eventually implicate himself in three of the women's deaths. But it wasn't until the disappearance of a well-loved nurse psychologist seven years later, and the discovery of her body in the remote wilderness of Wasilla, that two astute female detectives would finally bring the murderer to justice.

ICE AND BONE is the chilling, true account of how a notorious murderer evaded police and avoided conviction only to slip back into the shadows and kill again. Award-winning journalist Monte Francis tells the harrowing story of detectives' hunt for a serial killer, recounting a case that sparked cries of outrage and racial injustice, and reveals why the true scope the killer's savagery is only now, more than a decade later, coming into view.

Read More About ICE AND BONE At:

http://wbp.bz/iceandbone

www.WildBluePress.com

More True Crime You'll Love

From WildBlue Press.

Learn more at: http://wbp.bz/tc

www.WildBluePress.com

More Mysteries/Thrillers You'll Love
From WildBlue Press.

Learn more at: http://wbp.bz/cf

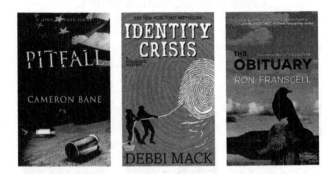

www.WildBluePress.com

Go to WildBluePress.com to sign up for our newsletter!

By subscribing to our newsletter you'll get *advance notice* of all new releases as well as notifications of all special offers. And you'll be registered for our monthly chance to win a **FREE collection of our eBooks and/or audio books** to some lucky fan who has posted an honest review of our one of our books/eBooks/audio books on Amazon, Itunes and GoodReads.

WILDBLUE
P R E S S
Audio Books

Let Someone Else Do The Reading.

Enjoy One Of Our Audiobooks

Learn more at: http://wbp.bz/audio

Please feel free to check out more True CRIME books
by our friends at

www.RJPARKERPUBLISHING.com